# MAKING
# CITY PLANNING
# WORK

## Allan B. Jacobs

**American Society of Planning Officials**
**Chicago**

The American Society of Planning Officials is consolidating with the
American Institute of Planners into the American Planning Association.

# Contents

To the memory of Mortimer Fleishhacker

# Preface

For 30 years from my vantage point in Berkeley—as a faculty member at the University of California, as a former San Francisco city planning director and mayor's deputy for development, and as a political activist in Berkeley and the metropolitan Bay Area—I have enjoyed the privilege of being an avid San Francisco city planning watcher. Thus, when Allan Jacobs accepted the invitation to come to San Francisco in 1966, after a nation-wide search by the mayor and city planning commission for the most promising young city planner in the country, I was eager to see him get established and to watch his leadership make itself evident. For me, his eight-year tour of duty proved to be a daily delight.

Between 1966 and 1974, the major city planning issues in San Francisco were widely recognized. They were thoroughly covered in the press and on television and vigorously debated both inside and outside of the formal structure of city government. Usually—but not always, of course—the outcome was favorable to the city planning point of view. As the spokesman for that point of view, Allan Jacobs helped the entire community raise its sights, act more thoughtfully, and make a stronger effort to provide for the environmental needs of both present and future generations. He was sensitive to the special qualities of San Francisco and the Bay Area. He had patience and impressive staying power. He was a strong public official and an influential community leader.

Since, in the pages that follow, Allan does not tell you very much about himself in a formal way, I will say something about his background and the experience he gained professionally before coming to

San Francisco. My purpose is to introduce him to as broad an audience as possible, including citizen planning commissioners, urban political leaders, and civic activists—from leagues of women voters to chambers of commerce to conservation groups to neighborhood associations—as well as to the city planning students and younger faculty members who will be entering the field in the coming decades. What I say may also help develop an appreciation for the fact that, although the experience reported in this book was gained in a city thought of by many Americans as being unique, there are good reasons for considering the 1966-74 San Francisco city planning case studies as having relevance and significance for cities throughout the United States.

A native of Cleveland, Ohio, Allan studied architecture at Miami University in Oxford, Ohio, graduating in 1952. At Miami he was encouraged by Rudolph Frankel, who was then developing a program in "city design" that was largely inspired by European ideas about cities and large-scale three-dimensional design. Another important influence at Miami came from teachers who were interested in the field of urban sociology. Allan studied at Harvard and, when Harvard professor William L. C. Wheaton went to Philadelphia, moved to the University of Pennsylvania in 1953 for his final year in the graduate city planning program. Here he studied with Lewis Mumford, Holmes Perkins, Robert Mitchell, Martin Meyerson, Jack Dyckman, and Charles Abrams. In 1954, he was a Fulbright Fellow at University College in London where he studied England's postwar New Towns Program, which at that time was entering one of its most exciting stages of development.

Between 1955 and 1963, Allan worked with Patrick Cusick, director of the privately financed Pittsburgh Regional Planning Association, and then served for two years in India as a senior staff member of the Ford Foundation's advisory team to the Calcutta Metropolitan Planning Organization. When he came to San Francisco in 1966, he had been a faculty member at the University of Pennsylvania for almost two years.

Jacobs knows big cities and is attuned to them. When he was young, on visits to relatives in New York City, he liked to walk, to explore, to sketch what he saw. He learned at an early age about Manhattan and the Bronx, Central Park, and the slums. Summer work in Cleveland in the early 1950s exposed him to the wit and wisdom of Ernest Bohn, director of the city's housing authority who also served as chairman of the city planning commission. And an assignment in the 1960s with Boston's redevelopment chief, Ed Logue, introduced Jacobs to one of the nation's most powerful and effective public development entrepreneurs.

When Allan Jacobs came to San Francisco, he had never worked in a city hall with an official city planning agency, and he had never studied or worked in the West. But he had had the best of educations, had made his mark with faculty members and fellow students, and had enjoyed a long and creative apprenticeship in Pittsburgh with Pat Cusick. He had studied in London and worked in Calcutta. He knew Cleveland, Pittsburgh, New York, Boston, and Philadelphia. Still, though, his ideas about cities and about the role of the city planning agency in a democratic city government were unknown. What was known about him was the very high regard that his senior coworkers, in universities and in the field, had for his creative abilities as a city planner, "city designer," and staff leader; his integrity; his social conscience; and his drive, stability, and sense of realism.

The San Francisco city planning program that Allan Jacobs assumed responsibility for in 1966 had been started in 1942. His predecessors during the initial years of the program had laid the foundations and prepared the way for the years of accomplishment and controversy that were to follow. In terms of a realistic historical perspective, therefore, it is important to appreciate that the outstanding record of the period from 1966 to 1974 is the record of only one portion—although a very significant portion—of San Francisco's modern city planning experience.

It probably will be surprising to many readers that experience in a major American city during the most turbulent periods of the 1960s and 1970s confirmed Allan's earlier judgment that city planning can in fact be made to work effectively in our society. To one who shares this view, and who also has had the opportunity to live and work in the practical world of local government as well as in the academic world, it is reassuring and refreshing to have carefully documented evidence for this judgment now made widely available.

The practice of city planning in the United States has been generously supported since the post-World War II period began more than 30 years ago. Throughout the country, whenever capable civic and professional leadership crystallized and understandable city planning programs were proposed, such programs almost invariably received

careful consideration and, in most cases, strong and continuing support. As a consequence, there are today a substantial number of city
planning programs that have 20 to 30 years of sustained and relatively
successful experience behind them. The time has come to examine this
work with a critical eye.

One of the merits of the book that Allan Jacobs has written is that its
presentation of specific cases is done in such a way that the reader can
develop a picture of the larger program within which each of the
individual cases took place. The book, thus, is more than a report on six
significant but necessarily limited city planning cases; it is a report on
the practice of city planning in the United States today. As such, it is the
first of its kind.

The American city planning tradition which the San Francisco city
planning cases illustrate was established by Frederick Law Olmsted and
his colleagues from several related fields in the decades between the
Civil War and the end of the nineteenth century. It was during this
period that the leaders of America's expanding metropolitan areas for
the first time began to give serious attention to the environmental as
well as the social problems that were being aggravated by the rapid,
haphazard growth of their cities. Largely as a result of the high quality of
the comprehensive city plans and the park and regional open space
systems and other key urban elements that Olmsted and his coworkers
designed and helped to create during an active practice of more than
forty years, a broad, firm foundation emerged as the basis for the future
practice of city planning in the United States.

The names and ideas of Burnham, Bettman, and Mumford symbolize both the continuity of the Olmsted tradition and the long period of
slow growth that was necessary before city planning staffs could be
successfully established in city halls throughout the country. Burnham's monumental city plans of the early 1900s dramatized the three-
dimensional setting of urban life, and his designs for public works made
civic leaders aware of the continuous, never ending, city-building activities of American municipal governments. Alfred Bettman's work as a
lawyer and city planner between the two world wars was largely
responsible for the acceptance of city planning as a normal activity of
local government in the United States. Bettman was a key figure in the
effort to clarify the scope and duties of the city planning agency and
hence of the profession. The definition of the public interest that he
formulated and successfully defended before the Supreme Court in

1926 subsequently enabled local governments to regulate private property for city planning purposes. It was a definition based on American
concepts and traditions. Lewis Mumford, with the publication in 1938
of his great book, *The Culture of Cities*, gave historical perspective to
American city planning and taught a new generation of city planners to
develop an awareness of the social and ecological implications of their
work as urban environmental designers.

The influence of these outstanding leaders on city planning in San
Francisco—and on the setting in which the case studies presented in
the following pages took place in the 1960s and 1970s, many decades
later—was more direct and has been more significant than is generally
appreciated. Olmsted's work with the city in the 1860s and 1870s
helped inspire the creation, design, and enhancement of Golden Gate
Park, a city planning accomplishment of the highest order that con-
tinues to amaze and inspire political leaders, citizens, and city planners.
The 1905 Burnham Plan for San Francisco educated and influenced
M.M. O'Shaughnessy and John McLaren, who, as city engineer and parks
superintendent, worked as a team for a 20-year period between 1912
and 1932. They were the first great city-builders of San Francisco.

When the city's present charter was written during the early
1930s, the Bettman definition of city planning as set forth in the Standard City Planning Enabling Act of 1928 was adopted almost word for
word. Restated and strengthened in a charter amendment in 1947, the
ideas of Bettman and his contemporaries continue to govern the practice of city planning in San Francisco today, 45 years later.

The writings of Lewis Mumford during the 1930s had a powerful
impact on the group of young men and women in the San Francisco Bay
Area who, largely inspired by Mumford and his colleagues from New
York in the Regional Planning Association of America, played a major
role in the revitalization of the San Francisco city planning program in
the early 1940s. Mumford's visits and support during this period stimulated and encouraged the creation of the environmental design group
that became known as "Telesis." His writings led to a new awareness of
the city's social and economic relationships with its neighboring communities and of their common interest in the resources and ecological
integrity of the dramatically beautiful geographic setting formed by the
nine Bay Area counties.

During the 1940s, Philadelphia, Seattle, Chicago, Detroit, New
York, and Los Angeles also made major changes in their city planning

programs, moving from token operations to the organization of the first modern city planning staffs and action programs, which led subsequently to major changes in city halls everywhere in the country. The postwar leaders of these new staffs, and their successors in the 1950s and 1960s, prepared the way for the second postwar generation of city planning practitioners, of which Allan Jacobs is an outstanding member.

In the pages that follow this preface, you will quickly become aware of Allan's concern for encouraging and producing professional work of the highest possible quality. The fact that this was a dominant concern during the period of central city riots and the surge toward participatory democracy is of special interest. On campuses throughout the country at this time, graduate students in city planning, like graduate students in other fields, were determined to deprofessionalize the practice of their professions to the greatest extent possible. The San Francisco city planning staff and its leaders did not, in any way, use their high professional standards to shield themselves against citizens' demands for more direct involvement. Indeed, Allan Jacobs may be said to be one of the profession's major demystifiers. His record clearly demonstrates his agreement with the views of Sir Patrick Geddes, expressed in 1915 in *The Evolution of Cities*, that town planning is "not something which can be learned in one place and imitated in another . . . . It is the development of a local life. . .capable of improvement and development. . .in its own way and upon its own foundations."

The cases presented in this book, being specific and related to one city, cannot be expected to convey Allan's ability and willingness to seek out and act upon basic issues of city structure that do not easily lend themselves to documentation by the case study method. It may be useful, therefore, for me to point out that San Francisco, during the eight years in which the case studies took place, never failed to support the potentially extremely controversial regional plan that was sponsored and nominally approved by the Association of Bay Area Governments during these years. Allan Jacobs not only judged the plan's proposal to put a definite limit on the outward spread of the metropolis to be necessary, but he subsequently concluded and stated publicly that there would have to be a limit to the size of the region's central district in San Francisco and to the residential density of the central city if families of all incomes and types were to be provided with decent living and working conditions. It is important, I believe, to appreciate his continuing concern with this larger context of ideas concerning cities and metropolitan regions within which case studies such as those reported here will always take place. Allan Jacobs is one of the few city planners I know who accepts and acts on the judgment expressed by Lewis Mumford in 1969 that there are "natural limits to urban growth, inherent in the very nature of city life, and that beyond these limits malformation, disorganization, and deterioration ... result."

Finally, one might gain the impression from the material presented in the interpretive chapters of this book that Allan believes that the political realities of American city life today are such that the ways in which we plan and work to improve the physical environment of our cities cannot be changed significantly in the foreseeable future. I have argued that this impression is correct, and that it may be misleading. American civic life, I believe, is more open to change than most Americans seem to recognize. It is important, therefore, for the members of each new generation of city planners to be encouraged, in effect, to ignore political realities—for a limited period of time, at least—and to say what they really think needs to be done. Without such uncompromised professional advice, political leaders cannot be expected to become fully aware of and to help the people of the United States face the social and environmental realities of our cities. The conditions of city life for a large proportion of Americans ought not to be considered acceptable. Today's local governments, by and large, either do not or cannot bring themselves to accept this judgment. And those few that have had to face reality, have not yet become determined enough to organize and carry out the long-term changes that will have to be made sooner or later.

City planners are servants of the people as well as of the elected and appointed citizens who are their official superiors. They must, therefore, anticipate possibilities that at any given moment will always be considered politically unrealistic. The great merit of Allan Jacobs's report on his San Francisco experience is that its honesty and directness will inspire civic leaders, students, and many younger members of the city planning profession to be true to their best instincts as human beings and to do so in ways that will be idealistic as well as tough minded.

In one form or another, the city planning profession will find ways to recognize and describe significant work, to present it within the personal and governmental contexts within which it was performed, and thus to gradually build a set of principles to govern practice and a set of concepts concerning cities that can be widely understood and openly judged. When principles and concepts of the sort suggested here do emerge, the work of reorganizing our cities and metropolitan regions and of governing their future size, structure, and shape will be immeasurably aided. City planners are dependent on the trust and support they are given by the elected officials who are their immediate superiors. Because of the attempt that has been made in this book to be straightforward and unsparingly honest, the San Francisco case studies that are presented in the following pages will be of incalculable value in making such trust and support possible for city planners everywhere.

T. J. Kent, Jr.
Berkeley, 1977

# Acknowledgements

Many, many people have helped to make this book possible. The people of a very special city come first. They and the land they inhabit gave me the substance with which to interact and about which to write. It would take forever to list all of them, for the list would have to include people from all over San Francisco, individuals and groups. Perhaps Reuel Brady, Alice Barkley, and Dorothy Erskine can stand as proxies for so many San Franciscans: Reuel as the dignified, active, independent citizen, concerned with his neighborhood, his people, and himself, but also with the city as a whole and with *what is right*; Alice as the militant organizer and worker, striving and shouting for her people and her area and working as hard as she expected others to work for the disadvantaged; Dorothy as the native San Franciscan, challenging conservationist, open space advocate, relentless in seeking the best for her city and region.

Mayors and supervisors also helped me to write this book, as did planning commissioners, appointed officials of government, developers and their representatives, and the press. They all put up with a lot from me over the years. To me, my colleagues at the department of city planning were (and remain) a special group of people without whom none of this book would have been possible. I hope I have done everyone justice.

Jack Kent has seen me through this book from start to finish. He read everything, more than once, and gave me the continual critical feedback I needed. We argued a lot over content, sharpening and reconsidering our positions about city planning and government, sometimes returning to the same points and the same arguments over and over again. Jack corrected me, made suggestions, and put me in my place more than once. He reminded me especially of the history of city planning and of city planners in San Francisco. His criticisms were always positive and he encouraged me when that was needed.

Peter Svirsky, too, has been a constant source of strength, help, and reference for my work. He reviewed and commented on everything and made any number of suggestions—which I followed. From the start of our relationship in the planning department in 1967, until now, he remains my idea of the consummate professional. When Peter says something is wrong, or right, you can (almost) always count on it. He told me I was wrong lots of times, and he smiled once or twice in what I think was approval. He has helped me enormously. Very few of our accomplishments in San Francisco would have been possible without him.

I needed financial aid to work on this book. Bill Brinton was the person, more than anyone else, who provided it. He also read and commented on some chapters. I could not have taken the summers to work on the manuscript or hired the research assistants without the financial assistance from Bill. His help, like that of everyone else, came without conditions. Janet Fleishhacker was also very helpful to me. I received additional support from the University of California and from Richard Goldman and his wife.

Sallie Walker would have liked this book, not necessarily because of its content but because she was so helpful in her role as administrative assistant of the Department of City and Regional Planning at Berkeley. And the help came to something. I'm sure she saw that as one of her roles—helping the faculty do whatever they want to do. Diann Miller and Susan Groff suffered through all my drafts and with the final manuscript—a lot of work.

Bruce Anderson and Michael Woo met with me early and helped shape the basic structure and format of the book. Bruce continued to review the work, to its improvement. Michael, as my first research assistant, helped to research and sort out all the events of my period as planning director, as well as of the times. He did some fine work on a case study of the northern waterfront as well. Michael's reviews of the early chapters were especially helpful.

I've had great help from research assistants. Phil Deters did the research on the Proposition J (open space) chapter. Leonard Salvato worked on the urban beautification and code enforcement chapters. Matthew Jacobs worked on citations and documentation. Amy Jacobs helped edit some early and all final drafts. Carola Sullam was most helpful as an editor and got me into the spirit of cutting rather than adding text.

Many people were kind enough to read and comment on one or more chapters. That group includes Tom Aidala, Donald Appleyard, Scott Blakey, Barry Checkoway, Bernie Cummings, David Dowall, Richard Gamble, Joan Hockaday, Warren Jones, Rosabeth Kanter, Tom Malloy, Calvin Malone, Roger Montgomery, Harriet Nathan, Don Nelson, Larry Orman, Don Perlgut, Janice Perlman, Lynn Pio, Laurel Robjohn, Stanley Scott, Charna Staten, Barry Stein, Bill Wheaton, George Williams, Frederick Wirt, and Marie Zeller. Howard Nemerovski read the manuscript, too, and helped me with some important changes. The book is better than it would have been without the contributions of all those people.

Bill Wheaton died while this book was in publication. Over a period of 25 years, Bill was my teacher, adviser, colleague, and close, loving friend. I am one of many fortunate people to whom he gave a lot. This book would never have been possible without him.

Beyond all of the above, so many other people in and out of government helped by answering questions and looking up information for me and my assistants. They did not have to. The offices and files of the planning department were always open to me and that was particularly helpful.

Within my family, Amy encouraged, Matthew tolerated, and Janet humored me. Jane was Jane, and that's fine, too.

Jack Sidener prepared the maps and most of the sketches of San Francisco. Barclay G. Jones gave permission to use the sketches that first appeared in a manuscript, *City Design Through Conservation,* Volume

1, that he and Stephen W. Jacobs prepared at the University of California, Berkeley, in 1960. The sketches from that source are on pages 10, 15, 24, 33, 37, 47, 48, and 302. The drawings on pages xix, 61, 71, 85, 116, 120, 204, 205, 210, 212, 215, 220, and 233 are reproduced with the permission of the San Francisco Department of City Planning. Heather Trossman drew the maps that Jack Sidener designed.

# Introduction

Early in 1967, G. Holmes Perkins, Dean of the Graduate School of Fine Arts at the University of Pennsylvania, suggested that I spend some time at the end of each day recording my thoughts as San Francisco's director of city planning. Presumably I would some day write about the experience. Although I never followed this suggestion exactly, I did have good records of my tenure when I resigned almost eight years later. I was not then thinking of writing directly and thoroughly about my experiences, however. Rather, I was intent on preparing a book of case studies that would consider the ways in which city planning responded to a variety of issues within the context of the formal and informal planning mandates given by local government. Using San Francisco cases, I wanted to explore the areas where city planning had been most and least effective and why, and what might improve it. Case studies of the Transamerica building, which I had unsuccessfully opposed, of the successful urban design plan, and of the citywide height and bulk ordinance were to provide the foundations of the book.

In 1975, I described my intentions to Chester Hartman and Ralph Gakenheimer. Chester suggested that I write instead on what it was like to be planning director of San Francisco. That sort of thing hadn't been done, to his knowledge. So Holmes Perkins's idea was recalled.

It was an idea that was consistent with what I had been hearing from students, young professionals, teaching colleagues, and interested nonprofessionals ever since my move to Berkeley. The questions, requests, and challenges I was hearing most often, especially from students, were on the order of "What is it really like?" or "How do things really work?" or "Can you really do anything to solve problems?" or "Did you finally get fed up with the politicians (I can't blame you; you must be glad to be away from it)?" or "Oh, you were one of those guys?" The inquiries have continued. The desire for first hand knowledge and information about urban problems, city planning, and the workings of government seems immense. It is accompanied by a high level of distrust and skepticism, some of which is deserved but much of which is not.

I decided to put the two ideas together into a single book. This book combines case studies of typical issues faced by a city planning department with a personal accounting of the professional, political, and administrative experiences that are bound up with city planning and with being the planning director of a major American city. The case studies, complete in themselves, are kept separate from the more personal "What it's like" chapters. The idea is for the two types of chapters to reinforce each other, so that while the case studies may stand alone, they also may be seen as a part of the larger world of activities, forces, and thoughts in which they happened. At the same time, my views, changing biases, and responses to the total environment stand amidst the more detailed examples of substantive city planning at work. It would be easy, too, to read the whole book as a single case study—of city planning in a generally beloved American city for a period of eight years.

I think the six cases are representative of the kinds of matters city planning customarily deals with at the local level. They range from plans for the physical development of the whole city, to neighborhood planning, to single-building development issues, to zoning, to specific programs for carrying out the plans. They deal with long- and short-range physical development in relation to social and economic issues of the city and its people. The cases also describe the kinds of interactions that take place between a planning department and other agencies, both at the same and at different levels of government. The points of view and roles of various actors who have an impact upon city planning and the development of the city are also considered—the elected and appointed officials, the people acting as individuals or groups, the developers, the press, and certainly the planners themselves.

I have tried to be objective in presenting the cases, recognizing both the strengths and limitations of a participant observer. The emphasis, understandably, is on the activities of the planning department.

Most of the cases represent successes, and in that sense the book is optimistic. That is what "making city planning work" is all about. Certainly there were failures, however, and we can learn from them. I have indicated some of them, and their lessons, in the personal chapters and in one case study. But my sense is that the failures of city planning and of city planners are much more than adequately represented in the other writings about the field.

Most of the case studies follow a similar format. First I define an issue or concern, such as whether or not to permit a specific building or how to best plan and insure quality housing for all. I am concerned here, too, with giving some background to the matter at hand and with pointing out its relation to other city planning matters. The core of each study is a list of questions that I have found useful in exploring a planning issue: How did the planning department respond to or deal with the issue? Were there other possible approaches, and were they considered? Was the matter related to the concerns of other agencies? Who were the most relevant actors in relation to the issue, and what roles did they play in its resolution? Did precedent help determine the outcome? How was the issue resolved (if it was)? Could it have been resolved in some other way (especially for the losers)? What have been its consequences for the development of the city? All of these questions do not apply equally to all the cases, nor does each case follow the format precisely, but that is the approach.

The case studies should be useful to people in other cities who are involved in solving urban problems and in planning and designing their communities. The cases address the potentials and limitations of city planning as they are determined by the particular location of city planning within government, the formal mechanisms that local governments have developed to guide their operations, and the growing influence of other levels of government upon local planning. I have tried to pinpoint the conditions that contributed to the success, partial success, or failure of each planning effort. The cases also speak to what was required to make city planning effective and what might be necessary to make it more so.

While the case studies deal with individual issues, the more personal subjective chapters cover many, many matters: the nature of the times in San Francisco and elsewhere, which is the background for the cases and the activities of the planning department; the political demands that are a part of city planning anywhere; administering a plan-

ning department; dealing with the bureaucracy; and the changing personal viewpoints, relationships, and style of a particular city planner. Many of the same important actors who figured in the case studies appear in these chapters, but here they are described from a more personal point of view. It is recognized that the style and relationships of individuals and of groups may be as important in determining what government does as its formal structure and processes. Finally, the personal chapters include short descriptions of any number of activities and mini-cases that exemplify the activities of the San Francisco planning department over an eight-year period. In short, these chapters try to convey the dynamics of a city planning office, while at the same time noting the conditions, biases, and points of view that affected the cases.

The basic sources of material for the book are publications of the San Francisco Department of City Planning, minutes of meetings, interviews, memorandums, correspondence, newspaper articles, appointment calendars, notes and scribbles, and my memory. That memory, often disturbingly refreshed by the other sources, as well as by colleagues, is the major source for the personal chapters.

I believe that cities ought to be magnificent, beautiful places to live. They should be places where people can be fulfilled, where they can be what they can be, where there are freedom, love, ideas, excitement, quiet, and joy. Cities ought to be the ultimate manifestation of a society's collective achievements. City planning, to me, is the art of helping cities to become and to stay that way.

My philosophy of city planning stems from a belief that a city and its people have both a right and a responsibility to say what they want their community to be—physically, socially, economically, culturally—and then to go out and achieve that community. What follows is an account of some attempts to do that in San Francisco.

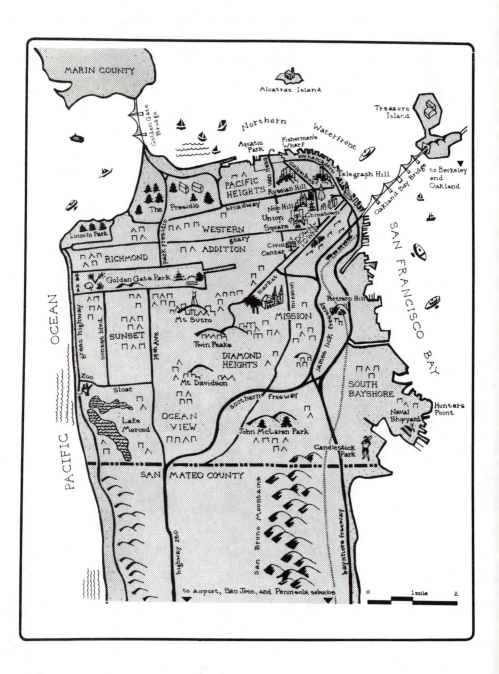

# Chapter 1
# Arriving on the Scene
# and Charting a Course

My first recommendation on a major city planning issue to the San Francisco City Planning Commission was a loser.

At a joint meeting of the planning commission and the San Francisco Redevelopment Agency, held in the formal, wood paneled, heavily draped chambers of the Board of Supervisors in late March 1967, I recommended against changing the plan for the Embarcadero Center section of the Golden Gateway redevelopment project to permit buildings of over 25 stories. The commissioners, who had only recently hired me, voted against my recommendation. Instead, they voted for changes that would permit one building near the waterfront to rise 60 floors and another to jump to over 40 floors. They also voted for a third building that would be exactly 25 stories tall but would stretch two blocks in length; it would create a new Chinese wall in small-scaled San Francisco. The only holdout was a new commissioner who had not been involved in my hiring. He abstained.

A few days later I flew back to Philadelphia, where I was winding up teaching at the University of Pennsylvania, and began to wonder why I had accepted the San Francisco job in the first place. During an earlier visit I had tangled with Justin Herman, director of the Redevelopment Agency, and John Portman, architect-developer for the Embarcadero Center project. We met at the San Francisco Museum of Art, around a model of the proposed project. Portman said that my opinion of his design was subjective and that he didn't see why he should have to be concerned with what I thought. My screaming reply—that as long as the project had to come before the planning department for my recommendation, he had goddamned well better be concerned with my opinion—was not considered friendly.

Then, too, on my first day in the city, I was greeted by a headline announcing that my department, without first informing either the planning commission or its new director, had just made public a report stating its opposition to any future freeway construction in the city. While the conclusion may have been reasonable, the report was less than perfect; and as a new boy in town I was not looking to make instant enemies among bureaucrats like the director of public works or the chamber of commerce.

At first glance, the staff seemed a mixed blessing in terms of quality and the caution with which they received me. After meeting with the head of Civil Service, I was left with the impression that he was serious about my not having any say over hiring and firing. Indeed, I was to learn very shortly that I might not even be able to fire an employee who was on probation, a period during which I supposedly had absolute authority.

The wonders of living in San Francisco were beginning to look overrated too. For a while it seemed as though it might be cheaper to move my $35,000 house from Philadelphia to the West Coast than to buy a house in the city. Why then was I leaving the University of Pennsylvania—where I had been tempted to stay with the offer of a tenured full professorship and a good deal of money—to become director of the San Francisco Department of City Planning?

There were reasons of course. Not the least of them was simple, old-fashioned ego satisfaction. In late 1966, when I was first contacted about the position, I was about to finish my thirty-eighth year. I felt that I had served my apprenticeship as a city planner. Twelve years earlier I had earned my graduate degree in city planning from the University of Pennsylvania. After studying new towns in England for a year, I had learned the nuts and bolts of my craft and art in Cleveland, Pittsburgh, and Calcutta. Teaching had permitted me the opportunity of reflecting upon those experiences, and I had an intense feeling—nothing more than that—that I knew how to do city planning. I had been fortunate to work with some inspired and outstanding people, and now it was time to try my own hand. I told my friend, Dave Wallace, an incredibly gifted city planner, that I wanted a shot at being boss. He was sympathetic, but he couldn't resist throwing in a gratuitous "You never are."

San Francisco itself had something to do with my decision to go there. I had enjoyed myself immensely on three brief visits in the late fifties and early sixties. The hills, the views, the climate, the water, the street activity, the bridges, the small-scaled but intensely urban development—all these created an impression of an extremely livable city, unlike so many of its eastern counterparts. San Francisco was a city I wanted to live in.

More important to my decision was the nature of the times. The middle and late sixties were days of urban riots and long, hot summers. After years of unfulfilled promises, the minorities and the poor were tired of waiting. They wanted their share. They were intent, too, on making such phrases as "maximum feasible participation" mean what they said. In 1965, on a French beach, on the way home after two years in Calcutta, I read about the rioting in Watts. Watts was followed by dozens of other riots in major cities, and San Francisco was not immune. A black teenager in Hunter's Point was fatally shot by a policeman on September 27, 1966. In the aftermath of that shooting, the city went through what some call its worst outbreak of racial violence, complete with shooting, the National Guard, fires, and looting. Eighty arrests were made. The violence subsided within a day or two, but the tension remained.

In 1966, then, it seemed more important to be doing city planning than to be teaching it. City planning had to be made meaningful to the lives of all the people of a community. It had to help solve their problems and help satisfy their needs, especially those related to social justice. I believed then that I should and could help solve some urban problems and that I could do this best by being where the action was.

Another issue concerned me as well. That was the matter of making planning relevant within the decision-making process of local government. In the early fifties, when I was in school, city planning seemed to be an important part of government in cities like Cleveland, Detroit, Philadelphia, Cincinnati, Chicago, New York, and Pittsburgh. I was left with the impression that real attention was given to the city planners' plans; that roads got built where planners said they should be; that parks, playgrounds, schools, and other public facilities had a good chance of being built if they were part of a public plan; that programs conceived by planners to help eliminate social inequities would become reality; and that city planners not only talked to but were listened to by mayors and councilmen, who sought and welcomed their advice on all sorts of matters related to the development and well-being of their communities. My early experiences in Cleveland, where Mayor Anthony Celebrezze regularly met with and listened to his planners (even young ones like me just out of school), supported my belief in the efficacy of planning. "Plans that gather dust on the shelves" was not yet a universally known phrase.

But by the mid-1960s things had changed. It seemed possible then to count on the fingers of one hand the communities where city planning was relevant to decision making. Urban renewal agencies, not planning departments, had the money and power and they "got things done." If a citywide plan existed, it was likely to be changed to conform to the dictates of a marketable redevelopment project. But the redevelopment project was rarely changed to carry out the policies of a master plan. Except in a few cities—Philadelphia was the shining example—planning departments were more often to be bypassed than consulted. That, at least, was the way it seemed to me in December 1966, when I was trying to make up my mind about this job. And so there was the challenge of making city planning work in San Francisco, a city where I had the impression, right or wrong, that it did not.

I had also heard from friends both in the East and in California that the staff of the San Francisco Department of City Planning was less than outstanding. Morale was low, the staff was occupied almost exclusively with zoning matters, and civil service regulations made it nearly impossible to hire competent people or to fire the incompetent ones. Although I wasn't sure that any of this was true—it simply could not be all that bad—I wanted the chance to build and to keep a high-quality staff.

Few, if any of these reasons were so clear to me during the period of initial contact, interviews, negotiations, job offer, and acceptance that took place between October 1966 and late January 1967. Some of them may not have been fully formed in my own mind at the start of that strange dance that takes place between employer and employee when each is eyeing and posturing for the other, deciding how close he wants to come or can afford to get. Certainly, however, the members of the planning commission were aware that they were considering a person whose self-image was that of a comprehensive physical planner and urban designer, strongly committed to responding to the needs of people, especially minorities, and greatly concerned about the changing physical shape of San Francisco.[1]

My own impressions of the position were mixed. Discussions with respected colleagues on both coasts did not suggest that San Francisco represented a golden opportunity for a city planner. It was considered a good place to live but not one in which to accomplish much profes-

sionally. The mayor, John Shelley, was not as strong or action-oriented as some would like. He had been a long-term congressman, and it was said of him that he had anticipated returning to the city he loved as an honored son and that he had not been used to an active executive life. On the other hand, T. J. Kent, Jr., then the mayor's deputy for development, held that Shelley wanted and would support a strong planning director. Jack Kent, who himself had been planning director in the late 1940s, was quietly enthusiastic about all the things that could be done. Justin Herman of the Redevelopment Agency, reigning power figure in the development-planning arena, was cordial at first, but he seemed suspicious of city planners. He neither encouraged nor discouraged me. The only person outside of government who was encouraging about the position was John Hirten of the San Francisco Planning and Urban Renewal Association (SPUR); he was said to be the person most responsible for driving out the previous planning director. I sought him out and concluded that city planning might have a much needed ally. He seemed to want strong planning, and he indicated that SPUR would be supportive.

Presumably, the planning commission had found in me someone who came reasonably close to meeting the requirements stated for the job: professional integrity, leadership, imagination, executive and technical ability, and respect for San Francisco's unique qualities.[2] But still, my negotiations with the planning commission were not entirely successful. Some of the most important considerations—those relating to budget, additional staff, and the power to make key staff appointments without screwing around with civil service—were vague. I had promises of support after I arrived, but these were not assurances of the sort one could put in a vault.

Clearly, then, ego satisfaction plus a sense of this being the right thing to do at the right time had to be the major reasons for my move to San Francisco.

It would be nice to report that a newly appointed executive of a major city department knew upon arrival what issues he would have to deal with and how best to organize himself and his office; in short, how to go about doing the job he was hired to do. Nice, but untrue. In the early going, desire, energy, and blissful ignorance of local methods and customs were more operative than knowledge of what to do and how to do it. That was the way it was during the first months as I tried to understand San Francisco and chart a course for the future amidst the flow of new and urgent issues that demanded my attention.

Any account of my early years in San Francisco is bound to appear much more orderly than in fact was the case. Unfortunately, major issues do not occur in sequence, let alone in an order that might be convenient. It is not always possible to determine the work program before dealing with an immediate land-use issue, and the development of programs in a minority neighborhood happens at the same time as a hundred other activities that are taking place in the planning agency and the neighborhood. Concurrent and often unrelated events are more the norm than a reporting of them might imply, and a decision as to how best to do the job may derive as much or more from an unordered sequence of experiences as from prior knowledge of what is required.

No one plans a city alone. It takes a good-sized staff to run a city planning department and to make the day-to-day decisions that are needed. In 1967, there were 62 permanent employees in the San Francisco Department of City Planning. My initial assessment, based on their resumes, comments they made at staff meetings, and personal contacts, was that they were indeed a mixed lot.

On the one hand, there were a few extremely bright, dedicated, experienced, and well-trained professionals. They were underpaid and overworked, and sometimes they were abused by the public and even by their colleagues. I wondered often what kept them at their jobs. Their presence, I concluded, reflected a value system, too seldom found, that says public service is the noblest calling and that it deserves the best. This group was augmented by four or five equally talented, although untrained and inexperienced, young people. They were full of social and environmental concerns and willing to try their hands at anything. Although sometimes it seemed that the charms of daily living, sailing, skiing, camping, and carousing, were at least as important to them as something called city planning, they were willing to learn.

Together, both groups—the top-notch pros and the eager novices—were knowledgeable about the legal and regulatory aspects of planning, about urban policy as it related to equity for minorities and poor people, about housing, and about analytical methods. I could see a budding strength in urban design and an appreciation of San Francisco's physical environment. But they knew little about transportation planning, economic analysis, fiscal planning, and comprehensive land-use planning—a real shortcoming, since the latter was our primary responsibility.

There was another strength worthy of note: the drafting and graphics people. Beaten down by years of abuse and lack of opportunity to show their stuff, they could nevertheless undertake major map-related research, prepare publications, and in general communicate graphically with the best. But they weren't advertising their skills. It would be up to a new director to recognize their abilities and prove himself with them.

So much for quality. It was matched by mediocrity and some incompetence. One planner insisted that it was impossible to analyze neighborhood traffic properly without having lived in the neighborhood for at least a year. A demographer related local population projections to famine in India centuries ago. Some had problems in writing the English language and in adding columns of figures. More numerous were those who could not follow directions, could not complete assignments, and could not direct subordinates. Among this group were senior people, some of whom seemed to have been there forever and to have reached their protected civil service slots by reason of endurance rather than merit. Other than dreaming about their removal, there was nothing to be done about these people. By far the largest group was made up of those who were neither good nor bad. Some simply suffered from an inadequate education. Others were showing the strains and insecurities that develop when talents are unappreciated and unrecognized. Years earlier, one staff member had proposed an underground freeway where the monstrous, never-to-be-completed Embarcadero freeway now stands. For his daring he was publicly chastised by his director with words to the effect of "How can I do my job when I have staff that proposes stuff like this?" So they came to work every day and did their jobs, but without spark or enthusiasm. Maybe it would be possible to light a few fires among them.

It was among the most senior positions that the highest levels of incompetence were to be found. The catch was that tenured employees could not be removed. Civil service practices gave them an insurmountable advantage for most higher level positions. Since most of the administrators found it psychologically impossible to dismiss unqualified younger people during their periods of probation—the time when they could be terminated—the staff was pretty much locked in, except for lower level positions and the few so-called specialty positions.

If one were to think hard about the problems of getting and keeping a high-quality city planning staff in San Francisco, one could reasonably conclude that to do so is legally impossible. It became clear that I would have to capitalize on low-level openings, filling them with top-notch young people who would forgo the better salaries paid elsewhere in favor of exciting and socially relevant work. I also would have to try to make the few new senior openings specialty positions that could be filled from the outside. I intended to elevate two of the most senior positions, which were then vacant, to the level of assistant director; the new positions would be equal with the one assistant director slot that already existed. In conjunction with this last move, and in order to have a semblance of power consistent with my responsibilities, it was decided to ask for an amendment that would make the three assistant director positions and the administrative assistant post appointive by the director, rather than filling them through civil service hiring mechanisms. That charter amendment was to be listed on the November ballot as "Proposition J."

Issues will not always wait until there is sufficient staff to give them adequate attention; as often as not, they must be dealt with on their own time schedule. It is also true that the only thing new about a city planning department with a new director is the new director. The old issues that require decisions and recommendations do not disappear as if by magic because of his presence. Neither do the staff members sit around doing nothing until the new director shows up; they are committed to and engaged in substantive planning efforts that must be understood and, if possible, directed.

There was no dearth of issues that required immediate attention and resolution in the last half of 1967. From late May until the end of the year over 100 official actions were taken by the city planning commission that required some kind of staff recommendation. They ranged from approval of a proposal for major rezoning of the downtown area ( it took two and one-half years of staff work to prepare for this decision) to disapproval of a plan for a downtown garage, to endorsement, with reservations, of the city-centered regional plan of the Association of Bay Area Governments. This says nothing, of course, of the myriad matters that required meetings with the mayor (about ways to modernize the municipal transit system), with the Board of Supervisors (O'Shaughnessy Boulevard should be rebuilt), with other city officials (about the accuracy of the information on housing vacancy that was being used to determine the pace of the redevelopment program), with developers and their representatives ("I cannot support the International Market Center as you propose it"), and with citizen groups (the Model Cities program seems reasonable in the South Bayshore).

The downtown zoning study, which had been prepared by the staff with the aid of consultants, was probably the most pressing matter to come before the planning commission during this early period. The zoning that it called for downtown was more restrictive and more finely drawn than the existing zoning.[3] Among the more significant proposals were these: allow less space for prime office and commercial development and direct such development toward planned transit improvements and away from residential and historic areas; offer development bonuses in exchange for such privately built conveniences as plazas and direct access to transit; reduce development intensities; and, for the first time, impose height restrictions in some critical areas. Although there was no explicit downtown plan to which the proposed zoning was tied, it soon became apparent that the zoning staff did have some kind of implicit plan in mind. It was clear, for example, that they were trying to create a more compact, transit-oriented downtown; that they wanted to maintain retail shopping continuity where it was strongest;

that they wanted to keep parking away from the center of downtown; and that they wanted to lower drastically the number and size of office buildings that could be built under existing zoning. In any case, it would be untoward for a new director to suggest that after years of staff work, adoption of the new ordinance should be postponed until a plan was prepared.

I learned quite a bit about San Francisco and its people during the public hearings and negotiations. For one thing, I learned that the chamber of commerce was extremely well funded and had a large staff. It had extensive associations with elected officials, commissioners, architects, and the media, and it was understandably opposed to constraints on development. Bigger is better was the prevailing philosophy at the chamber. Government should keep its hands off. Although that position was predictable, the chamber's strength was a modest surprise. More surprising was the philosophy of the committee of the local chapter of the American Institute of Architects that was monitoring the proposed ordinance. Its chairman and some of its members seemed philosophically in tune with Ayn Rand's Howard Roark and were at heart opposed to any zoning. Later, I was to find that this committee was not wholly representative.

Others voiced opinions too. Chinatown business interests were looking ahead to opportunities for future development (and profits) by

replacing modest structures (that housed poor Chinese) with new high rises. They were not above claiming, through the Human Rights Commission, that the proposed height restrictions would cause hardship to low-income people. Organized labor demanded that the new zoning eliminate the low paying, nonunion garment shops of Chinatown. Over and over I was surprised to learn that this property owner and that lawyer knew individual planning commissioners, not necessarily in any improper or conspiratorial sense, but as schoolmates, club members, neighbors, or old acquaintances. It seemed a very small city.

Hundreds of people and organizations made their views known, but only a few, notably SPUR and the Telegraph Hill Dwellers, tried to speak for the whole city, or for good planning, or for moderation. To a city planner who had previously paid little attention to zoning and who had spoken in favor of all possible discretion being given to planning commissions and their staffs, it now seemed that perhaps zoning was indeed very important in San Francisco and that, given the kinds of pressures that could be brought to bear in favor of development, the less discretion the better. In the end, the staff members who had been assigned to the zoning issue had done their homework and had solid responses to most criticisms. It was not too difficult for a new director to champion the proposals, and after what seemed like minimal compromises, to achieve unanimity by the commission. In June it approved the proposed downtown zoning ordinance and sent it on to the Board of Supervisors for more hearings and for final action.[4] That action was to take some time in coming.

The downtown zoning issue was only one of many city planning issues that were to be publicly debated during 1967. The widening and realignment of a narrow, winding road through a canyon excited the vehement opposition of neighborhood residents. The Department of Public Works had once sited this canyon for a freeway. It made no difference to the residents that the Department of City Planning had in fact significantly reduced the scale of the traffic engineers' proposal, required additional landscaping, and redesigned the road in a way that would make a future freeway impossible. The residents were against the road, period. And some didn't believe that the city would build it in accord with the new drawings in any case. Another brouhaha occurred over the prospect of either a tunnel or a second bridge to parallel the Golden Gate Bridge. Just about everyone, except perhaps the state highway engineers, agreed that that was a lousy idea.

Sometimes decisions slipped by almost unnoticed. That was the case when the site of a new multistory health center was approved. It was to be located over a street and in the air space over a tunnel entrance, thereby blocking some fine public views of San Francisco Bay. A planning director, however new, should have known better than to approve such a site; he should have cared less about being overruled by one of his commissioners, the city's chief administrative officer.

The staff and the commission joined in opposing a large parking garage near the new Bank of America building on the grounds that its location in the downtown core would increase congestion. Similarly, the commission and ultimately the Board of Supervisors agreed with the staff that the city should purchase for a park the dramatic and historic Sutro Baths/Cliff House area at the city's western extreme, rather than allowing it to be developed privately. But when the park was placed on the ballot, supporters could not get the two-thirds majority needed to carry a bond issue. During the same period the planning commission approved a staff application to the Department of Housing and Urban Development for Urban Beautification funds, and it approved my attempts to have the South Bayshore area designated as a Model Cities area under the new HUD program. But the people of the South Bayshore, at least those who represented the community in meetings, would have nothing to do with the Model Cities program. To them it was just another name for urban redevelopment, or it was being rammed down their throats, or they were not guaranteed enough control. So, in November 1967, when 63 of 193 applicant cities were designated as Model Cities areas, San Francisco was not among them.

At the beginning of that same summer of 1967 (people have described it as the "summer of love" in the Haight-Ashbury), the Landmarks Preservation Advisory Board held its first meeting. Few realized at the time that it was an indication of growing concern for preserving the unique character of the city.

Less public, in the sense that no immediate public decisions were required, was a series of planning studies that accounted for most of the time of the staff. Taken together, these studies represented the department's work program although no such formal designation may have been given to what the staff was doing.

One of these studies was a major planning study of the northern waterfront area that was under way during this time by two consultants to the planning department, John S. Bolles Associates and the Arthur D.

Little Company. The northern waterfront was by far the most visible, accessible, and controversial stretch of San Francisco's shoreline. It was still an active maritime center, albeit one with less than adequate port facilities and a number of rotting piers. In addition, it was the site of such prominent landmarks as the Ferry Building, Fisherman's Wharf, and the Ghirardelli Square shopping complex. The waterfront was under the jurisdiction of the Port Commission, a state agency. However, the California attorney general had ruled recently that nonmaritime uses being contemplated in this area would have to comply with the city's land-use restrictions. A citizens advisory committee had been assembled by the consultants and the staff to guide the planning efforts. In this controversial area, an early and continuing battleground between conservationists and developers, it was clear that staff direction of the consultants who had already been hired to conduct the study was meek and inadequate and that the matter would require considerable personal involvement.

The South Bayshore study had also been committed before my arrival, but it was more to my liking. Located at the extreme southeast corner of the city, the South Bayshore is one of the least known parts of San Francisco although it contains Candlestick Park, the big naval shipyard, and Hunter's Point, the scene of the 1966 riot. The area was also the site of a major new redevelopment effort. Approximately 35,000 people lived in the South Bayshore area, most of them black, many of them poor.

Staff involvement, encouraged by Jack Kent in the mayor's office, represented a very recent commitment to neighborhood planning and citizen participation and an attempt to do planning in areas where it was most needed and might prove most relevant. The first staff-initiated general community meeting, arranged to seek people's involvement and to introduce the new director of city planning, was informative—many people in attendance had never heard of the Department of City Planning. Many of those who had seemed to think it was part of the Redevelopment Agency. They assumed that our object was to expand the local redevelopment projects already in the planning stages and to ensure the removal of additional families. The nature of the questions and the demands led me to conclude that few high ranking city officials had ever been to a neighborhood meeting. Indeed, one speaker said that I was just there for the publicity and that people had better make their demands known then because they weren't likely ever to see me again. It was a long, noisy meeting with lots of shouting, insults, testing, and some hostility. It was the first of many such meetings.

The planning department staff was involved in a number of housing studies during this period. One was an analysis, requested by the mayor's office, of the statistical accuracy of a Redevelopment Agency report on the availability of housing for people displaced by redevelopment projects. On its own, the staff was preparing the first yearly report on changes in the city's housing stock. The report "Changes in the San Francisco Housing Inventory—1967," issued in March 1968, proved to be successful in pinpointing the kinds of housing that were in fact being eliminated as well as the housing that was being provided throughout the city.

One member of the staff was working on an elaborate computerized "housing model" that was part of a large, federally funded undertaking of the mid-1960s. It was supposed to show policy makers how their proposed actions would affect housing in San Francisco. Although it was pronounced operational in late 1966, the model was extremely complicated and very expensive to run. There was some question as to just how useful it was. Moreover, the model was understood by only one employee, Peter Groat. He was trying to simplify the thing and work out the bugs, and patiently explain the whole matter to a skeptical new boss.

Aside from a major effort to prepare a citywide transportation plan, virtually no comprehensive planning was going on. The existing master plan was outdated and inadequate, although its preparation and maintenance were supposed to be primary reasons for the existence of the department. There seemed to be very little demand for a revision and probably not enough staff talent to undertake such a big project. Instead, I began exploring possible sources of financial support for a citywide urban design study.

Closer to the action, the planning department, which had worked with the Bureau of Building Inspection to designate the city's first Federally Assisted Code Enforcement areas, was now consulting with area residents on the detailed planning and design of the public improvements that would coincide with private housing rehabilitation.

During this period the assistant planning director was heading something called the Market Street Transit Task Force. This was a small group specially organized to coordinate city relations with the Bay Area Rapid Transit District (BART), as it prepared to build San Francisco's

share of the new regional subway system, tearing up Market Street for new tunnels and stations. The task force was responsible for the work of a team of consultants that was preparing plans for the design of a new Market Street, to be realized when construction was completed. The task force worked under the direction of a group that included the heads of all city departments that might have anything to do with construction of BART. The group, which met every Tuesday morning, included the planning director as one of its members. I was assigned by Mayor Shelley to act as client on all design matters related to the Market Street construction. I took this assignment to mean that I was to have the last word, as far as the mayor was concerned, on matters of aesthetics and also that I could participate directly with the consultants in design.

Boredom was not a problem during those early months in San Francisco.

In addition to finding out what the staff was doing and beginning to direct its efforts, it was important to get to know San Francisco and its people. I learned about the city more in weekend walks and quick visits to particular sites that were at issue than by making use of the blocks of office time that I reserved for that purpose. Unscheduled—but always "urgent"—meetings with this official or that group often intruded on time scheduled for field trips.

Getting to know the people of San Francisco seemed no task at all. Their attendance and participation at planning commission meetings, especially at hearings on zoning issues, was remarkable, much greater than I had experienced elsewhere. They even attended general meetings and committee meetings of the Board of Supervisors in considerable numbers. Once there, they had few reservations about speaking their piece, not hesitating to castigate the processes of government that denied them adequate participation. Beyond these formal meetings, many people acting as individuals or as part of a group found no problem in telephoning their concerns to the planning director or in coming to the office for meetings. Accessibility was as important for me as it was for them.

Many of the neighborhood associations that abound in the city sought out the new planning director either to ask him to speak or to let him know early in his tenure what their problems were and what they might want. I do not recall declining an invitation to a neighborhood association meeting during the period. I tried to be as informal as possible, to ask and to answer questions about the concerns of the residents, and to find out what they thought the department should be doing. The only problem with the neighborhood meetings was that there were few invitations from minority or poor neighborhoods. But even so, these meetings taught me more about the city than any other source.

The press was a major source of information about San Francisco. Not noted for quality in their national or world news coverage, the *San Francisco Chronicle* and *San Francisco Examiner* nonetheless gave reasonably thorough and accurate coverage to local events and concerns. I would later find out, however, that the general astuteness, accuracy, and fairness of the stories about the planning department were not necessarily repeated in the coverage that other departments and issues received.

From all these sources, as well as from discussions with public officials, reflections on the results of recent elections, and observation of the actions of the Board of Supervisors, it was possible over a four- or five-month period to get a sense of the major issues in San Francisco. Most significant was the issue of citizen distrust. Simply put, it appeared that there were very few public officials that people trusted. The reason for the distrust was not entirely clear, but it had something to do with promises unfulfilled; with a growing awareness that the data and projections of the technicians were sometimes inaccurate and always subject to divergent interpretations; and with a sense that the process of physical, social, and economic change was almost out of control.

Housing was a major issue. There simply was not enough housing at prices that people could afford, especially for the poor and for minorities—in San Francisco mainly blacks, Chicanos, and Chinese. The problem was made worse by the dislocation of low-income, minority families, especially blacks, that was brought about by freeway construction and the redevelopment program. The excesses of the redevelopment program were in large measure responsible for the coalitions of moderate- and low-income people organized to stop it, for the alertness of the neighborhood associations to anything that smacked of renewal, and for the high degree of public awareness about all housing matters.

Transportation was another issue. San Franciscans had made it clear that they wanted no more freeways. In what has been called the country's first major freeway revolt, the Board of Supervisors rejected a federal expenditure of some $280 million to complete two of them, the Embarcadero and the Central.[5] The anti-highway forces looked at almost any proposed roadway change with jaundiced eyes—"It's a freeway in disguise!"—and were convinced that improved public transit was the only solution. At the same time, the city's gridiron street pattern, together with what seemed to me as excessively wide streets with little or no landscaping, invited auto traffic and made many streets unpleasant and unsafe places to be. Neighborhoods with streets like that seemed less than totally desirable places to live and therefore vulnerable to competition from the suburbs. I said as much at early neighborhood meetings.

In perhaps no other major American city was urban design a significant issue. For those few not already aware that this was an extremely attractive and joyful place to live, well-publicized surveys showed San Francisco to be just about every American tourist's favorite city. Residents, especially those living in the most favored locations, were alert to building proposals that offended them, and they were prepared to do public battle to stop them.

Unemployment was another issue. As in other central cities, manufacturing was giving way to service or office industries, leaving blue-collar workers without jobs. Again, the hardest hit were the minorities, who were also the least mobile. Union representatives called for a major effort to stop the outward flow of manufacturing industries.

Finally, zoning was a continuing issue, not in a citywide sense but in that many, many individual proposals for change, often initiated by someone wanting to develop property at a greater density than was permitted under the zoning code, were hotly contested. These contests involved considerable effort by all parties concerned, including representations by lawyers, architects, and other professionals, and they often filled the hearing chambers to overflowing. Five to 10 cases were heard at the first planning commission meeting of each month.

The backdrop for these issues was a governmental and political structure that was new and strange to me. It seemed a naive and cumbersome government, hardly suited to efficient, contemporary methods of management, and incapable of being responsive to the kinds of issues that demanded attention. Nor was it clear in this supposedly nonpartisan government whether top elected officials were void of strong leadership qualities or if they were indeed without significant power. Mayor Shelley's staff was unusually small, with four or five assistants at best. In my few meetings with the mayor and other department executives, he gave few orders and was undemanding of actions or programs. Although department heads seemed knowing and confident when I met with them alone, many appeared uneasy in the mayor's presence, and I wondered what, if anything, was going to happen as a result of the decisions made in that office. By far the strongest presence was that of Chief Administrative Officer Tom Mellon—red-faced, white-haired, the epitome of everyone's favorite, kindly, political father figure. A goodly number of the city's operating departments were under him, and, as an ex officio member of the planning commission, he was reserved a seat of honor, which he usually filled, at meetings of the Board of Supervisors.

If public officials appeared strong and confident in the mayor's office or in meetings with their peers, they were clearly less confident when asked to testify before the Board of Supervisors. Despite their reputed job security they often stood mute before outlandish attacks by a few board members. Perhaps power did not reside with the civil servants. Or were they just being smart by holding their tongues?

The 11-member Board of Supervisors, with six or seven conservative downtown business and development-oriented members, might have been quite typical of the governing boards of many large cities, but it also seemed rather incongruous in a city that was then giving birth to the "hippies." Except for their antifreeway position, most of the supervisors did not see the issues I did during this period. Although members of the board were then without individual staff aides, most of them were remarkably accessible. One phone call was usually all that was required.

Most notable to me were the rules under which all these people operated. The *Charter of the City and County of San Francisco* is a long document.[6] It goes on for over 300 pages, dealing with such matters as the cable car routes and the compensation to be given planning commissioners for their attendance at meetings ($15). It requires a line-item budget form that tells a citizen how much a department will spend for janitorial services but says almost nothing about the duties and responsibilities of that department. Departments did not have the flexibility to transfer allotted funds from one purpose to another. I was reminded that the charter says that elected officials may not meddle in the affairs of a department under penalty of being removed from office. Over and over again one heard, "The charter says . . . ," in response to "Why doesn't someone do this or that?" It took a vote of the people to change any part of the document. I read the parts related to the department of city planning, but I have to admit that I never got around to reading the rest.

I was coming to the conclusion that no one had much power in San Francisco. This was a situation that did not coincide with my preconceptions about government, especially the need for local government to be responsive. There was a naive, textbook nature to it all, hardly "big city." It was the kind of government about which a newcomer might shake his head in disbelief and smile, as yet unaware that he was comfortable within it.

I end my account of the period in November of 1967—but not because there was a local election in that month, or because the honeymoon was drawing to a close. There was no honeymoon. If anything, my first months in San Francisco might be termed a period of discovering new hurdles at every turn, each one apparently invented to keep a new planning director from doing his job. But I was much too busy, working much too hard, experiencing too much that was new, and too full of energy and thoughts of the future to be anything but optimistic.The period ends in November because the department's work program and budget were due for review and approval by the planning commission at the end of the year. In San Francisco fashion, this work program was not to take effect until the following July. It would take that long to run the budget maze. Nevertheless, its preparation was a chance to say where I wanted the department to go and how I proposed to get there.

The work program and budget that I presented were directed as much as possible to the issues as I had observed them, toward being relevant to the extent that the planning department could have an impact on the issues without slighting ongoing responsibilities. To do this, we would have to be responsive to immediate issues as well as to matters that could be addressed only over a period of many years. Also, we would try to address the issues at the geographic scale that would be most appropriate and that promised the greatest results, from a city-wide scale, to projects for individual neighborhoods, to improvements for one block.[7]

The budget reflected a major commitment to planning and to the development of action-oriented programs at the neighborhood or district level. Our South Bayshore effort would continue as our most important neighborhood work because it set a pattern for future department projects. We proposed to undertake major new planning studies in the mixed residential, commercial, and industrial area south of downtown, as well as to become actively involved in Chinatown. Neighborhood improvement plans and programs would be utilized as extensively as possible, using federally funded conservation and beautification programs as the basis for needed public and private actions. Our increased face-to-face involvement with people at the neighborhood level would also address the issue of citizen distrust.

At a citywide scale, at least nine proposed studies were directly or indirectly related to housing issues. These ranged from surveys to determine the vacancy and turnover rates of all types of housing units to the drafting of policies and programs that would serve as the housing element of a new, citywide, comprehensive plan. Our involvement with urban redevelopment projects would be minimal. I was convinced that the Redevelopment Agency's approach to renewal was unsound, and clearly there was growing citizen disenchantment and fear of the program. Nevertheless, the agency had all the marbles. It had a large, high-quality staff; it had money; it had political and media support; and its staffers knew their way around city hall. Unfortunately, there was no way of becoming a colleague of the agency's director without also becoming his servant. We would, therefore, try to stand apart from the city's redevelopment efforts, instead assembling information about housing that anyone could use and developing separate programs, such as those related to slum prevention. Slowly, we would attempt to build a fence around the Redevelopment Agency's power and influence.

In response to the issues that were related to the city's appearance, we proposed to prepare an urban design plan for the physical development of San Francisco.

Other items in the work program that we proposed were directed to additional issues that had been identified. We did not propose to solve all the problems we saw, but we would keep our senses alert for opportunities to solve them.

The budget we proposed for the 1968-69 fiscal year was almost $1,300,000, as compared to the existing $772,000 allotted to the department for the 1967-68 fiscal year. I felt reasonably confident that we would get the new professional, secretarial, and drafting staff that we needed. It would be possible, I hoped, to infuse the new as well as the existing staff with enthusiasm. The passage of Proposition J, which would amend the city charter at the upcoming city election, would make it possible to select my key professionals and administrators. Only one or two labor representatives had spoken against the measure, and their arguments were unconvincing. Any number of officials had supported it. There were good reasons to feel confident about the future.

Proposition J lost handily. I was told that a local state assemblyman, John Burton, or his congressman brother in Washington, Phillip, had included a "Vote No on J" statement in a mailing sent the weekend before people went to the polls. Apparently, I had sponsored an anti-labor measure in a very prolabor town. On the brighter side, the election resulted in a Board of Supervisors with a six-member majority that was expected to be sympathetic to city planning as an important activity of government and to a planner's point of view. Finally, San Francisco would have a new mayor, Joseph Alioto. I knew nothing about him and was not to meet him until late November. The mayor would have the opportunity to select a new planning commission and with it a new planning director if he chose. It was reasonable to expect that some commissioners would change, but I did not expect to lose my new job and gave the matter little or no thought. I was more interested in looking to the future.

# Notes

1. The point is made clear in a letter from the author to T. J. Kent, Jr., on November 10, 1966. Jack Kent, then Mayor Shelley's deputy for development, was helping the planning commission in its search for a new director. All contacts at this point were with him.

2. "City Planning Commission Policy Statement on Qualifications of New Director of Planning," September 22, 1966, prepared by Jack Kent.

3. San Francisco Department of City Planning, *The San Francisco Downtown Zoning Study Final Report,* December 1966. For a more detailed description of the downtown zoning ordinance, see "San Francisco: The Downtown Development Bonus System," in *The New Zoning: Legal, Administrative, and Economic Concepts and Techniques,* Norman Marcus and Marilyn W. Groves, eds. (New York: Praeger, 1970).

4. City Planning Commission Resolution No. 6109, June 29, 1967.

5. "The Freeway Crisis Is Back," *San Francisco Chronicle,* February 20, 1966.

6. *The Charter of the City and County of San Francisco,* 1972 printing.

7. San Francisco Department of City Planning, *Proposals for the San Francisco Department of City Planning,* December 1967.

# Chapter 2
# City Planning in the Context
# Of Local Government

It is important to understand that city planning does not happen in a vacuum. For the most part it happens as a part of local government. It is an activity of government in the sense that city planning is done by a government or its agents, and in the sense that government is intimately involved in encouraging, permitting, denying, modifying, or putting conditions on what individuals, groups, or institutions plan and build. The purposes, responsibilities, and constraints of city planning are stipulated by local governments acting as agents of the state. To a considerable extent, then, the approach, methods, process, and ultimate effectiveness of city planning are determined by a local government. And at least some of the powers and limitations of local government are inherent in its organizational structure. That is the case in San Francisco.

San Francisco is a small city. Its 45.4 square miles make it about one-tenth the size of Los Angeles, one-fifth the size of Chicago, and less than one-sixth the size of New York. It is not surrounded by suburban development in the usual city-suburb sense. Rather, it is bounded on three sides by water and on the fourth by largely undeveloped hills. The boundaries of the city are thus remarkably clear. It is delineated and visible as an entity within the much larger Bay metropolitan region. It is the cultural and economic focal point of the Bay area, with its roughly 4.6 million people.[1]

The population of the city hovers around 700,000. That makes it the second most dense city in the country, with almost 16,000 people

per square mile. That's a lot less than New York's density of over 26,000, but slightly more than Chicago's and Philadelphia's. The density is achieved, by and large, by intense but low development of small parcels.

San Francisco's people are known to be diverse, ethnically, racially, and a lot of other ways as well. The proportions of older people and of young adults are higher than in most cities. Its people are tolerant of new ideas and diverse living styles yet feisty over issues that bother them. They are active in their own government.

It is relatively easy for San Franciscans to know all or most of their city. It is a small, understandable whole that is easily thought of as a unit as well as in terms of many small, overlapping neighborhoods. City hall can be reached quickly from most parts of the city by public transportation. This means that government is physically accessible and visible and in turn may help account for people's willingness to participate.

San Francisco operates under a charter whose primary concern appears to be honesty. When it was adopted in 1931, the charter was both a response to the issues of the time (most notably corruption) and a product of the notions about the desired nature of local government that were generally held then. Under the previous charter it had been possible for members of the Board of Supervisors, the policy-making arm of government, to conduct city business themselves, directly, and they apparently availed themselves of that opportunity. There were no central purchasing or accounting mechanisms—in short, the process of government was open to manipulation of a questionable nature and to mismanagement.[2] It was understandable that the voters, in approving a new charter, wanted to prevent future corruption. At the same time, this was an era when it was held to be possible and desirable to keep partisan politics out of local government and a time when many people looked to the prospect of efficient, professional management of their governments, management that they thought would resemble that of large corporations. A commitment to prevent the excesses of the past combined with a desire for a more ideal structure and process of government to produce the present charter.

It was a charter designed to keep public officials from going astray. It produced what could be termed a no-power-to-anyone form of government. The most significant powers that the mayor has relate to appointments and the budget. Other executive powers are widely dispersed among a host of elected and appointed officials, apparently to prevent the accumulation and abuse of power by any one person or department. We will see that any number of checks and balances are built into the process of government in order to assure deliberation and honesty. Under conditions of the late 1960s and 1970s, power was so dispersed that some might have called San Francisco's government a mild form of institutionalized anarchy.

An opposite view to the no-power-to-anyone form of government would also be accurate: the San Francisco charter could easily be seen as providing for a mixture of a strong mayor-council form of government and a strong city manager form of government, plus a few citizen-directed agencies.

To the extent that the charter concentrates power and responsibility anywhere, it is in management, from a chief administrative officer, controller, manager of public utilities and other appointed department heads to manager-technicians hired and advanced by merit under a civil service system. While it is presumed that the professionals, whether managers or technicians, will be competent, efficient, and honest, a considerable number of limitations are also placed upon them. However, the most significant check is placed upon elected officials, particularly the 11 members of the legislative body, the Board of Supervisors: by charter (section 2.401, Non-Interference in Administrative Affairs) supervisors are forbidden from interfering with the administrative functions of the various departments and commissions.

The charter-prescribed budget, and the process of its yearly adoption, is geared more to honesty than to its use as a management tool for achieving certain objectives or for assessing the cost effectiveness of government programs. A line-item budget is called for, one that might designate the number of tires a department can buy during the year but that would not explain why the car is needed in the first place. Municipal executives have little flexibility in the use of budgeted funds. If, for example, money is not used for specified personnel, it may not be used to hire consultants.

Responding to excesses of the past, the charter leaves little to chance. It is long, running over 100,000 words, almost twice the length of the California constitution. By 1969 it had been amended some 400 times, and it contains sections that would be more likely to appear in legislation than in what is essentially a constitution for the city. Thus the charter not only assures citizens that the cable cars will remain in San Francisco, but, in section 3.595 (Regulation of Street Railways), also sets a minimum schedule that cannot be changed without a vote of the people.

It is hard to measure the extent to which the charter encourages citizen involvement, especially in comparison to other cities. On the one hand, the sheer length, legalistic style, and complicated nature of the document, after so many amendments, keep it a mystery to most people. On the other hand, the continual voting on charter issues, the number of citizen-directed agencies, and the public hearings required before legislation can be passed all speak to considerable public participation in the affairs of government.


The 11 members of the Board of Supervisors are elected for overlapping four-year terms. Until 1977 they were elected at-large. (In that year the supervisors were elected by district, following a 1976 amendment to the charter.) The board is the fundamental policy-making arm of government: it has a high degree of control over the budget, public programs, and improvements and is the final authority on the use of public and private land. In this capacity, it adopts the zoning ordinance and is ultimately responsible for changes to it.

The board meets weekly. No matter, except for emergencies, can be heard and acted upon unless it has been first heard in a public meeting by a committee. Committees have published agendas, as does the full board. Committee meetings take the form of open hearings at which anyone can speak. Representatives of city departments spend a lot of time at these meetings presenting, defending, and commenting on pending legislation and public projects. The process encourages citizen

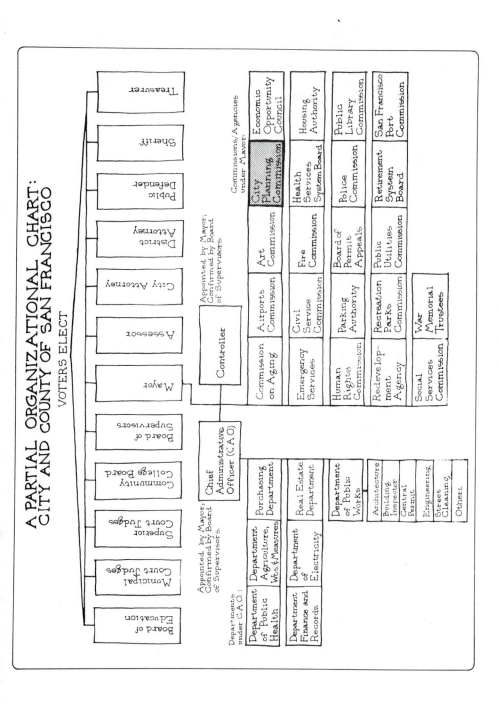

A PARTIAL ORGANIZATIONAL CHART:
CITY AND COUNTY OF SAN FRANCISCO

VOTERS ELECT

Board of Education

Municipal Court Judges

Superior Court Judges

Community College Board

Board of Supervisors

Mayor

Assessor

City Attorney

District Attorney

Public Defender

Sheriff

Treasurer

Appointed by Mayor; Confirmed by Board of Supervisors.

Chief Administrative Officer (CAO)

Controller

Departments under CAO:

Department of Public Health

Department of Agriculture, Wts.&Measures

Purchasing Department

Department Finance and Records

Department of Electricity

Real Estate Department

Department of Public Works

Architecture
Building Inspector
Central Permit
Engineering
Street Cleaning
Others

Appointed by Mayor, Confirmed by Board of Supervisors.

Commissions/Agencies under Mayor:

Commission on Aging

Airports Commission

Art Commission

Economic Opportunity Council

Emergency Services

Civil Service Commission

Fire Commission

Health Services System Board

Housing Authority

Human Rights Commission

Parking Authority

Board of Permit Appeals

Police Commission

Public Library Commission

Redevelopment Agency

Recreation Parks Commission

Public Utilities Commission

Retirement System Board

San Francisco Port Commission

Social Services Commission

War Memorial Trustees

City Planning Commission

involvement: people do come to the meetings and they do speak on issues that concern them. A single speaker, with a new twist on a much discussed issue, can cause a postponement of a decision for weeks while new answers are sought. However, inadequate public notice is often a problem, one not remedied by the usually excellent coverage given to both committee and board meetings by the local press.

Over the years, the committees most concerned with city planning matters have been the Planning, Housing, and Development Committee; the Streets and Transportation Committee; and the Finance Committee. If there is one committee more important than others it is the last. Most matters involving the expenditure of funds come before it, and it is responsible for presenting the city budget to the Board of Supervisors for enactment. This is an endeavor that requires review and approval of every department's detailed budget proposal at many long public hearings, all within a short, prescribed period of time. The full board rarely examines the budget package in detail before taking a vote, fearing perhaps to open a can of worms. Thus, the conclusions of the committee are extremely important in determining what does or does not get funded. Since, of course, the board has the final say in approving the annual budget and any supplemental funding requests throughout the year, the importance of its role in not only determining but also effecting policy is evident, although as we shall see, the controller also has a major say over the expenditure of funds.

Historically, the board has operated with a small staff headed by a board clerk. Members of the board have not worked full time at the job, nor have they been expected to do so. In recent years, however, with the growth of government in general, their personal and collective staffs have grown. Since the early 1970s the board has had the services of a budget analyst to assess the efficiency of the city departments and their programs and to advise it on fiscal matters.

To a considerable extent, the effectiveness of San Francisco's government depends on active and involved supervisors. Yet during the period from 1967 to 1974, supervisors received an annual salary of only $9,600. Almost all of them had other sources of income. Unless they are prepared to put considerable effort into their roles, supervisors can easily be coopted and left ineffective by knowing and better prepared executives, especially those in a growing mayor's office. The supervisors' awareness of this potential threat to their powers and the degree to which they protect their position depend on any number of factors; not the least of these are the personalities of the supervisors themselves and their relationship with the mayor.

San Francisco's mayors are elected in nonpartisan elections for four-year terms and may serve a maximum of two successive terms. On paper, the position is not one of great authority, but like so many others, it can be, depending on the person who fills it. The major powers of the office are conferred by the charter: to appoint commissioners, to approve the budget, and to coordinate the activities of the various departments. The mayor also speaks for the city in relationships with regional, state, and federal governments.

The citizen-commissioners responsible for setting policy for 21 departments, commissions, authorities, and boards are appointed by the mayor. Once appointed, most, although not all, serve at the mayor's pleasure. The commissions are intended to be independent of political pressure. Whether or not they are, of course, depends upon the nature of the agency and its commissioners, when it was established, and whether the commissioners serve at the mayor's pleasure. It is to be expected that the departments whose commissioners are appointed by the mayor will reflect the incumbent's ideas, values, and approach to government. In general, it is true that the fewer the members, the easier for a mayor to control a commission. It is noteworthy that executive officers are appointed and dismissed by the commissioners, not by the mayor; in order to fire a department director, a mayor may have to fire his commissioners. The mayor does, however, have the power to appoint a chief administrative officer and controller when these positions become vacant. These appointments are confirmed by the supervisors.

At the earliest stages, the mayor has little more than a negative control over the budget. Budget requests come to him from the departments and through the controller. He has the power at this early point to decide whether or not a matter is to be sent on to the Board of Supervisors. That veto or approval power gives the mayor more than merely passing influence in advising the departments and the board of what he will approve and in suggesting to the departments what they should propose in the first place, especially in regard to new positions. Few mayors have taken advantage of this potential influence in any comprehensive way, perhaps because the size of their staffs has always been limited.

The mayor is responsible for coordinating the activities of the various city departments through the many formal and informal coordinating devices that have been established over the years. Until 1975, for example, the mayor's deputy for development saw to the coordination of the Department of City Planning with the Housing Authority, Parking Authority, and Redevelopment Agency. (Under Mayor George Moscone, in 1975, there was no position of deputy for development. Rather, there were program managers. The manager for community development handled housing, redevelopment, and matters that related to the Office of Community Development.) The task of coordinating is more easily assigned than carried out, however, because of the semi-independent nature of the various agencies and because many departments, such as Public Works, are not under the direct control of the mayor, as are the departments responsible to commissions. Because of his budget veto power, there is a greater chance for the mayor to coordinate when budget-related issues are at stake than when they are not.

Like the Board of Supervisors, the mayor has had a small staff; it amounted to 32 people in 1967. Of these, nine were appointed by the mayor and served at his pleasure, and another five were in nonclerical positions related mostly to budget review. During the early 1970s, the staff grew, largely because new positions were funded in whole or in part by federal programs. By late 1974 the League of Women Voters reported that approximately 170 positions in city government related directly to the mayor's office. If staff size is taken as a measure of power, then by the mid 1970s, it can be said that the power of the mayor's office was growing in relation to the board and to the various departments.

Day in, day out, the most powerful person in San Francisco's government is the chief administrative officer (CAO). Appointed by the mayor and confirmed by the Board of Supervisors when the position becomes vacant, the CAO can be removed only "for cause" by a two-thirds vote of the board. No CAO has ever been removed. At least nine large departments are under the direction of the CAO, including Public Works, Public Health, Purchasing, and Real Estate. The city architect, city engineer, and superintendent of the Bureau of Building Inspection are, in turn, under the director of the Department of Public Works, although they are ultimately responsible to the CAO. Over 7,000 of the city's employees were in agencies under the CAO in 1974, according to the League of Women Voters. The CAO's influence goes beyond the agencies directly under him. Public improvements for departments nominally under the mayor must go through the CAO by way of Public Works for cost estimates, engineering, and, often, construction. Moreover, the CAO, unlike any other officer of government, enjoys discretionary control over a large amount of money, namely that part of the city's hotel tax that is used to support cultural activities. With the position of CAO goes chairmanship of or membership on any number of committees, including membership on the planning commission and on the committee of appointed city officials that makes final recommendations on capital improvements. In essence, the CAO is a modified city manager, but one who is appointed for life. It is no coincidence that his salary is only slightly lower than the mayor's.

The controller is appointed and tenured by the same process as the CAO. Although usually less visible than the CAO, the controller, too, can wield considerable power. He is responsible for establishing the tax rate, based on the annual budget and estimates of income, and he advises the mayor, Board of Supervisors, and voters of the tax implications of proposed legislative programs or of changes to the charter. A nod or frown from the controller to the chairman of the board's finance committee, signifying that money is or is not available, can spell life or death for a department's pet program. Most important however, is the controller's power, even after an expenditure has been approved, to withhold payment if he does not think adequate funds are available. In the day-to-day operations of government, the controller's willingness to advance money or to define an expenditure as being in keeping with the initial legislative intent affects a department's ability to pursue its objectives. Such is the essence of real power in local government.

Of the other offices and officers that make up San Francisco's government the most notable for our purposes are the city attorney and the Public Utilities Commission (PUC). The city attorney is elected (although deputy city attorneys are not) and by tradition serves in a semijudicial capacity. Since he represents San Francisco in the courts and advises elected and appointed officials on legal matters, his written opinions carry a special weight. These opinions represent the city attorney's interpretation of the law and thus indicate what he will pursue or defend on the city's behalf. A department will not readily propose anything that stands in contradiction to an opinion of the city attorney. Therefore, his conclusions can represent considerable constraints to its actions.

The five commissioners who, together with the general manager of utilities and his top staff, direct the Public Utilities Commission oversee a municipal enterprise that goes far beyond the city's boundaries. The Hetch Hetchy water system that serves San Francisco and other Bay Area communities is part of the PUC; it extends as far as the Sierra. A reservoir that supplies San Francisco is in Yosemite National Park, and the city even runs a family camp there. The PUC also controls considerable land in neighboring San Mateo and Alameda counties, as well as land in San Francisco itself. Any plan for recreation and open space at the metropolitan or county scale might well start with land owned by the city.

Within the city boundaries, the PUC is responsible for the San Francisco Municipal Railway and the Water Department. The municipal railway is a public transit system that includes streetcars, buses, electric trolleys, and the cable cars. It is one of the more extensive local transit systems in the country, serving some 500,000 passengers a day. The general manager of utilities directs, therefore, a considerable establishment. (In 1976 the PUC had 3,836 permanent employees, of whom 2,923 worked for the municipal railway.) The charter designates the general manager of utilities or his designated alternate as one of the seven members of the city planning commission.

San Francisco has very few appointed employees. In order to keep politics out of municipal employment, the vast majority, some 80 per cent, are hired through the civil service system.[3] Positions are secured by examination. Advancement is supposed to be on the basis of merit, although incumbent employees who pass the exams are given preference over outsiders. Until the mid-1970s, the person who scored highest on an exam was automatically offered the position; management had no choice. Since then, department heads have been able to choose from among the top three scorers. In an effort to keep the examinations as objective and "clean" as possible, the emphasis has traditionally been placed on written examinations, almost always of a multiple choice or true-false variety. Oral examinations are also given, though usually as part of a written-oral exam. Recently, however, oral exams have become more common, to speed up the examining process. Even so, the process, from job description to job announcement to exam to scoring and hiring can be time-consuming. Sometimes an employee may be hired conditionally, on "limited tenure," while the examination process takes its course. It is difficult to fire anyone once hired. In what is generally acknowledged to be a very strong union city, civil service activities are closely monitored and organized labor's presence is continuously felt in all personnel matters.

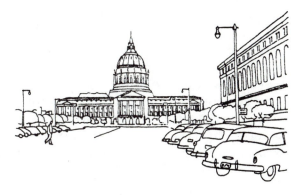

San Francisco's "classicist Baroque" city hall was built under an earlier charter for a different government. Nonetheless, there is much about its physical design and the organization of activities within it that reflects the nature of this government. On the second floor, along the front of the building, which was erected as an expression of faith that the city would rise from the ashes of the 1906 earthquake and fire, are the offices of the mayor, the chief administrative officer and the manager of public utilities. The central door leads to the mayor's suite— grand, formal, heavy. The long hall leading to the mayor's office sports the portraits of previous incumbents. The CAO's offices are directly adjacent to the mayor's, but there is no connecting door. Smaller than the mayor's, they are no less formal or well appointed. Next in line are the PUC offices. They are larger than the CAO's but are less grand and more businesslike. The controller, city attorney, assessor, and head of the Civil Service Commission have offices that are far less visible; they might even be called hidden, although they occupy strategic corners of the building. They are harder to get to than the first three. In all cases, however, the offices of the top executives are spacious; sitting in them, one knows that they are meant for important people.

But the place of honor in the city hall, the room that is the focal point of the grand staircase that starts under the dome and leads across the building from the executive offices to the second floor, is the chamber of the Board of Supervisors. The layout of this exquisite, rectangular room, some 90 feet long and 45 feet wide, puts government in perspective. From the central entry door along one of the long walls, the room is divided into two almost equal areas. The larger of the two is for the public. Over 200 people can sit on long, finely crafted wood benches. There is room for standees. The officers of government and the members of press are seated to the left of the entry, separated from the public by a low railing. A citizen speaking at a public hearing would stand in the middle of the room, facing the railing. The raised place of honor against the far wall is for the president of the board. The table at which the president sits is large enough to accommodate another chair, reserved for the mayor if and when he chooses to sit with the board. Slightly behind and to either side of this central point are seats for the CAO and controller. They are out of the spotlight, but they are clearly present. In front of the president, but still raised above the floor of the

chamber, is a place for the clerk, perhaps symbolic of the role of the bureaucracy. The central space between the railing and the dias is reserved for the 10 other supervisors, who sit at two facing rows of desks where they can see each other, the people, and the president. There is room for everyone—supervisors, public officers, the press, and the people. They all have their places. It is a very diverse government that meets in this grand space.

This brief outline of the basic structure and organization of San Francisco's government does not take into account the processes that have been established over the years by legislation and tradition for getting things done, for making government work. Perhaps the best way to get an idea of how things work is to examine briefly three key areas: the budget process; the relationships that exist between departments, elected officials, and the people; and some of the mechanisms that exist to facilitate relationships among government agencies.

The preparation of the annual budget starts more than six months before its adoption with the individual budgets at the departmental level. The basis for the budget depends on the department: it may derive from one department's assessment of what seems possible or urgent in the coming year, from the work program the department has proposed, or from the availability of state or federal money. A department's perception of what the mayor or supervisors want may also affect its budget proposal. Although departments rarely hold public hearings on their proposed budgets, they usually have enough contact with the public to enable them to anticipate what people want. But by far the strongest determinant of a department's future budget is the current budget. Rarely will an agency propose to have less of anything, especially personnel. The individual department budgets are approved by the various commissions, the CAO, or the elected heads of other offices and sent to the controller by a given date.

The controller assembles the budgets submitted by all the departments into a comprehensive document, which is then forwarded to the mayor. The mayor may cut, but, with the exception of capital improvements, he cannot add. This part of the budget-making process usually involves a considerable amount of give-and-take between the mayor, his staff, and department heads.

The next step finds the budget in the hands of the board's finance committee, which, like the mayor, can cut but not add. The public hearings that are held by the finance committee are primarily for departmental defense of a budget that has now had one cut. Attention is focused most often on justifications for new items rather than on objectives to be reached by the expenditures. In tight budget years, departments try to hang on to what they have. The budget passed by the finance committee then goes to the full board for final action, with or without further consultation with the mayor, after which the tax rate is set. The controller handles the disbursement of funds, including payments for programs in the departmental budgets. During the late 1960s and early 1970s the lineal budget process that went from the departments, to the controller, to the mayor, to the finance committee, to the full Board of Supervisors, and then back to the mayor for signature was accomplished with little communication or back-and-forth negotiations between the board and mayor (or their staffs) along the way. This situation has changed in recent years, as the mayors have inserted their views more forcefully while the budget is with the board so that the resultant expenditures will come closer to reflecting what a mayor wants.

The process does not necessarily end with the formal passage of the budget. Throughout the year, emergencies arise; departments may need additional funds for any number of purposes. Requests for supplemental funding follow the same lineal process as the annual budget, with the same veto possibilities along the way.

Despite recent improvements, the whole budget process is long and more than just a little cumbersome. Notwithstanding the considerable influence that both the mayor and board have upon the budget, the departments remain the initiating force; they must prepare the proposals for the expenditure of public funds related to their responsibilities before the mayor or board considers them.

Relationships between San Francisco and other governments at local and other levels are usually, but not always, orderly. On the one hand, formal mechanisms exist to provide for local representation in such regional and state agencies as the Association of Bay Area Governments, the Air Pollution Control District, and the Bay Conservation and Development Commission. The city has maintained legislative representatives at Sacramento and Washington, and the State and National

Affairs Committee of the Board of Supervisors, together with the mayor and the CAO, attempts to coordinate policy and maintain relations with those levels of government. At various times, the Board of Supervisors has been represented on at least eight regional agencies: Bay Area Sewage Services Agency, Bay Area Air Pollution and Control District, Golden Gate Bridge Highway and Transportation District, Metropolitan Transportation Commission, Bay Area Rapid Transit District, Bay Conservation and Development Commission, Association of Bay Area Governments, North Central Coastal Commission.

On the other hand, local departments generally have been free to pursue their own interests, establishing relationships with agencies at different levels; for example, the Department of Public Works maintains close contact with both the federal Department of Transportation and the state Division of Highways or Metropolitan Transportation Commission. Any number of local departments have dealings with the federal Department of Housing and Urban Development, just as many federal agencies have separate relationships with the Department of City Planning. An outcome of all this has been that policies and programs are not always coordinated between San Francisco and other levels of government.

Relationships between city departments can be as complicated as those between San Francisco and other governments. As a rule, departments establish relationships out of necessity: when jurisdictions overlap or when there is something to be gained by acting together. Any number of mechanisms have been established over the years to ensure smooth relations among departments and to facilitate decision making: the Capital Improvement Advisory Committee to coordinate capital improvements; the Transit Task Force to interrelate the many departmental interests involved in the redesign of a major street; an interagency committee on urban renewal to coordinate activities of the

Department of City Planning, the Redevelopment Agency, and the Housing Authority. It must be said, though, that when it comes to day-to-day matters, the many agencies of government get together only when they have to, and that their relative power—determined by age, size, level of expertise, location in government, and political and popular support—determines the nature of their interaction.

There are apparent faults with San Francisco's political structure. Although the government has been largely free of corruption for the past 40 years, in 1969 the citizens' group organized to revise the charter pointed out that the achievement has too often been at the expense of responsiveness and efficiency. The fragmented government established in the long, difficult charter inhibits action, if only because the required legislative processes take so much time. Reformers also have argued that the system, with all its checks and balances, is overly expensive. Some hold that San Francisco's civil service, with its built-in job security, also brings about a lack of responsiveness in city employees. Others express misgivings about the inflexibility of the city's government—a result, they feel, of the cumbersome charter—and about the amount of power that resides with nonelected officials. Operating departments, say the critics, frustrate the will of the electorate and their representatives simply by postponing action on policies and programs or by making "slight changes" that accord with their own desires rather than with legislative intent. There is continuous disagreement as to whether at-large or district elections encourage greater participation of citizens in their government. After two previous tries, a charter amendment to establish district elections passed in 1976. It was challenged and defeated at the polls by another proposal in 1977.

The other side of the efficiency coin, to some, is twofold: that democratic processes are never efficient and that efficiency is not necessarily a purpose of government anyway. Moreover, few matters that come before a city's government are pressing, unless they have been put off for so long that they have become pressing. The second point is that if it is true that San Francisco's decentralized government is slow to act, it also permits deliberation and participation, and it is generally agreed that San Franciscans want to take part in their government. A 1969 attempt to rewrite the charter, which would have placed more power in the hands of the mayor, was defeated soundly at the polls. (The vote, as reported in the *San Francisco Chronicle*, was 108,002 against and 64,146 for.)

However distinctive San Francisco's government may be in some of its details, its similarities to other major cities in the United States are stronger. Most cities have mayors, councils, and operating departments. Many have the equivalent of a chief administrative officer. They all pass laws and adopt budgets, even though the process may be less attenuated. Federal and state programs, mandates, and court decisions have an impact upon all of them. And they all engage, in one way or another, in city planning.

Unlike the overall structure and organization of San Francisco's government, the location, responsibilities, and powers of city planning within it are classic, if not downright old-fashioned. The Department of City Planning is responsible to a commission, five of whose seven members are appointed by the mayor and serve at his pleasure.[4] The commission hires and can fire the director, who is the administrative head of the department. The staff, under the director, is responsible to the commission, which gives policy direction to the department. The overwhelming majority of staff actions and recommendations—from long-range plans for the city's future physical development, to changes in the zoning code, to decisions about declaring a building a landmark, to the location of urban renewal projects—must be acted upon by the commission. As we shall see, some of the commission's actions are final in that policy is determined by its action. In most cases, however, its findings and recommendations are forwarded to other arms of the government, such as the Board of Supervisors, where final action is taken.

Like other city planning agencies fashioned from the standard city planning enabling legislation of the late 1920s, San Francisco's is supposed to be fairly independent of day-to-day political pressures and the demands of government in guiding the physical development of the city.[5] Thus, the commission, even though almost all its members are appointed by the mayor, is somewhat removed from that office and even more removed from the control of the Board of Supervisors.

The commissioners who are appointed by the mayor generally represent political views that are similar to his, at least at the time of their appointments. They are, however, supposed to exercise independent judgment when it comes to decisions about what is best for the city over the long run. Through the years commissions have been representative of a balance of the interests that the incumbent mayor considered important. These interests have usually included downtown business, labor, and civic groups. Most of the commissioners have come from San Francisco's white, male establishment. Before 1975, blacks, Chicanos, Chinese, conservationists, and representatives of the neighborhoods were rarely appointed. This usual composition changed somewhat with the 1975 commission, under a new mayor, to appear more representative. To some extent, it can be argued that the planning commission was intended to be elitist from the outset. Size alone has always kept it from being representative. The strength of the bureaucracy in San Francisco's political structure is underscored by the fact that the two commissioners not appointed by the mayor come from the operating departments. In fact, these two ex officio members, the CAO and general manager of utilities, have more power on the commission than appointed members in that they alone are permitted to send voting alternates to meetings.

San Francisco's organizational model is by no means the only one available. Efforts in some cities to increase the effectiveness of city planning by placing it in a more pivotal position with regard to day-to-day development issues have resulted in planning staffs being directly responsible to mayors or to city managers. Commissions, if they continue to exist in this type of arrangement, are usually advisory to the staff.[6] In some cases the commission serves the same role as it does in San Francisco, but the director is appointed by the mayor. In Los Angeles the planning director is hired by exam and holds a civil service, tenured position under a commission. Other communities in California place city planning under the city manager. When city planning is under a chief executive, zoning responsibilities are often handled by a separate agency. Sometimes city planning is combined with a redevelopment agency (as has been the case in Boston) or a public housing department, or it becomes part of a large planning and development agency that is in the mayor's office. Offices of community development that include city planning have proliferated as a result of changing federal preferences for centralized administration.

Another view holds that since city planning is primarily a policy-setting activity it should be part of the legislative branch of government.[7] However intriguing the idea, it has not been put into practice in any major American city. It will be seen, however, that much of what San Francisco's Department of City Planning actually does is more related to the Board of Supervisors than to the mayor.

The responsibilities and powers of the planning department reflect a primary concern with the physical environment, particularly with the uses of land and of buildings, and with transportation planning, zoning, and public improvements. Some are established by the charter; others by local legislation, with a push from the state; and still others by local tradition and custom. The responsibilities mandated by the charter are taken to be the most basic.

The major responsibility of the planning department is the preparation of the master plan for the city. The charter spells out the requirements for a "comprehensive, long-term, general plan for the improvement and future development of the city."[8] The master plan is to "present a broad and general guide and pattern constituting. . . recommendations . . . for the coordinated and harmonious development, in accordance with the present and future needs, of the city." It is supposed to include "a land-use plan showing the proposed general distribution and the general location . . . of public and private uses of land, and recommended standards of population density and building intensity, with estimates of population growth." The master plan must include the commission's proposals for any handling, acquisition, sale of, or changes in public land or buildings, including streets. Master plans are now required by state legislation as well. By 1975 no fewer than nine distinct general plan elements were mandated by state laws.[9]

Unlike the charters or state statutes that mandate them, master plans have often had a visionary character. Although they are presumably grounded in physical, social, and economic reality, they have nonetheless attempted to envision and then achieve a desirable, indeed utopian, urban physical environment in which to conduct human affairs. It has been expected that San Francisco's master plan would, among other things, serve that visionary role.

The charter does not stop at requiring the preparation of a master plan. There must be public advertisement and public hearings before the plan is adopted or changed. But, although copies of the plan must be sent to the mayor and to the Board of Supervisors, in San Francisco, unlike other California municipalities, the board is not required to adopt or the mayor to endorse the plan. The formal process of adoption stops at the planning commission. The reason, presumably, is related to the charter makers' fear that the politicians might refuse to adopt a plan whose policies might conflict with their own day-to-day decisions.

Charter provisions attempt to ensure that actions regarding public lands and buildings conform to the plan.[10] Any acquisitions, sales, or changes of public lands or buildings must be referred to the planning department for reports to the supervisors and to the controller on the conformance of such action with the master plan. The process is called master plan referral or mandatory referral. Although the supervisors may not act without such a report, the department's report is not binding on anyone. Except in the case of land subdivisions, the finding is advisory. Again, the charter requires that planning considerations be made part of a decision-making process but stops short of giving them any special priority. Similarly, plans for public housing projects and clearance or redevelopment of blighted areas must be referred to the department under the referral process.

Capital improvement programming is another function given to the planning department by the charter and other legislation.[11] Departments are required to submit any proposals for projects for the budget year plus another five years to the city planners. It is the responsibility of the planning department to decide whether individual projects accord with the master plan and to prepare a capital improvements program for the budget. The department is supposed to work with other agencies to eliminate conflicts and may, if it wishes, make its own recommendations.

The actual role of the planning department in capital improvement programming has been considerably smaller than that defined by the charter. What at first glance might appear as considerable responsibility—earmarking and coordinating the use of public money to carry out a plan—is much less in practice. Of the long lists of projects presented to the mayor and supervisors, precious few at the top have been funded out of normal tax revenues. Earmarked funds, such as those set aside for roads by the state gasoline tax, have created their own priorities, often divorced from local planning considerations. Funds for major improvements have been secured more often through single-purpose bond issues than ad valorem taxes. Furthermore, the planners' role in capital programming is circumscribed by the Capital Improvement Advisory Committee, a high-level coordinating committee chaired by the CAO. It is responsible for setting priorities among the proposals that have been presented to the Board of Supervisors.[12] Given San Francisco's political structure, it would be difficult for the planning department's position to hold sway if it differed from that taken by the advisory committee's leadership.

Zoning, the use of the police power to regulate the uses of (primarily) private land is probably the most sacredly held and widely known of all the responsibilities that the charter gives the planning department.[13] Zoning is determined, administered, and enforced in large measure by the department. The responsibility is a time-consuming one. In 1973-74, for example, there were hearings on 15 proposed changes to zoning districts and on 80 proposed conditional uses. Almost 8,000 building applications and 1,700 sign applications were reviewed to determine whether they conformed to the zoning ordinance. There were 48 applications for variances and 400 enforcement cases to be investigated and determined.

Considerable power goes with the zoning responsibility. The commission must hear and decide proposals to change zoning, as well as proposals to allow certain uses that may be permitted only under specified conditions—"conditional uses." It takes a two-thirds vote of the supervisors to overrule the planning commission's refusal to change the zoning. Within the planning department, the zoning administrator, who is at the level of assistant director, has all the power to administer and enforce the zoning ordinance, with the exception of the cases that come to the commission. He determines that proposed uses conform or not to the zoning and issues permits and cease and desist orders, for example. The power to hear and to decide upon variance requests—the minor deviations to the existing zoning, usually associated with hardship—is his alone, not the commission's or the director's. His decision may be appealed to a Board of Permit Appeals.

There are other charter mandates that are worthy of note. The department may undertake whatever research and issue whatever reports it deems necessary to prepare and promote the master plan. It is also authorized to advise the mayor, supervisors, and others on matters affecting the physical improvement and development of the city.[14] Following passage of a charter amendment in 1974 ("Proposition J," described in detail in chapter 11), the department is also intimately involved in the acquisition and development of open space and in park renovation, with funds assured through the amendment.

In addition to responsibilities given to the planning department in the charter, there are a number of others that derive from local or state legislation. For example, the department prepares the environmental impact reports that are required by state and local laws to assess the environmental consequences of any significant public or private development project. In urban renewal projects the department is not only supposed to be involved in designation, but also in the preparation, together with the Redevelopment Agency, of preliminary renewal plans. Supposedly, it consults with the agency on final plans. In reality, between the middle 1960s and the early 1970s, preliminary planning was largely in the hands of the Redevelopment Agency. By local ordinance, the city planning department staff is also responsible for designating and recommending to the CAO and to the Board of Supervisors areas in which to concentrate efforts to enforce the housing code.[15] Another responsibility of the planning staff is to assist the Landmarks Preservation Advisory Board in researching and recommending both individual buildings and historic districts for landmark status.[16] The planning commission has the power to defer demolition of designated landmarks for an initial six-month period, and for an additional six-month period if the supervisors concur. Any number of other "official" tasks and powers have fallen to the city planners as a result of local and state legislation or resolutions. They involve such activities as reviewing building permits to ensure conformity with Bay shoreline regulations, serving on a regional planning committee, representing San Francisco in intergovernmental studies, and serving on local committees. Some of these activities last and others come and go. In most cases, however, they derive from basic responsibilities found in the charter.

Some observations regarding the formal, legislated responsibilities of the city planning department can be made. First, city planning as defined in San Francisco, is concerned primarily with the physical environment. Next, the planning department, like those in most other cities, acts in an advisory capacity on most matters; it advises the Board of Supervisors, the mayor, and other departments. It does not build anything itself, nor does it normally operate direct service programs. Realization of its primary product, a plan or plans, is in large measure dependent upon a decision-making process that makes constant reference to the plans but rarely requires that they be followed, especially in regard to public projects.

There are difficulties in carrying out the department's coordinating and priority-setting functions. Others also have the responsibility for coordinating, most notably the mayor, the CAO, and the controller. Other departments have at least as much stature and official power as the city planners, and they are directly responsible for their projects and their programs. Their autonomy makes coordination difficult.

The planning department does have regulatory powers. The main one might in fact be called a negative power—the ability to say "no." While it is true that the "no" to a public building proposal is no more than advisory, that same "no" on a zoning issue related to the use of private land carries considerable punch, since a two-thirds vote of the board is necessary to override the commission. If a developer is contemplating something that is not specifically permitted and is convinced that the planning department will turn him down, then he is much more likely to find out what the public officials are likely to approve. A positive, persuasive power is exercised; the city planners can advise developers of what they are likely to approve, sometimes in considerable detail. The ability of city planners to be negative has a positive side in relation to public improvement proposals, although this is not as strong as with private projects. Heads of departments do not like to hear their projects criticized in public, especially by fellow bureaucrats as part of the mandatory referral process. That possibility can result in sound, cooperative planning. There is also increasing opportunity for city planners to affect public projects through environmental review.

The charter mandate to prepare a master plan, capital improvements program, and zoning ordinance is broad enough to encompass a wide range of city planning activities. Particular activities and responsibilities of the planning department at any given moment, however, might not stem directly from legislative mandate. Custom, the interests of the staff, the demands of the times, the availability of funds for specific kinds of planning, and chance all help in determining not only which of the formal responsibilities receive most attention but also the less formal activities. It was the interests of the staff plus the demands of the times that generated a major neighborhood planning program in the late 1960s. The historic concern of city planners with housing, together with community pressures, helps explain the emphasis the department has put in that area. Similar reasons explain the department's involvement in the area of transportation and its work on city planning at the state level.

Many other activities of the planning department are not recorded in any official list of duties. They include assuming the role of advocate for various groups and interests and geographic areas; generating new ideas about the physical environment and testing them before the public; and giving citizens a forum for voicing their complaints. Research into local physical, social, and economic conditions and the continuous provision of timely, easily understood information, regardless of whose cause it might help or hinder, can bring prestige and a measure of influence to those who provide it. It may be inherent in the nature of government that the more informal or voluntary activities serve the citizens as well as those that are required by law.

The charter clearly recognizes what can be called a city planning process. After mandating a master plan, it speaks to a method of making amendments to it and to a way of "systematic effectuation."[17] The mandatory referral of public actions having to do with lands and buildings and the preparation of a capital improvement program are further steps. The charter strongly implies that zoning should be a part of the process. What the charter calls for, basically, is a process that will ensure that both public and private development will be consistent with (or at least considered in light of) some overall objectives and policies that are directed to a concept of what the community should be.

In addition to the general planning process suggested by the charter, each of the functions that are mandated operates according to a process of its own. Changing the zoning ordinance, for example, involves a process that starts with a formal application by an individual or a group, or a resolution of the planning commission or the Board of Supervisors. It goes on to require public notice, public hearings, decisions by the planning commission, and ratification by the Board of Supervisors. The board hears appeals of commission disapprovals. Other processes, all directed toward public decision making, take place when changes to the master plan are proposed, when environmental impact reports are filed, and when renewal projects are designed.

Within each process, there are places where city planners, plan-

ning commissioners, and supervisors may use their discretion to change, to grant, or to withhold something. In some cases, but not all, guidelines help determine how much discretion to exercise. Of course, the charter makers had to make a choice initially in deciding whether or not to have the board adopt the master plan, pass a zoning ordinance, or enact any of the other laws related to city planning. That is one level of political action—determining the nature of the laws that will guide the physical development of the city. In this regard, except for zoning, San Francisco is like most other cities in that it has chosen not to give extensive powers to the planning department to carry out its plans directly. This seems consistent with the general approach to government in the city.

Another level of discretion is exercised within any formal process, such as the process of zoning. To the extent that there is a high degree of flexibility or discretion on the part of professional staff, the planning commission, and the Board of Supervisors, there is an implied willingness to have political involvement in the decision-making process. The decision to exercise more or less discretion might be based on an assessment of the relative strengths, honesty, and responsibility of the actors involved and the relative need for flexibility in dealing with unknowns and avoiding arbitrariness. The issues are similar to those that were relevant in deciding the nature of San Francisco's government in the thirties.

Increasingly, in the United States, city planners have leaned toward greater use of discretion, especially as it applies to zoning. This may say something about the way that the city planning point of view is perceived in comparison to other forces at work in political situations; that is, people anticipate that the planners will have considerable influence. On the other hand, people might believe that if planners are intent on using discretion at every turn, there is *no* city planning point of view in the first place. Perhaps, they say, planners are incapable of working out standards in advance and so look to discretion as the easy way out. In San Francisco, during the late sixties and early seventies, the trend was toward minimizing the use of discretion by the major actors involved in city planning processes, a direction that also seems consistent with the point of view of the people who wrote the city's charter.

An additional point in relation to the process of city planning should be noted: the planning director is required to make his recommendations on most issues publicly, at scheduled and well-reported open meetings. It goes without saying that the views of the director and his professional staff often differ from those of the mayor, the supervisors, and the commissioners. When the city planners disagree with the commission or with the mayor, there is always the question of whose point of view will be presented, and with how much passion, at the next level of government, for example at the Board of Supervisors. Thus, the process builds in the likelihood of public disagreement and conflict between the commission, elected officials, and their city planning employees.

What can be concluded about the role of city planning within the government of San Francisco? First, the planning department, responsible to a commission, exists within a political structure that attempts to distribute power broadly. If the department seems rather distant from the central decision-making process, that may be because none has existed. Nevertheless, the department is in a position to come into frequent conflict with the mayor and the supervisors. Given the decentralized nature of the city's government, it would appear difficult for the department to coordinate physical development in pursuit of its plans.

Second, the master plan is not adopted by the Board of Supervisors or endorsed by the mayor. There is nothing, however, to keep the city planning commission from requesting them to do so.

Third, while on paper the planning department does not appear to be in a position to be a direct, strong, moving force, there are any number of mechanisms that ensure that city planning considerations are voiced in the decision-making process.

Fourth, there is a certain freedom attached to being a semi-autonomous agency within government, as the planning department is. This freedom allows the department to engage in certain activities of its own choosing, to take a long-range view of the city's development, and to advocate particular causes and the ideal.

Finally, the formal process of city planning encourages a considerable degree of citizen participation.

Any number of questions are raised by such a brief description of the mechanisms that govern a city the size and importance of San Francisco. The most significant for us, here, are these: Can the city planning process work to produce effective, responsive plans? And to what extent does this process help or hinder the achievement of plans? We will try to shed light on these questions in the chapters ahead.

## Notes

1. U.S. Census, 1970, for the nine-county Bay region. The counties are Alameda, Contra Costa, Marin, Napa, San Francisco, San Mateo, Santa Clara, Solano, and Sonoma.

2. *Report of the San Francisco Citizen Charter Revision Committee,* June 1969, pp. 1-4. For a more detailed account of the conditions and circumstances that led to the present charter, see F. M. Wirt, *Power in the City: Decision Making in San Francisco* (Berkeley: University of California Press, 1974). A short, general description of San Francisco's government may be found in *Inside City Hall: A Guide to San Francisco City and County Government,* by the League of Women Voters of San Francisco, 1974.

3. Estimate from an employee of the Civil Service Commission. In its 1974 study the League of Women Voters also estimated that out of the almost 28,000 positions surveyed, 23,226—80 per cent of the total—were under civil service.

4. Sections 3.520 and 3.521 of the San Francisco Charter.

5. Advisory Committee on City Planning and Zoning, U.S. Department of Commerce, "The 1928 Standard City Planning Enabling Act."

6. Robert A. Walker, *The Planning Function in Urban Government* (Chicago: University of Chicago Press, 1941). The Walker model remains the basic reference for this type of arrangement, just as "The 1928 Standard City Planning Enabling Act" remains the basic model for planning commissions.

7. T. J. Kent, Jr. *The Urban General Plan* (San Francisco: Chandler Publishing Co., 1964).

8. Sections 3.524 and 3.525 of the San Francisco Charter.

9. For a more thorough discussion of local planning that is required by the state, see Paul Sedway and Thomas Cooke, "Local Planning Laws and Agencies," *Land and the Environment: Planning in California Today* (Los Altos, California: William Kaufmann, Inc., 1975). This study was prepared for the Planning and Conservation Foundation.

10. Section 3.527 of the San Francisco Charter.

11. Sections 3.529 and 6.202 of the San Francisco Charter and portions of chapter 3 of the Administrative Code (the body of administrative laws passed by the Board of Supervisors).

12. Section 3.06 of the Administrative Code lists the membership of the Capital Improvement Advisory Committee as the chief administrative officer, controller, director of public works, director of planning, manager of public utilities, and general manager of the Recreation and Park Department. The mayor's deputy for development has often sat in on the weekly meetings.

13. Sections 7.500 and 7.503 of the San Francisco Charter and article 3 of the City Planning Code (more commonly known as the zoning ordinance).

14. Sections 3.526 and 3.529 of the San Francisco Charter.

15. Section 301.A of the Housing Code.

16. Article 10 of the City Planning Code.

17. Section 3.526 of the San Francisco Charter.

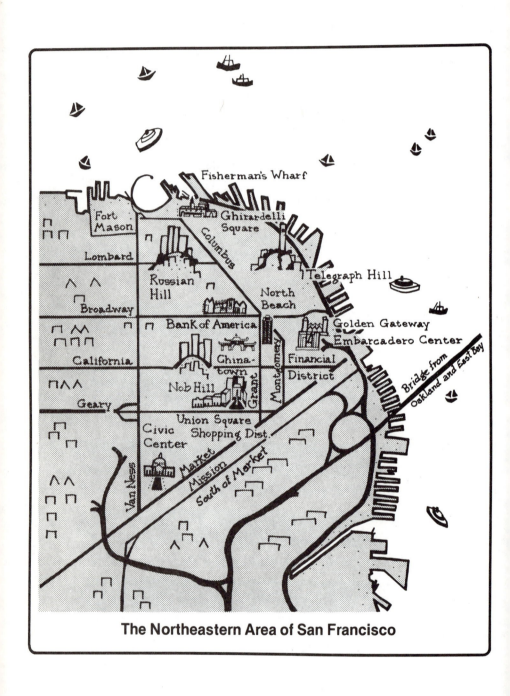

**The Northeastern Area of San Francisco**

# Chapter 3
# 1968: Getting Going, Staffing Up, Responding to Issues

Nationally, 1968 was not a particularly good year for the United States. The light at the end of the Viet Nam tunnel went out with the *Tet* offensive, and President Johnson withdrew as a candidate amidst increasing discontent with the war. Martin Luther King and Robert Kennedy were murdered. Continued attempts to solve long-standing social problems through civil rights and social equity legislation and massive funding programs were often overshadowed by the violent nature of the times. The Kerner Commission report blamed racism for the riots that continued throughout the year in cities like Cleveland, Seattle, Gary, and Peoria. Most notable and noticed were the confrontations at the Democratic National Convention in Chicago. As the year drew to an end, Richard Nixon was elected President after an end-the-war-with-honor and law-and-order campaign.

The mood in San Francisco was both reflective of and distinctly different from the national mood. As in other places, antiwar demonstrations were commonplace. And the militancy of the nation's poor, especially the blacks, who were demanding their fair share of rights, privileges, and wealth was mirrored in San Francisco. But unlike other major cities, San Francisco had three big minority groups: blacks, Chicanos, and Chinese. Whether this meant that San Francisco was three times or one-third as militant as other cities is hard to tell. It made no difference to the poor that San Francisco's slums were not as bad as Detroit's or Pittsburgh's. They wanted jobs, they wanted good housing they could afford, and they were tired of being pushed out of their homes for public works and redevelopment projects. They expressed their anger at every turn. One had merely to appear in public to be called a racist or bigot.

At the same time, however, this was the era in San Francisco of the hippies, the flower children, and love. It was a period of serious, youthful questioning of old values and life styles and of experimenting with new ways. It was a time for "dropouts," bare feet, and parents searching for missing children in the Haight-Ashbury district. It was a period of antifashion fashions that soon became fashionable, a time when people were nice to look at. On Sundays, thousands went to "be-ins" at the Speedway Meadows in Golden Gate Park to eat, drink, look at each other, dance to rock bands under a low haze of pot smoke, and be watched by city police, who stood leisurely at the edges of the crowd. The flower children, it seemed, were a San Francisco invention, perhaps by way of Berkeley. Their love existed side by side with anger about social inequities and the war. San Franciscans tolerated, even nurtured them all.

However bad the problems were, the mood in San Francisco in 1968 was hopeful. One had a sense that the city was not nearly as bad off as its eastern and midwestern counterparts, that here problems could and would be solved. And no one was more optimistic or exuded as strong a "can do," "will do," and "things are not so bad" aura as the new mayor, Joseph Alioto. A bright, energetic, eminently successful lawyer and New Deal-type Democrat with strong labor backing, who could and would talk with enthusiasm, passion, and compassion on just about any subject, Alioto was accessible to everyone. He listened and seemed to understand the problems, and he gave promise of solutions. He had access to the Johnson administration and he was admired by local liberals, who appeared to have his ear. His deep roots in the Italian community stood him in good stead with most ethnic groups. His enthusiasm was contagious. San Francisco might have problems but they could be solved. There was no better place to be.

For reasons that I will never fully understand, I seemed to have had it "made" with the mayor from the beginning. Perhaps he and his staff had been advised, although I'm not sure by whom, that his city planner was one of the better department heads around and that he had a sense of the important issues in the city. Or it might have been because the planning department was quick to produce a list of 40 possible sites for mini-parks when he needed the information in a hurry. When the mayor asked for my professional opinions, I gave them to him without mincing words. When I first met him, I had the opportunity to recommend a new planning commissioner. I had not known that Mortimer Fleishhacker had supported the mayor's opponent, and I cannot even be certain that my strong recommendation had anything to do with his appointment, but Alioto did appoint him. Maybe we got along in those early days because we were both learning and because my lack of concern with what he might want to hear was matched by this own desire to hear and learn as much as possible. In any case, I was considered to be "one of the team" or "one of the inner circle," as a mayor's aide put it. I liked it. To be sure, I was not kidding myself about Alioto's being a planner's mayor. He was not. My initial sense was that he was highly development-oriented, even when development might be ill placed, and that he would not be terribly concerned with long-range views. His early addresses, in which he talked about his "Darwinian theory of urban development," confirmed my fears. But then, how many mayors are planners' mayors? One could wait for a long time for that happy situation.

In the meantime, it was personally pleasant and professionally important to be in the mayor's good graces. There were things to be done. This would be a year of responding to immediate issues while establishing a solid professional base in the community; of attracting high-quality staff; of establishing good working relationships with the Board of Supervisors and with the planning commission; of citizen involvement in citywide and neighborhood planning; of looking for opportunities to make planning more relevant, effective, and responsive; and of starting to roll on long-range programs. It would be much easier to get things done if the relationship with the mayor and his office were friendly rather than hostile or neutral.

In large measure, 1968 was a year of responding to immediate issues in a "best as can" way while simultaneously staffing up and initiating policies that might provide a better basis for day-to-day decisions and programs. We were still inadequately staffed, although we had added some people in 1967, and the quality of existing plans was, to my taste, less than adequate. So we "winged it" a lot in 1968, although not as much as in the previous year. We looked for opportunities to address the issues we had identified, to make city planning more relevant. And there were plenty of immediate issues.

During the year about 100 zoning cases came before the planning commission. Each one required a staff recommendation. They included proposals to change the zoning on a hilltop to prevent apartment house development and to convert the basement and garage of a home in a residential area to medical offices.[1] Although some cases were more important to the whole city than others, each one was critical to the applicants and the contestants and had to be responded to in that light.

By far the most significant zoning matter was one that had been previously decided by both the staff and the commission: the proposed major changes to the city's zoning ordinance, which would affect the downtown and adjacent areas. The proposal had been lodged in the planning committee of the Board of Supervisors since July 1967 and would finally be acted on in May 1968. The man who chaired the committee in 1967 was known as a proponent of increased downtown development. He was hard to contact and seemed uninterested. In 1968, the chairman was Ronald Pelosi, who was sympathetic to the ordinance and to city planning in general, but he was the minority member of the committee. We met with him whenever possible to bring him up to date and to convince him of the rightness of our course, hoping that he would persuade other new supervisors. On the whole, though, I was not confident. What I feared was that the supervisors and the city planners would become involved in a game, spending years shuttling amendments and changes back and forth. Meanwhile the passage of time would make the proposals meaningless and the staff would be debilitated. If that were to happen, all of my worst fears about zoning would be confirmed.

By chance, one or two developments that would be permitted under the proposed ordinance were not permitted under the existing zoning code. The sponsors of the new developments wanted some kind of action and helped persuade the committee to bring the matter before the full board for a debate and a vote.

The breakthrough came when the committee recommendations finally came out on May 10. The majority (two to one) proposals were in the form of a series of amendments to the new ordinance that would make it less in keeping with good planning than the old. I suspected the fine hand of the chamber of commerce had been at work.

Our views did receive public attention. On a totally separate matter I had called the chief editorial writer of the *Chronicle* to express my disagreement with the paper's position, but also to express my appreciation for the fairness and accuracy with which the paper had reported the views of the planning department. The writer, unaccustomed to such calls, thanked me and asked what I thought of the committee's proposed changes to our ordinance. I blurted out that I thought they were so bad I'd rather not have any ordinance at all. Both the editorial and the news story ("High Density Plan Hit by Alioto, Planning Chief") that appeared in the paper borrowed heavily from a memo we immediately sent to explain our position.

Mayor Alioto, although never briefed by me as to the details of our proposal, endorsed it rather than the committee's version after I explained to him that I thought it was reasonable. Personal conversations with supervisors indicated we might have a chance, especially if at a later date we would agree to include two or three of the small changes suggested by the committee. When the measure came to the floor of the Board of Supervisors, the most critical first vote was six to five against postponing action. This was followed by a string of six-to-five or seven-to-four votes against weakening amendments and finally by a six-to-five vote for the ordinance.[2] It was a major city planning victory, one that for the first time established a strong liberal block on the board. It was also the first time I had ever been in the position of strongly advocating a planning proposal that I had not prepared personally in the first place.

The biggest conflict of the year erupted over a proposal for development in the northern waterfront area at the foot of Telegraph Hill, the so-called International Market Center. The initial proposal was for a complex of buildings that would cover eight blocks and approximately 17 acres. It would include a wholesale home furnishings and apparel market center and a hotel that would be as tall as the nearby Coit Tower, a San Francisco landmark. Building the complex would require the closing and public vacation of some unused or unimproved streets. I was concerned that such an overall massive development was unsympathetic to the character of that part of the city. Together with our northern waterfront consultants, I also was concerned that new development not block historic views from or to Telegraph Hill, and, further, that it allow room for a waterfront roadway we were contemplating. We advised the developers and their architects that we would oppose any street vacations unless they would comply with what we called "urban design terms of reference" for the site. They didn't take us too seriously.

One well-known architect gave me a lecture on what was best for San Francisco, to which I replied that as long as he had a client in tow I was not interested in his views, since his interests were those of his client, not the city. He had trouble speaking to me again for six months.

The development proposal was announced with hoopla. I immediately denounced it and soon found myself in a meeting with both the developers and the mayor. The mayor, who was sympathetic to my concerns about views and about Coit Tower, advised the developers to pay attention to me. After that it was downhill. The developers agreed to most of our conditions, and we built them into a strong legal document that would govern all street vacations. Except for some residents of Telegraph Hill, everyone was happy. In a 12-hour public hearing that didn't end until two in the morning, the Board of Supervisors approved the projects subject to all of our proposed conditions.[3] The irony is that the project was never built. A lawsuit by Telegraph Hill opponents held up the project, and, by the time the suit was settled, changes in the financial climate made the project impossible. In any case, it had been a nice fight, and it provided yet another lesson about the nature of San Francisco.

By no means were all of our positions negative. As I noted earlier, I was a member of the Market Street Transit Task Force, which was involved in planning for the two-mile stretch of Market Street that would have to be reconstructed after the new subway was in place. The design proposed by the task force, with considerable aid from its consultants, included widening the sidewalks. But the public works people valiantly fought almost any proposal that would in any way hinder the automobile. They lost, though, and a $24 million Market Street bond issue—Proposition A—placed before the voters in the June election passed by almost 70 percent of the vote (146,657 in favor and 65,158 opposed). I wondered whether the people in any other city would vote, by that margin, to spend that kind of money to beautify two miles of street.

In 1968 the federal government declared Alcatraz Island to be surplus property. The rapidity with which public officials became public entrepreneurs was wondrous to behold. The city was supposed to be given first chance to buy at a cheaper price if it wanted the land for public purposes. But the feds, all in favor of selling to the highest bidder for a commercial venture, seemed to discount the possibility that the city might be interested. I tried to impress upon the mayor that it was the Board of Supervisors, not he, that was responsible for setting the kind of policy that would determine use of the island, and I also reminded the federal folk that the city, not they, would determine its ultimate use (and thereby influence its price). Although it was a practical impossibility, I remarked to one federal employee that we could zone the island for single-family housing, which would of course have a devastating effect on its value. He seemed to get my point.

Once the matter was in the hands of the supervisors they had to be convinced that it was proper to refer it to the planning department for a recommendation. They and the mayor preferred to deal directly with developers, one of whom, Lamar Hunt, wanted to build a space museum complete with an observation tower in the form of a space capsule. We got proposals from any number of would-be developers, and we had to hear them all. There were many trips to the island amidst proposals for a western Statue of Liberty, hotels, colleges, housing, and the inevitable gambling casino. An ex-guard who was working on the island as a custodian and guide thought it would make a good prison.

Our report, prepared with our consultants, called for retention of much of the open space and preservation of the older structures underlying the newer prison buildings. It also included a number of commercial recreational uses of the sort usually associated with tourism.[4] I had some personal misgivings about this part of the proposal and was angry with myself for not thinking of the idea that planning commissioners Kearney and Fleishhacker came up with: they favored just letting it be. The other commissioners agreed with them (and passed Resolution 6425 to that effect on September 12, 1969). But the mayor and the Board of Supervisors were running hard to find a use that would make the city lots of money. As the controversy continued into 1969, a local dress manufacturer, Alvin Duskin, placed a full-page announcement in the local newspapers opposing any commercial development of the island. His campaign was very successful; the public response forced the federal officials to take a go-slow attitude. Ultimately, Alcatraz was invaded by Indians and the government took it off the market.[5]

Another policy matter for the Board of Supervisors came up in 1968. Agents of the federal government planned to release three old fort sites, Forts Mason, Miley, and Funston. In part, it was intended by them that the property be used to solve local housing problems, although not necessarily for low-income people only. But it was hard to convince the mayor and his staff that this was indeed a policy matter. In fact, one of the mayor's aides, Jack Tolan, was negotiating directly with possible developers. In the meantime, the planning department was studying the best uses for the sites. Our report, *Forts Mason, Miley, and Funston,* proposed a combination of open space, housing for low-income and moderate-income people as well as market-rate housing, preservation of historic structures on the sites, and a major public educational use for one of the sites.[6] When the matter finally did get to a board committee, its members were furious that they had been by-passed and that a mayor's aide was negotiating directly with a developer. They voted to keep all of the sites as open space. Committee chairman Pelosi advised me, in an aside, that any proposal for development would have been rejected on principle. It was one of the first defeats by the board of a proposal by Mayor Alioto. Since our mixed-use proposals had been turned down, and since some socially oriented housing would not get built, I did not view it as a victory for city planning.

There were many other immediate issues to be dealt with in 1968. We were not lacking for things to do.

About a dozen of the professional staff members who were on hand when I arrived were proving to be as competent city planners as anyone might hope to meet anywhere. A few, such as Peter Svirsky, Bob Passmore, Peter Groat, Jim Paul, Jim White, Phoebe Brown, Tom Malloy, and Lynn Pio, were a lot more than competent. But overall, the staff was still not up to the caliber I wanted: there were too few people trained as city planners or as specialists in the areas of expertise that city planning required and too many people who looked at planning differently than I. Our staff did not have the technical skills to hold its own with other bureaucrats, especially those in the Department of Public Works, and we were not nearly as sharp as the staff of the Redevelopment Agency. Public presentations by staff members were too often weak and unsure, and we lacked experienced leadership and managerial skills. If we were going to establish a solid professional base in the community and get on with our work, we needed to attract good people to fill unstaffed positions as soon as possible.

There were two parts to attracting and hiring good city planners: finding them and persuading them that San Francisco would be a

productive place in which to work, and getting them on the staff despite the civil service system. That system was to prove a much more formidable hurdle than attracting good people in the first place.

San Francisco's civil service system was and is incredibly cumbersome and time consuming. It is not geared to attracting top people. The process of agreeing on qualifications; getting out announcements; preparing, administering, and grading written and oral exams (with appeals permitted and common at every step along the way) took forever. Exam questions, to be "fair" and "objective," were either of the factual or multiple choice variety. Questions like, "In what direction does the Seine River flow through Paris?" became famous. It was extremely difficult for anyone living outside the Bay Area to take exams. Employees' unions even protested required minimum qualifications for entry level positions on the grounds that those standards might later be used to prejudice minimum standards for promotive positions. If they passed the exams, existing employees almost always had priority over outside candidates when higher level openings occurred. The time between the announcement of an opening and the appearance of a list of those who passed the exam often was more than a year. In the interval, the most qualified people had long since taken other positions. I concluded that the good people who were already on the staff were there despite, not because of, the system.

Once a list of passing candidates was established, I had no choice in hiring, a policy that made it difficult to seek out and hire minority employees. That law has since been changed so that now a director may choose from the top three scorers, but back then the top scorer got the job. It was only during the six-month probation period that every employee served that I had the authority to fire anyone.

All of this was taking place during a period when jobs in city planning were plentiful, and the best applicants could pick and choose. For opening positions, the salary structure in San Francisco was any-where from $1,000 to $3,000 less than was being offered by other big cities.

Although our approach to overcoming hiring barriers was by no means original (sometimes a system includes mechanisms, however dreary and time-consuming, to overcome its own excesses), our dog-gedness and perseverance may have been noteworthy. We hired people on what was called a "limited tenure" basis. This meant hiring, with Civil Service permission, on a temporary basis to fill vacant positions for which examinations were not yet in progress. We tried to get exams delayed so that people already hired would be better prepared to take them. Some exams would be postponed for years. We also tried to change the emphasis from written to oral exams. When exams were announced for positions that were already filled with top-notch but temporary professionals, we tried to influence the Civil Service staff to make the filing periods as brief as possible. I tried to create specialty positions to get the people I wanted.

Representatives of the employees' unions watched us carefully, and our moves were countered by their moves—appeals, attempts to do away with limited tenure hiring, and the like. I had shouting matches with them in front of the Civil Service Commission, most of whose members I felt were overly sympathetic to the unions. At one Civil Service Commission meeting, attorneys for an employees' union ac-cused me of cheating and lying. During one short period I made arrangements to have a lawyer—my personal attorney from a presti-gious office—represent me. He would stand next to me and silently pass his card around. His presence seemed to inspire the Civil Service Commission to treat me more gently.

On one or two occasions we requested and received Mayor Alioto's assistance in influencing the staff of the Civil Service Commis-sion to do things our way. One of these times involved an exam for my administrative assistant. The administrative assistant position was a professional position created at my behest. Bruce Anderson was filling it magnificently on a limited tenure basis, and he more than met the criteria that were important to me: compatibility, trust, and the ability to attend to the myriad details that are associated with the job of director. Ultimately, however, Anderson had to take an examination, and he feared that he had failed the written part because the questions were unrelated to the position (which was often the case on such exams). But I was not about to have anyone in that position who was not totally acceptable to me professionally and personally, and I told the mayor as much. Although Anderson's fear later proved ill founded, I requested that the passing score be lowered by five to ten points. It took the mayor's influence on the head of Civil Service to do that, and it took more influence to get an oral examination board that was likely to listen to my admonition not to pass anyone who was unlikely to be personally acceptable to me.

The battles with Civil Service over testing, hiring, firing, promoting, setting qualifications, and determining proper salaries were continual and enervating. The rules always seemed to change, but they almost never became more flexible. I knew even then that hassles with Civil Service would be one of the reasons for ultimately quitting.

During this period, I went to an evening meeting of a supervisors' committee dealing with salary standardization to argue for higher pay for my staff. The chambers were jammed with city employees and their union representatives. I was the only department head present. At one point my ear tuned in on a union official making a case for the same pay for category X-1234 (or some such number) "Laundry Marker" as for Y-5678 "Laundry Packer" (or some such title). My mind skipped around; I wondered what a laundry marker looked like and whether he thought of himself as such. It occurred to me that in 1968 San Francisco was in the final stages of fixing a caste system not too dissimilar to the one that had dominated India for thousands of years. And the results might turn out to be the same. It was a depressing evening.

The immediate job was to attract bright, eager, challenging city planners. If a sense of purpose could be communicated to prospective employees, the Civil Service barriers could be overcome. Pat Cusick, my boss in Pittsburgh, had taught me years earlier never to promise or imply anything you can't deliver. And because I was dealing with other people's lives, I tried to be extremely cautious, even negative, in explaining the terms and conditions, and the pitfalls, of employment with the department. I suspect that people figured that things couldn't be as bad as I had pictured them, so they decided to take a chance. I must have given my speech about what brought me to San Francisco a hundred times: to have a chance to address real people's problems in a direct way, to try to make city planning more relevant than it had been in the operations of the city, and to build a high quality staff. The promise of being given responsibilities equal to their talents was influential in attracting good people, as was the prospect of working on housing, neighborhood planning, and urban design issues—areas of concern to many city planning graduates at the time. The fact that we made little differentiation between long-range and immediate planning concerns, that people would be working on both together, was also attractive.

A lot of fine young people responded. Most of them were very inexperienced, and I had to keep reminding myself that at their age I had been inexperienced too, and that I still was, as far as being a planning director was concerned. I met and interviewed applicants at conferences; they came with recommendations from friends; and they walked in off the street, attracted by the prospect of living and working in a city that was something of a mecca for young people in the sixties. In 1968 I think I personally interviewed every job applicant.

Coincidence and good fortune played a role in the makeup of the staff. During the summer, two just-graduated city planners from the University of Pennsylvania, former students of mine, were in my office asking about jobs. One didn't interview Trixie Farrar and Dennis Ryan so much as they interviewed you. They were bright, questioning, suspicious, and frustrating. They also seemed to have zillions of other job offers. In response to a question, put in the form of a demand actually, about what we were doing in the areas of neighborhood and minority planning, and tiring before their barrage of unanswerable queries, I suggested that they come to a meeting that night in the largely black South Bayshore area to see for themselves. We were to present alternative plans for the shoreline area and review the adequacy of local shopping facilities. The meeting was going well and was reasonably tranquil until one young man, in front of the crowd of 50 or so people, tried to take over. I sensed that if we were to be respected and effective in the community, I had better not back down. Shouts led to screams as we got closer to each other. Stupidly, I returned his threat of violence with a challenge, and the man left the room, to do what I'll never know. We may have "made it" in the community that night. I suspect that Trixie's call the next day, saying that she and Dennis would like to have jobs if they were available, was related to the previous night's theatrics. (Years later, in January 1977, Adam Rogers, the young man involved, was murdered in South Bayshore.)

Attracting a new assistant director proved to be more difficult. Both the Civil Service Commission and the Board of Supervisors had to be convinced to raise the status of the position, and its salary as well, and to postpone the exam for two years. The money to pay moving expenses would have to come from private sources, and two planning commissioners agreed to help out. Of course, finding the right person was the big job. It had to be an experienced big-city planner who was well grounded professionally, especially in comprehensive and project planning, and who could operate knowingly among other high-level city hall technicians. Above all, I needed someone who could lead, inspire, and manage people, since almost half the staff would be under his, or her, direction on a day-to-day basis. Finding such a person took about a year. Finally, after turning the job down once, Dean Macris, with 10 years of experience in Chicago, where he was then assistant commissioner of development and planning, agreed to move to San Francisco.

Establishing and maintaining working relationships with the Board of Supervisors and the planning commission, as well as with the mayor and his people, ranked in importance with the development of the professional staff. They, along with the people of San Francisco, represent clients, and I looked at them in that way. They make decisions; they endorse policies and programs; in the short run, they are the keys to the effectiveness of city planning (the people as a whole being the keys in the long run). They can give and they can take away; and it was good to remember that the planning commission, figuratively, signed my pay check. It was important for the people who made up the board and the commission, and who held key positions in the mayor's office, to know the planners, to value us, to respect us, and to like us if that was possible. It would be beneficial too, if they sensed that we could help them.

I had no special program for endearing myself with the city's major policy makers. Our approach was simply to respond quickly and thoroughly to their requests and to say what we had to say regarding the physical planning of San Francisco in a clear, straightforward, and forceful manner. Our job was not only to present decision makers with thoughtful and clear alternative courses of action, based on as much research and data as we could put our hands on, including assessments of the consequences of the alternatives, but also to advocate, as strongly as necessary, what we thought was good city planning. If we had an ax to grind, it was for city planning. That meant that I was going to give my professional opinion often, regardless of the political ramifications. I assumed that was what my clients—the policy makers and the people— wanted. Besides, I was also a client to be satisfied. I did not want rotten decisions to come back to haunt me, especially if I knew they were politically rather than professionally inspired. It was important to be able to sleep well at night. I felt that a city planner should say what he had to say and have his bags packed in case his client didn't like the advice.

My wife and I did invite individual supervisors to small social gatherings. It seemed reasonable to get to know them and for them to get to know us. But if this was a strategy to gain influence, it wasn't a very good one. I never got around to inviting the supervisors I didn't like, and I didn't need influence with those we saw. The dinners did help form some lasting friendships, as did social evenings with the planning commissioners.

Another exception to my "professionalism" stemmed from the fact that many of the decisions, judgments, and recommendations that we were called upon to make were of marginal significance for city planning or physical development. A permit to use a vacant lot for a fair, the expansion of a grocery store in a residential area, the conversion of an unused church, surrounded by houses, to a small, neighborhood-oriented dance center, or even minor changes in zoning are a few of many examples. My rule was not to compromise on issues where an important planning idea or principle was involved. But I was not opposed to deciding marginal or insignificant items in a manner that would gain for the planning department the most currency—by which I might mean support, stature, friends, future influence, or good will. There were any number of groups or individuals with whom to gain currency, and at any one time one might be more important than another. These would include individual property owners, neighbor-hood groups, elected officials, planning commissioners, fellow bureau-crats, design professionals, and others. The trick was not to fool yourself into concluding that something of importance was really of no signifi-cance.

Our approach seemed to work with the supervisors. Their meetings, in committee and at the full Monday afternoon sessions, were relatively open, and individual supervisors continued to be accessible. So long as we presented our material forcefully and clearly distinguished between fact and opinion, they were prepared to listen. Neither did they respond negatively to our taking strong advocacy positions. One or two supervisors were noted for their propensity to berate, insult, interrupt, and otherwise publicly abuse representatives of various departments. I found that it was not necessary to take that abuse and that it was acceptable behavior to match insults and false assertions with interruptions, denials, and assertions of one's own. As long as one was not discourteous to start, the board seemed to enjoy a scrap. Sometimes the scrapping was humorous. Supervisor William Blake took every opportunity to remind his fellows, and the public, that the board had paid my moving expenses, something unheard of, and that it would do well to pay my expenses back East. I told him that I expected him to come up with the money on the day after he got the planning commission to fire me.

Contacts with members of the mayor's staff were more than cordial. They were approachable and helpful. It was a straight and uncomplicated relationship. They assumed that I knew my field, and they sought my counsel on matters that were related to city planning. The most significant element in the relationship may have been the fact that most of the mayor's staffers were newer to city hall and knew even less about how things worked than I. I helped them learn as I was still learning, answering their questions about the city's government, the people, and the issues that were important to the community. They were as amazed as I at the difficulty of getting things done. The only clash that I recall, and that was only a momentary one, was with the mayor's deputy for development, Jack Tolan, who seemed to be suggesting, one day, that there were better ways to run my office—in particular, ways that would give him more direct access to my staff. I recall walking around my desk, taking a seat next to him, and suggesting that if he wanted to fill the now vacant seat of planning director, fine, but if not, then he should stop telling me how to run the office.


My views about the planning commission began to change. During the first year, I had tended to view the commission as a cumbersome layer between the professionals on the one hand, and the people, the mayor, and the Board of Supervisors on the other, a carryover from the days when city planning was an elitist activity of high-minded do-gooders who believed that the long-range view and development of the city had to be independent of both politics and day-to-day decisions. Julia Porter, one of the commissioners, had me sized up correctly when she said that I secretly wished I could do away with all the commissioners and be free to do as I wished. The commissioners were not necessarily nonpolitical in their decisions about the future of the city, and they were often out of tune with what was going on in certain areas. For no good reason, their meetings, especially the zoning hearings, were lengthy, and preparing for and sitting through them took inordinate amounts of staff and personal time. Commissioners often gave greater weight to the views of other department heads than to those of their own director and too often represented a potential hurdle for the staff.

Nonetheless, the commission did serve positive functions as well. Some members had knowledge of the city and its people that the staff did not have. Commissioners sometimes acted as a buffer between the staff and the public, taking a lot of heat off the staff. They advocated for the staff, especially before the board and with individual supervisors. One or two commissioners, like Fleishhacker and Walter Newman, took the devil's advocate role before issues came to a hearing, thereby allowing the staff to focus its research and sharpen its recommendations. Commissioners could provide easy entry to certain segments of the community, and their judgment was usually sound and therefore to be respected, especially when no political issue was involved. Perhaps most important, they were quite supportive during this period, and one felt that they would be helpful on most matters.

As we had promised, in 1968 we increased our efforts in the area of neighborhood planning and encouraged more citizen involvement. We still had no preset formula for neighborhood planning. We just went out and did it, understanding that it was both desirable and necessary to involve residents.

Our efforts in South Bayshore increased significantly. Three people were assigned full time to the project. They were all white, and their leader, Phoebe Brown, was a brahmin type who lived in a most exclusive part of town. In retrospect, it is anyone's guess as to why the neighborhood had anything to do with any of us, including me, or why people came to the community meetings we called. But they did come. Perhaps they sensed, as I soon did, that Phoebe Brown was a plain-speaking, no-nonsense professional, who worked tirelessly and would meet with any group, was clear about our abilities and limitations, and radiated dignity and a desire for a better community.

Following the pattern started in 1967, we would call occasional community meetings to present our work and to discuss topics of areawide concern. We didn't produce much in the way of written reports, mostly because the talents of the junior staff did not lie in that direction, but following our hostile reception in 1967, we began to communicate better and, over time, we fought and shouted less and saw and heard more. We learned, among other things, that the South Bay-shore community was in no way a slum, that there was no inherent reason for it to be any less pleasant a place to live than any other San Francisco neighborhood, that it was isolated from the rest of the city and therefore ignored, that it had a bad image, and that there were any number of opportunities to improve the neighborhood. One of the things we could do was to tell other city departments about problems that residents relayed to us. And so, on occasion, I would call the Public Works director or a high-up police official to relay a complaint about street cleaning or public protection. In time, we became known; there were no more confrontations like the one in early summer. It helped that we could produce, by means of reimbursements from the urban beautification program, about $100,000 for a long-promised recreation center. For me, the real turning point came the morning I was called upon by the community to help mediate a disagreement between the Housing Authority and the Redevelopment Agency. I began then to feel that we were accepted in South Bayshore.

Chinatown was another matter. I knew I didn't know anything about the area, and I suspected that most staff members didn't either. One heard all kinds of stories about "The Real Chinatown"—stories of extreme crowding in terrible housing, sweat shops, gang wars, illegal immigrants, and of the influence of the Chinese Six Companies and the family associations. One also heard that the Chinese bought buildings with cash.

J.K. Choy, elderly banker and activist, called Chinatown a slum and said the height limits should come off. He regularly said something to the effect that if I couldn't stand the heat I should get out of the kitchen, and he called for a plan. Alice Barkley, quite Chinese despite her name, swore at just about everyone in wonderful four-letter words while working incredibly hard to solve housing problems, open space prob-. lems, public service problems, and the social and economic problems of the elderly and young Chinese. She, too, wanted a plan.

Jim Paul was assigned to spend about a month walking around Chinatown, getting a sense of the place, and then to suggest what we ought to do. Our conclusion was that assigning a full-time planner, committed to the area for an extended period and charged with solving immediate problems and developing programs and projects, would be more useful than doing a plan. Late in the year, we presented the alternatives to a lively, everyone-is-welcome meeting in Chinatown. The community wanted both!

In November, our Northern Waterfront consultants produced a plan.[7] It was the culmination of what had been a frustrating experience from the start. The planning had begun before I was hired and at first I had no good understanding of the reasons for making a plan to begin with or of what it was to accomplish, the kind of understanding that comes from living with a problem for a while before attempting to solve it. Moreover, I was uncomfortable in the role of official overseer of a planning contract; I would rather have been doing the planning than trying to relate to the consultants and to the major interests that constituted the client. For the first time, I was exposed to some of San Francisco's more feisty urban conservation advocates, like those who purported to represent Telegraph and Russian hills. Their intransigence was matched by the development-oriented port commission, our own highway-centered Department of Public Works, the waterfront land-owners, and the commercial developers. No matter whom we met with—and we had regular meetings to test our proposals—we seemed to be missing some group, or else a new group sprang from nowhere. It was not just that we couldn't please everyone. Rather, I got the sense that we could please no one.

In other parts of the city, we were becoming more involved in the Federally Assisted Code Enforcement program (FACE). The program was already in effect in four areas where residents were beginning to take part in detailed planning of public improvements. In 1968 we worked actively to get three more areas to a point of start-up. We still had to convince many people that FACE made sense, that subsidized rehabilitation of homes combined with a public improvements pro-

gram was a natural for San Francisco, where most housing was basically sound. Also, FACE associated us with a positive action program that could be used to carry out plans. It was positive in that it didn't take away property or demolish buildings or dislocate people (or at least not many) but provided public improvements and subsidized loans instead.

I learned a lot about the federal government, the local redevelopment program, and the Bureau of Building Inspection through FACE. Federal representatives wanted two of the three new areas we were considering to be renewal projects under the auspices of the Redevelopment Agency. I came to realize just how committed the feds were to a bulldozer approach to city problems. Their propensity to question the judgment of local officials on what was or was not appropriate in San Francisco was also more than a little disconcerting.

I learned, also, just how fearful people were of redevelopment. At first, we had to convince them that we were not the Redevelopment Agency and that we were not proposing a renewal program. But later, the residents of a block where there was a real possibility of significant displacement of people—because of elimination of illegal units and rent increases—nevertheless asked that it be included in the FACE program. They reasoned that FACE was better than the alternative of doing nothing, since doing nothing was in fact an invitation to more redevelopment operations.

Before I came to San Francisco, I had never had much use for building inspection operations. In most cities that I knew of, the housing codes were rarely enforced in any serious way, and one frequently heard rumors of payoffs. Nor were building inspection departments noted for having the brightest employees in the world. San Francisco was different. Not only did the guys in the Bureau of Building Inspection know their business, but they knew what the laws said and didn't say, and they knew how to organize and run a program. The inspectors involved with the FACE program were serious, straight people, and they were terribly competent pros. Their curt, uncompromising manner before neighborhood groups and elected officials did leave something to be desired, but when they told you something, you knew you had been told. Al Goldberg, the head man, came on as the epitome of a nasty know-it-all who would send his mother to jail over a leaky faucet, but he and his top staff seemed honest beyond any question. And they made the FACE program work. The staff of the bureau was to be an ally in the years ahead.

This was a busy time. One day's calendar, such as the one for January 30, 1968, might include a meeting with the mayor's deputy for development on the Model Cities program, a meeting with staff and would-be developers over use of the shoreline in the South Bayshore area, 40 minutes of paper work and telephone calls, a meeting with the mayor regarding the Embarcadero Center renewal project, and 20 more minutes of private work time before a lunch meeting with local architects to discuss a comprehensive urban design plan. Lunch might be followed by a two-hour meeting with key staff on salaries, job classifications, and recruiting; a review of the proposal for the International Market Center; and a meeting on northern waterfront planning. Miscellaneous telephone calls and one-minute consultations were sandwiched in somewhere. At 6:30 I would go home for dinner. If there was no evening meeting, I would spend a couple of hours reviewing the material that had piled up on my desk during the day. I could have named at least half a dozen other people who were just as active.

The primary responsibility of the planning department is to prepare and maintain the master plan. The existing master plan, completed in 1945, had been amended many times since. It was a small mimeographed document that might have served well for its time but was now out-of-date. Some local planning buffs considered it a kind of embarrassment. However, I was not all that anxious to redo the plan. I had had disheartening experiences with comprehensive, master plans both in the Pittsburgh area and in Calcutta, and the volatile times seemed to call for immediate solutions to crisis conditions. I succumbed to the academic criticisms of comprehensive physical planning that were then widespread: irrelevant, elitist, anti-social equity, and God knows what else. Further, a major revision of the master plan would cost a fortune, and there was no new money for that purpose. The planning commission was not interested and the department did not have the staff on hand for preparing a new plan. But despite all the negatives, a course of action did evolve from our research and information-gathering activities, from our work on the issues that we had identified as being of critical importance to the community, and from the interests and expertise of the staff.

The San Francisco simulation model of the housing market was one of those back-burner activities that was, unfortunately, visible, and it was important to decide what to do with it. Both the model and the Community Renewal Program that it came from were in bad repute around city hall. Although the model had been declared operational by someone, no one was operating it in public. Requests for new positions or for funds to undertake new studies were met with, "Are you nuts? So you can build another model?" Peter Groat, who was in charge of the model, had spent hours on end explaining it to me—how it was supposed to test the effects of various public policy programs upon the city's supply of housing, what went into it, how it worked, its status, and the like. They were painful hours for him. There were a lot of things wrong with the model, including very questionable accuracy, difficulty in interpreting its output, the high cost of operation, and its ability to answer only questions no one was asking. A new terminology had to be invented to deal with computer limitations (a "fract"). In September we published a report that described the model, its potential, and its shortcomings, and put it to bed.[8]

More positively, we produced the first of our *Changes in the San Francisco Housing Inventory* reports in 1968. If housing was an issue, then knowing the amounts, locations, types, sizes, and costs of the housing that was being added and subtracted from the overall stock of the city would help to develop policies and programs to address the issues.

Because housing issues were so significant in the late sixties, because housing is by far the biggest user of land and in large measure its nature and quality determine the character of the city as a whole, and because new and unassigned staff had expertise in the subject, we elected to prepare a comprehensive plan for residence. In making that decision we were really committing ourselves to an element-by-element preparation of a new comprehensive plan for San Francisco. To the challenge that this was not a comprehensive way to prepare a comprehensive plan and that we could not be sure that this or any element would relate properly to another, we responded that we didn't have funds to do the whole job at once, that we were attacking the most important issues first, that in San Francisco it was probably more important for other issues to relate to housing than vice versa, and that later we would make adjustments to completed work if that proved necessary. I might have added that, for me, any plan for San Francisco that I had a hand in was likely to be oriented toward protecting and maintaining the basic character of the city. We would build upon the city as it was. In any case, we had started to roll on long-range, citywide plans.

We also began an urban design study in 1968. After almost a year of preparing study outlines and work programs, estimating costs and personnel needs, tracking down funds, and getting necessary approvals, we started on a plan that was primarily directed to the appearance of the city, to the way San Francisco should look. It would be a major undertaking.

It had been a busy year. There had been more winners than losers. I think we were establishing, or strengthening, a respected professional base in the community. We seemed to be doing relevant work, and we were doing long- and short-range city planning, which is supposedly what we were paid to do. If there was a loser of the kind that stays in one's mind for a long time, and causes a twinge whenever he sees it, it was the pedestrian bridge from Portsmouth Square over Kearny Street to the so-called Chinese Cultural Center, which was really an arbitrarily shaped Holiday Inn. Although I am convinced that I could not have stopped that pompous, shadow-producing, space-reducing bridge—the Redevelopment Agency had managed to convince every public agency that was involved that the others were for it and that there was no turning back—I could have and should have said "No" in the loudest voice possible. Instead, I gave some kind of a wishy-washy, Mickey-Mouse, "only if" type of recommendation that did nothing to hinder the abomination. In truth, I was a little intimidated in those days by the Redevelopment Agency and its director, Justin Herman. I didn't like him. I knew he had little use for city planning, thought he was devious, and didn't know how to beat him. I felt that way about no one else in San Francisco, an open, free, no-holds-barred, welcoming city that would give all sorts of new people and new ideas a chance and an audience.

Feeling as I did about San Francisco, it seems inconsistent that I would support a study that was aimed at simplifying the existing charter and centralizing power and responsibility with the mayor. The good-government types, especially the liberals, were unhappy with San Francisco's cumbersome, inefficient, slow-to-respond, no-power-to-anyone form of government. The government did not appear to have a very rational structure, if getting things done was a major criterion. The only thing that could be said for it was that it was relatively honest, but that might mean spending $100 to be sure no one could steal $5.

The drafters of the new charter wanted to take power from the entrenched bureaucrats—who ever heard of a chief administrative officer with a lifetime appointment?—and make government more flexible, efficient, and responsible by placing that power in the hands of a strong mayor. City planning would be directly under the mayor, and the planning commission would become merely advisory to the staff. It seemed to be an arrangement that would help city planning increase its effectiveness and its relevance. It would put it closer to the driver's seat. It made sense to me. It was the way things were being done in the smart, eastern cities that I still held as models. Besides, I liked Mayor Alioto and foresaw no problems with being closer to his office, although I did say at the time that if a much-expanded planning operation were to move to the mayor's office, I would resign. My reason, however, was not related to the location of city planning within government. Rather it was the nature of the job that bothered me; it would be much broader than planning and guiding the physical development of the city and more concerned with the planning and coordination of social and economic policies and programs—general purpose governmental planning and coordinating. It would also be less fun and less interesting for me. I did not see at the time the relationship between San Francisco's existing governmental structure and the growing effectiveness of city planning. So I encouraged the efficiency-responsiveness-centrality directions of the Charter Revision Committee in 1968. Their deliberations continued through 1969. In the meantime there was plenty to do.

Whether or not we saw or grasped all the available opportunities to be effective is hard to say. We tried.

It was important to understand the significance of the small day-to-day matters that came to the commission regularly—each with a direct effect on only a few people. In sum, they would prove to be a measure of our effectiveness and relevance. Each of those small zoning and referral cases deserved a well-thought-out and reasonable recommendation. I don't think I understood that very well when I first came to San Francisco, but I was learning.

We viewed the subsidized code enforcement-rehabilitation program, coupled with modest public improvements, as an opportunity to be immediately effective. We also gained points for the department through the federally sponsored urban beautification program, which seemed equally important at the time. We had put the program together in the first place and had considerable influence over its use. Although the amounts of money involved were relatively small compared with other programs, their use helped to raise the visibility and effectiveness of the department. The simple ability to offer something tangible, however small, was enough to suggest to people that planning and "those planners" might hold some immediate pay-offs for them. Much of the money was spent in less-advantaged neighborhoods. That summer we developed an employment program, putting 300 young people to work rehabilitating an almost forgotten area of Golden Gate Park.

The mini-park program was another program that increased our visibility. The planning department staff found sites for the parks on extremely short notice. That meant that we were directly associated with providing things that people wanted in their neighborhoods. On the other hand, the speed with which we had to select the sites was not always consistent with good citizen participation practices. In one South of Market area, especially, people were furious that we had selected sites without talking to them. They let me know with a vengeance that the sites we had chosen were too small, too few, and too poorly located. Their anger was compounded by the fact that they were being dislocated by the Yerba Buena redevelopment project. During two of the most raucous meetings I ever attended—meetings where I was held responsible for the death of a child, the Viet Nam War, and just about everything else, meetings that had no order beyond the opening sentence, meetings that were full of crying kids and adults screaming filthy language and threats of physical violence, meetings that were nothing but nastiness, meetings where I learned to give as well as I got—during those meetings we somehow hit upon an approach that resulted in the building of two mini-parks in the South of Market area. Somehow, through all the shouting and anger, we must have shared a common purpose and common objectives.

# Notes

1. The hilltop zoning case was reported by Maitland Zane in "Supervisors Reject Pleas of Mt. Olympus Residents," *San Francisco Chronicle,* July 17, 1968. An example of a case involving a residential conversion appears in the minutes of the San Francisco City Planning Commission for November 7, 1968, Case CU 68.27.

2. The supervisors lined up the same way in all of the six-to-five votes, including the vote against a delay and the final vote of approval for the Department of City Planning proposal. Voting aye were Pelosi, Boas, Francois, McCarthy, Mendelsohn. Voting nay were Von Beroldingen, Tamaras, Blake, Ertola, and Maillard. On the seven-to-four votes against certain amendments, Maillard switched his vote to aye.

3. Ron Moskowitz, "Supervisors OK Market Center," *San Francisco Chronicle,* July 15, 1968.

4. Actually, the San Francisco Department of City Planning produced two reports: "Draft Report—Alcatraz Island," August 22, 1968, and *Development Criteria and Policies for Alcatraz Island,* September 12, 1969. The consultants were Sedway/Cooke, Urban and Environmental Planners and Designers.

5. "As Big a Steal as Manhattan Island," *San Francisco Chronicle,* October 3, 1969; "Alcatraz Not for Sale—U.S.," *San Francisco Examiner,* December 3, 1969.

6. San Francisco Department of City Planning, *Forts Mason, Miley, and Funston,* November 1968.

7. John S. Bolles Associates, *Northern Waterfront Plan,* 1968.

8. San Francisco Department of City Planning, *Status of the San Francisco Simulation Model,* September 1968.

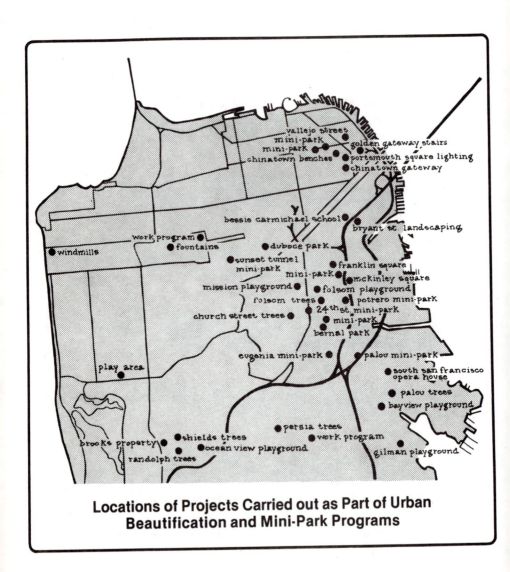

**Locations of Projects Carried out as Part of Urban
Beautification and Mini-Park Programs**

# Chapter 4
# Case Study: The Urban
# Beautification Program

San Francisco's Department of City Planning has a charter mandate "to secure understanding and a systematic effectuation of the ... master plan," but it has few direct powers that would enable it to carry out the plans it produces. Located where it is, under a semi-independent and semi-isolated planning commission, the department has difficulty "making things happen." This is particularly so in regard to public programs and projects, as compared to its role in regulating the use of private property. If city planning in San Francisco has a problem in this regard, it is one that is shared with planning agencies in many other cities.

However, city planning can be effective within a governmental context that would seem to augur against that probability. San Francisco's urban beautification program is a case in point. The planning department used its knowledge of government, its informal powers, and the interests of its staff to help carry out a plan and to deal successfully with community issues. The case is an illustration of the considerable opportunities that exist in most cities for city planning to be responsive to issues. It shows that one program, with modest objectives, can help address other, more significant problems. It also suggests that local government can usually adapt its organizational structure to take advantage of federal programs that it considers desirable and that a change to a structure that is favored by the federal government is not necessary.

In March of 1965, President Johnson sent a message to Congress on housing and urban problems. He spoke of cities "where men and women can feed the hunger of the spirit for beauty and have access to the best of man's work."[1] The federal Urban Beautification and Improvement Program was born of that message and of the Housing and Urban Development Act of 1965, which provided the authority requested by the President "to help American communities to improve the quality of their urban environment and to replace ugliness with beauty in our urban areas." The legislation encouraged local governments to establish beautification plans and programs. Beautification could take the form of development of existing public open spaces with landscaping, walkways, and recreation and exhibition areas; or it could mean making public streets more pleasant by installing planting, decorative paving, benches, and lighting.

Funding of the beautification program was somewhat different from others run by the Department of Housing and Urban Development in that it was directed not so much to individual projects as to encouraging sustained efforts by communities. A community could obtain a federal grant for up to half the amount by which it exceeded its usual yearly expenditures under an approved beautification program. In other words, once a community established a base level of expenditures for urban beautification, the federal government was prepared to pay for half of any extra efforts. Overall, the program was not large by federal standards. The maximum that a community could receive under it was $1 million yearly. Not much at all compared to federal subsidies of up to 100 times that much for a single large redevelopment project.

For purposes of federal funding, an urban beautification program had to begin with a plan, which included a statement of its overall scope and objectives, a description of the organization for putting the plan into effect, and a summary of existing and proposed activities, including costs and completion schedules. One other feature is worth noting: any department of a local government was eligible to apply. This meant that with proper local approvals, the San Francisco Department of City Planning could be an applicant.

The modesty of the federal funding was consistent with the relative unimportance of urban beautification in San Francisco in the 1960s. Although there was evidence to indicate San Franciscans cared about the sensuous nature of the city, they seemed to be less concerned with what could be viewed as the cosmetic nature of the federal program. Residents spoke of how pleasant it was to live in the city, and they were aware of its attractiveness to tourists. They were prepared to fight against new freeways on the grounds of urban aesthetics. And there were indications that they cared about how well or poorly an individual building proposal would relate to the rest of the city. They continually expressed concern about the maintenance of public parks and open spaces. But generally they were satisfied with the city.

Voters might support a major project such as the beautification of Market Street, the main downtown thoroughfare, but there was no generally accepted and endorsed effort to beautify the city as a whole, at least as implied in the federal beautification program. There was no commonly understood notion of what such a program might be. San Francisco was certainly not unique among American cities in this regard.

Most large cities do, however, have at least a small coterie of people concerned with what might be called urban beautification. San Francisco is no exception, and groups like San Francisco Beautiful have existed for some time. Individual block clubs and neighborhood associations might also initiate beautification and tree planting programs from time to time. In government, too, there are people concerned with the subject, most notably in the Recreation and Park Department, those responsible for street trees and roadway landscaping in the Department of Public Works, and a number of people in the Department of City Planning.

In the mid-1960s there were at least two senior staff members,

Ruth Jaffee and Sam Jung, with long-term interests in urban landscape and beautification. One was involved in citywide planning and the other was in charge of the department's capital improvement program efforts. Both were familiar with the charter's admonition to carry out the master plan, with the city's governmental structure, and with key city personnel. They were aware of the federal beautification program and knew that both the Public Works and Recreation and Park departments might have valid claims on possible grants. The staff of the other two departments knew this as well, and thus they understood the need for coordination, as well as the need for knowledge of all budgeted beautification-related funds, and for a plan. Planning department involvement and leadership in the program was therefore considered reasonable. As for the city planners, they saw an opportunity to get federal funds that could be used to enhance the quality of the physical environment in a modest way, through beautification.

During 1966 and early 1967, the planning department analyzed both current and previous budgets to determine what local expenditures might qualify as allowable under the beautification program guidelines. The staff also prepared a local beautification plan with other departments and was engaged in preparing the application.

The previous years' budgets would reveal beautification expenditures which could be used to establish a base amount from which an accelerated program could benefit by way of federal grants. The agency that was most knowledgeable about all applicable projects and expenditures would be the most important in relations with federal representatives. That would prove to be the planning department. A meticulous search of the current budget established that beautification expenditures were about $688,000 higher than the average of previous years. The city would be eligible for a federal grant of approximately $344,000. (Later, the figure was raised to $369,050.)

In preparing the program and application, the staff decided that it would only include fully funded projects that would go forward regardless of whether a federal grant was received. The grant money would not be necessary, then, to reimburse the city for half of its "accelerated" expenditures, but it could be used for additional projects. Basically, the staff was proposing to make maximum use of already budgeted programs to get additional money from the federal program and to apply it to an accelerated local effort. No additional local funds were to be involved.

The beautification plan consisted of a series of objectives and goals, together with a five-year program of projects taken largely from the proposed capital improvement program. The objectives and goals were couched in general terms. They spoke of enhancing "the unique visual qualities of the City"; enriching the "quality of outdoor living spaces" and introducing "amenities into . . . working areas"; embellishing the "transportation system with landscape treatment"; providing for "attractive development . . . of public parks, recreation areas and school grounds"; and encouraging "neighborhood groups, merchants' associations, and other citizen participation in the beautification program."

The formal application for federal funds was prepared and submitted by the planning department. The authorized signator to the application was the planning director. This was probably the first time that the planning department had applied for capital improvement funds, an act that would enable it to exert considerable control over the allocation of the grant monies.

The first plan, "The Beautification Program for San Francisco," was approved by the planning commission on July 13, 1967, and adopted by the Board of Supervisors only 18 days later.[2] The speed with which the matter passed the board was related to the fact that no new local monies were required. The planning department was simply applying for a grant. The controller had been briefed by the planning staff so he was ready to endorse the application. Mayor Shelley's approval was immediate. The grant, of $369,050, was approved in Washington in March 1968, about six months after it was requested. It would later be raised by over $250,000 for a special project. By October 1968, the planners had met with the mayor and the finance committee of the Board of Supervisors to review the department's proposals for spending grant monies. The planners proposed that the funds be used primarily for projects that could further the beautification program, thereby ensuring sizable future grants. The new mayor, Alioto, and the supervisors agreed. With a few modifications, the process established with the first year's program in 1967-68 was continued until 1972.

City planning was able to determine the use of the beautification funds in large part because the department and the director had been designated as the "official agent" of the city in regard to the program. In addition, the staff got along just fine with Sam Weinstein and Bob Boalt, the local HUD representatives who were responsible for the program in its early years. They were knowledgeable, sympathetic, open, and helpful. They made decisions about including a particular project in the program on the basis of a simple telephone call. At times they made suggestions as to where funds could be found for particular projects. Their questions were clearly to get information, not to challenge. There was a feeling of mutual trust between the federal employees and the city planners, and it resulted in a considerable shortening of the time needed for bureaucratic paperwork. In the early days of the program, the federal checks were mailed directly to the planning director. One was for over $200,000. He handled them like a hot potato, getting them to the controller as quickly as possible. All of this helped the department in influencing the direction and speed of the beautification program, and the mere fact that the checks came to the planning department increased its stature around city hall.

The explicit criteria used to determine the allocation of the federal beautification grants were, for the most part, quite general. Perhaps the most important was the policy, endorsed by the mayor and the Board of Supervisors, that the added funds be used to augment existing beautification efforts. The most helpful aspect of the approved plan was the inclusion of broad principles for the kinds of projects that should be undertaken.[3] They left room for a wide variety of projects throughout the city, allowing a considerable amount of leeway in the choice of specific projects.

In preparing the list of projects for approval by the mayor and board, the planning department had to take a number of considerations into account. It was generally understood that many small projects were preferred over a few large ones. One or two large projects would be harder to plan, approve, and execute than small undertakings. Choosing small projects would also mean that no one department was likely to benefit at the expense of another by using the lion's share of the funds on one favorite project. Need was of course another factor. The planners worked with the staff of other departments, primarily Public Works and Recreation and Park, to decide which of their projects should be funded. Projects that were not likely to be funded through normal budgetary channels were given priority. The city planners also initiated their own projects.

Visibility and probable impact of projects were other considerations. Street trees surrounding a barren school site in a low-income area were visible, and they were desired by nearby residents. New equipment at a playground could be expected to have a positive impact.

Money spent to make the old fountains work at the Music Concourse in Golden Gate Park, where thousands of people went every weekend, was certain to have a noticeable result.

Both the planning department and HUD were inclined to give priority to lower income, minority areas. But this tendency had to be measured against a need to distribute projects throughout the city. The department was of two minds on this, because it wanted a citywide program, but it also recognized a need to serve disadvantaged areas first. In the end, more projects were located in poorer sections than in the more affluent parts of town.

Three other kinds of projects were favored: those in areas where the planners were heavily involved and committed; those that might be of particular interest to the mayor or the supervisors; and projects advocated by neighborhood organizations. Since there was not all that much money available, and since there would be no attempt to force a project where it was not wanted, expressed neighborhood desires were especially influential, and the department tended to pay most attention to those areas where it was involved in ongoing planning.

The urban beautification program was clearly a plus for the mayor, the supervisors, and the planning commissioners; consequently, it enhanced the image of the planning staff in their eyes. Mayor Alioto had not really known much about the program, because he was not in office when the application was made. Here now were new and unanticipated funds that could be used for all sorts of projects. The planning staff was careful to give the mayor's office the information on forthcoming grants so that the mayor could make the announcements. It was easy for the mayor and his staff to perceive the planning department as one that could make things happen, one that could deliver.

Similarly supervisors, individually and collectively, were impressed, particularly since some of their favorite projects could be included in the program. Moreover, the board's finance committee, highly influential in determining the size of the department's budget, saw city planning in the positive light of bringing in money to the city. However irrelevant and unnecessary it seemed to the planners to have to justify their existence by producing income, they did not miss the opportunity of comparing the size of grants received with the size of their proposed budget. Also, planning commissioners, so much of whose time and energy went to controlling the uses of private property and to the public controversies so often attending those efforts, could not help but feel positive about activities that were carrying out plans they had approved. With some justification, then, public officials could view the department as being effective in regard to the beautification program.

To other departments, such as Recreation and Park and Public Works, the planning department was now a source of funds for projects that otherwise might not be carried out. Although the planning department worked cooperatively with the others, it was soon apparent that the planners had the most to say about how the funds would be used. Sometimes it was a case of the planners' almost forcing funds on a department. Public Works, for example, resisted some funding for street trees on the grounds that there was no assurance that residents or anyone else would maintain them, and it did not wish to commit its resources for this purpose. The planning department saw to it then that some of the grant money was allocated for maintenance. Another time the poor maintenance of a previously funded project led the planning director to question his staff about the wisdom of a new Recreation and Park project. Within two weeks, the area in question had been brought up to par.

To the planners, an important payoff of the program was the enhancement of their ability to do comprehensive physical planning in neighborhoods, especially those composed largely of lower income minorities. People who are concerned with immediate issues—jobs, housing, violence, health, education—might be excused for their minimal interest, disinterest even, in urban beautification. Other things concern them. But when the results of a planning effort become immediately apparent, then they may learn to consider time devoted to such planning as worthwhile and relevant. Thus, the planners' ability to help produce a long-sought and promised recreation center, to improve a playground, to purchase the threatened, historic South San Francisco Opera House for use as a community center—all as part of the program—may well have convinced residents of the South Bayshore district that participating in planning was likely to have payoffs.

Saving the opera house is an example of the use of beautification grants to achieve community objectives. Planners working in the area discovered that the building was to be destroyed and replaced by a gas station. No city funds were available to purchase and rehabilitate the building. Besides, the Board of Supervisors had never earmarked funds for that purpose and were not likely to do so anywhere, let alone in the South Bayshore. The planners were advised by federal officials that federal historic preservation and open space funds could be found to cover up to one-half the costs, but that still left over $80,000 to be raised locally. The planners made quick calls to neighborhood residents who had been active in local planning efforts to confirm that they would rather spend beautification grant funds for saving the opera house than for neighborhood landscaping. So the city used beautification funds, which some people felt were really federal funds in the first place, to match the federal preservation and open space grants. Ultimately, the South San Francisco Opera House and an adjacent block were purchased for public use, in conformance with the department's plan for the area.

The planners were not trying to kid either themselves or the residents that the beautification program would solve basic problems like unemployment, low incomes, and high-priced housing. Within their considerable limitations they were trying to address those matters on other fronts.

When the beautification program started, there was no anticipation that it could be used to provide jobs. That possibility was raised by local HUD officials in early May 1968 when they informally advised the city that about $250,000 in special beautification funds might be available for the coming summer. The money was part of a national effort to give jobs and training to young, low-income people and thereby avert what had become known as "long, hot summers." The initial response of the operating departments to the prospect of running a new youth-employment program was lukewarm: the summer was only a month away; there were no appropriate projects; the kids would present more problems than they were worth, and the city's strict civil service hiring rules and purchasing procedures might not permit such programs. But the staff of the planning department was enthusiastic: here was a chance to help solve a pressing problem. They found a site and, together with Recreation and Park Department and labor union staffs, developed an employment program. The planners prepared and shepherded the application through city hall by mid-May. The application went to HUD as a second amendment to the first urban beautification application. By the end of the summer an overgrown section of Golden Gate Park had been restored, and approximately 300 young people from low-income areas had been employed and had received a modest amount of training in landscaping skills. There was a similar but smaller program in 1969.

The mini-park program was another area that involved the active participation of the planning department. During a trip to Washington, Mayor Alioto was assured that up to $750,000 was available from HUD and the Bureau of Outdoor Recreation to create small parks, especially in low-income areas. Apparently, Vice President Humphrey had made a commitment to support the new Democratic mayor during Humphrey's campaign for the presidency in 1968. Again, however, the operating departments were not too enthusiastic. The relatively high per-unit costs of such facilities, plus chronically inadequate maintenance budgets for even existing parks, made those departments gun-shy of new, small open spaces.

The city planners were enthusiastic, though. Mini-parks were needed, and the neighborhoods wanted them. At the request of the mayor, the planners, led by veteran staffer Sam Jung, came up with over 100 potential sites in a period of 30 days. They quickly produced some prototypical designs for the HUD program and then prepared two applications for federal funds for 33 sites. The applications were signed by the director of the Department of Public Works.

The mayor's staff soon found out that applying for and receiving funds did not create mini-parks. Active departments did. At the planning department's urging the short-term position of mini-park coordinator was established in the mayor's office and filled by a planning department staff member. Planning staff continued to work with neighborhoods and to be the program's foremost advocate in city hall. Such advocacy might include finding and presenting new sites in land-scarce Chinatown to lethargic negotiators in the Department of Real Estate, or convincing the Board of Supervisors that a vacant site in a Spanish-speaking commercial area was appropriate. It included intense involvement with residents of one area who were dissatisfied with the first, hurriedly designated site and who wanted more and larger parks.

During the six-year period from 1968 through 1973, San Francisco received almost $2.5 million in urban beautification and mini-park funds. Almost three-fourths of the total was from the federal urban beautification program. The money was used for approximately 71 projects, of which 24 were mini-parks. Other projects included rehabilitation of park areas through youth employment programs, planting street trees, restoring old windmills in Golden Gate Park, providing play equipment and park benches, landscaping and lighting parks, constructing a recreation building, and putting up an ornamental gateway in Chinatown.

For all intents and purposes, San Francisco's federally funded beautification program came to an end with the final grant of approximately $143,000 in 1972-73. The program's demise can be attributed to changing priorities of the federal administration, decreasing local expenditures for projects related to beautification and increased paperwork associated with growing federal requirements. The federal government was becoming more centralized, and programs were being consolidated. These changes were reflected in pressures for San Francisco to consolidate local programs as well. Ultimately, the beautification program was included in the categorical grants to local governments that became known as "community development block grants" and would disappear as a distinct effort of the planning department.

The urban beautification program was established under the Democrats. The Nixon administration was not especially sympathetic to many of the programs it inherited, and even less so with their size and cost in an inflationary period. Furthermore, the beautification program was strongly associated with Lady Bird Johnson, reason enough perhaps for the Republicans to look at it with suspicion. Despite congressional mandates to the contrary, the early 1970s marked the start of a period when appropriations for various programs were often withheld or frozen. Although one cannot say for sure that San Francisco's 1970-71 application for beautification funds was rejected because of a new view of the program in Washington, the local effort was nonetheless caught up in a changing federal perspective. The city's own expenditures for urban beautification also dropped in the early 1970s. Its 1972-73 program amounted to only $287,000, as compared to approximately $1,232,000 some six years earlier.

What had started out as a remarkably simple and easy-to-administer program became more troublesome by the fourth year. The federal pessures to spend the monies in certain low-income areas became more intense. Although most of the projects were in fact located in lower income neighborhoods, the city planners objected to the federal pressures, pointing out that there would be a reaction against the program from the middle- and upper-income majority if some funds were not spent in other parts of the city.

The number of hurdles blocking a project's ultimate approval increased. For example, it became necessary for the federally recognized regional planning agency, the Association of Bay Area Governments, to review plans for San Francisco projects. The review may have been perfunctory, but it was another delay. With a change in HUD personnel, the informal, verbal commitments that had marked earlier contacts were replaced by less trusting relationships. Written requests, responses, and justifications began to take the place of phone calls. By the time the beautification program ended, the files were two or three times bulkier than they were in earlier years, although the program was only one-fourth as large as it had been. For the city planners, too much time was being spent in federal accounting exercises and far too little in planning and doing.

The federal trend toward more centralization of power and administration continued, bringing with it an attempt to consolidate the many so-called categorical programs. There were pressures from HUD to imitate the federal model. By 1971, local HUD staff had made it clear to the planning department that they wanted to deal only with a single, central agency with full responsibility and authority, from inception to completion, for programs related to urban beautification, open space, and historic preservation. They based their rejection of the 1970-71 beautification application on the need for "changes in operational responsibilities and accounting procedures."[4] HUD wanted the city to put the total urban beautification program either in the hands of the mayor or the Department of City Planning. It was difficult for the HUD staff to understand that neither alternative was reasonable within San Francisco's governmental framework, that the charter specifically vested operational responsibility and authority with the various departments, and that not even the mayor's office could have full control over them. To solve the problem, the Board of Supervisors carried out a planning department proposal to create an Open Space Coordinating Committee, made up of relevant department heads and chaired by the planning director.[5] The planning staff continued to provide project leadership. Thus, San Francisco's government displayed an ability to adapt to a new requirement, even a rather foolish one. In 1972, urban beautification became part of what was called the Legacy of Parks program. About a year later, in the federal game of wordmanship, it became known as the Open Space Land Program. By the end of 1975, it had effectively disappeared.

San Francisco's urban beautification program illustrates the positive use of a small, federally sponsored program to help carry out a plan and to increase the effectiveness and relevance of the planning department. The case provides a counterpoint to the lack of formal powers delegated to the planning department within San Francisco's governmental framework. It is a situation that is familiar to many local city planning offices in the United States.

A plan needs to exist before it can be carried out successfully. The planning department had prepared and the commission had approved such a plan. The contents of the beautification plan and accompanying program are not significantly different from what might be found in a section of a master plan. Also, the Board of Supervisors adopted the beautification program when it authorized the application for federal funds.

Given a plan that was related to a source of funding, a number of conditions were present that contributed to its being carried out. First, there was an aggressive planning staff with considerable interest and expertise in the subjects at hand—recreation and open space and beautification. The staff was prepared to do what was necessary to get the program into operation, including running it once it started. At the same time, relations with other departments had to be such that they perceived benefits rather than threats resulting from the planners' leadership. An intimate knowledge of the city, including available sites for small open spaces and for desirable and desired beautification projects was essential. Without that knowledge, uniquely held by staff with years of experience, the choice of sites might have been so controversial and so time-consuming as to be self-defeating. A mature and knowing staff was central to these choices, as was the knowledge that came from experience with neighborhood planning activities.

To grasp the opportunities that were presented by the federal programs, someone had to know about them—and the planners did. Such knowledge was reinforced by the existence of entrepreneurial opportunities in government that permitted individual departments to benefit from their own aggressiveness. Whether the planning department would have been as enthusiastic if another agency or some central office had the major say in the use of funds is difficult to say. San Francisco's government was flexible enough to permit a nonoperating agency to apply for funds, a condition that was important to carrying out the program and to the department as well.

A perception on the part of residents that planning could bring substantive improvements to their environment increased both their willingness to spend time in such an activity and the ability of the department to prepare plans with them. If employment issues could also be addressed, however modestly, as a result of an improvement

program, that was so much the better. The urban beautification program therefore proved important to the department in that it made planning easier than it would have been otherwise.

One measure of city planning's effectiveness is whether or not claimed achievements occurred as a result of the presence of the planning department. It is almost certain that an application for federal beautification funds would have been prepared and submitted even if the planning department had shown no interest in it. The prospect of funds to enhance their programs would have encouraged the Recreation and Park Department and the Department of Public Works, together or separately, to find ways of applying for funds. Somehow, they would have found a way to meet the requirements of a citywide beautification plan. It is unlikely that the planners would have stood in the way of funding applications. Once the program started, however, it is probable that the department's presence was essential to its size and duration. The department, at this point, had more at stake than the others: it was helping to achieve its own plan, the amount of money involved was more significant to it than to the other departments, and it had a more extensive view of potential funding sources. It was also better able to seek and direct funds for other governmental agencies, such as the Housing Authority.

Over half of the projects are likely to have been funded and completed regardless of the department's presence. Improvements to existing parks and playgrounds, new play equipment, benches and lighting, improvements to the Golden Gate Park fountains, funds for rehabilitation of old windmills, the Chinatown Gateway, and street trees and landscaping for major thoroughfares would probably have happened anyway. These are consistent with the normal needs and interests of Public Works and Recreation and Park, and there were people in those agencies who were prepared to act. On the other hand, projects in the South Bayshore area are less likely to have been undertaken. The recreation center, a mini-park, some of the street trees, and preservation of the old opera house—all grew out of the involvement between the city planners and the community. Moreover, these were not projects in which the other departments would be particularly interested had they even known of the possibilities. Street tree and playground improvements in the Ocean View area are also attributable to planning staff activity and interest. Finally, the two employment programs in the summers of 1968 and 1969, as well as many of the mini-parks and trees on minor streets, can be attributed in large measure to the department's presence. Other departments showed no great interest in these types of projects.

Four questions are of particular interest in regard to the department's role in the urban beautification program: Did the planning department increase its effectiveness by inching its way into the role of an operating department? Why was it necessary to increase the department's effectiveness; in other words, does this small program underline the general ineffectiveness of city planning in regard to public improvement programs? Did the planners have effective control over the urban beautification program mainly because it was small, and would they have had as much control over a larger multipurpose program? If it is desirable to have aggressive, entrepreneurial departments, as it is implied here that it is, then why should the planning department any more than another—the mayor's office or the chief administrative officer, for example—be responsible for coordination?

For the most part, the planning department did not act in an operating capacity in regard to any of the beautification projects: it was not involved in detailed designs of projects, in letting contracts, in construction, or in operating any facility. The exceptions were the purchase and rehabilitation of the opera house and the summer employment programs, whose detailed operations did involve the planning staff from time to time. (During the summer of 1968, for example, the planning director found himself trying to moderate a dispute between two unions fighting for the dominant role in supervising and teaching summer employees. He was terrible at it.) On the other hand, the department did play a stronger role in proposing, advocating, and then pushing the projects it generated than was normally the case. It was because the department had considerable control over the funds involved that it could take charge and could more easily "make things happen."

While the beautification program shows that under some conditions it is very possible indeed for the planning department to be effective, it also underlines the rather ineffective role of the department in determining the nature, size, and location of public improvement projects. Still, even though the funds involved in the beautification program were small compared to those at stake in a redevelopment project or a new sewage treatment system, the case shows the possibility of more effective city planning and of carrying out plans on a larger, citywide scale.

It is no doubt true that the department could exert leadership over a continued period at least partly because of the small size of the urban beautification program. Had the program been significantly larger, it would have drawn more public notice and with that the likelihood of greater involvement by the mayor, the Board of Supervisors, other departments, and the general public. Indeed, if the program had expanded to the point where it included funding for public projects more diverse than beautification, then it would have been similar to the local capital improvement program. The role of the planning department in relationship to capital improvements is clearly defined by the charter. We have seen, however, that the department has not in fact had as great an influence on capital improvement programming as might be expected, in part at least because of the presence of the CAO, the controller, and the heads of older, larger departments on the coordinating committee, which sets the priorities.

The urban beautification program was similar in some respects to the larger, federally sponsored community development program, in that blocks of funds were turned over to cities for a variety of possible uses, to be determined in detail locally. In a larger program, however, there seems to be a need for greater political involvement and greater citizen participation in determining how the funds are allocated. It is likely that the planning department could have provided the mechanism for greater political involvement in an expanded beautification program. It should be noted, however, that with increased political involvement in a larger program such as community development, funds are more likely to be sidetracked to meet day-to-day government expenses (as the capital improvement program funds are), than to support earmarked improvement programs. It is reasonable to conclude that the department would lose some control and effectiveness with a larger program, and that is indeed what happened with urban beautification under the community development program.

The city planning department played such a strong role in the coordination of the city's physical development because, by definition, that is a significant part of what city planning is all about. This does not lessen the desirability of considerable entrepreneurial freedom by all departments of government. Enough checks and balances are built into the structure of the city's government (or can be) to prevent one department from running roughshod over others. Even if another operating department had been in charge of the beautification program, citywide planning interests could have been protected by the mandatory referral process, particularly if the Board of Supervisors agreed to consider the planners' findings as more than advisory. To be sure, if strong control and coordination of all public development are paramount objectives, they can probably be achieved more easily in the office of the chief executive. But it would be no less desirable for individual departments—including the planning department—to have the freedom to invent and develop programs and to pursue funds.

The centralized control and accountability of the urban beautification program—preferably in the mayor's office—that HUD pursued in the early 1970s may have been consistent with federal philosophy, but it was inconsistent with certain traditions of local government. The beautification case points to the actual flexibility of San Francisco's supposedly rigid system of government. The planning department undertook new responsibilities in applying for and then directing a program—responsibilities that were not set down in black and white—and the city adapted to new federal requirements. The department did that by going through all the necessary steps of talking to each of the departments involved in the program and then going to the legislative and executive branches to seek their concurrence. The feds were looking for accountability, and they got it. The stronger chief executive's office that they had envisioned was not necessary.

In sum, then, the planners saw that new opportunities existed and took advantage of them. But they cannot be accused of the kind of opportunism that can be the antithesis of city planning. They were working within a set of policies adopted by the planning commission and the Board of Supervisors—within the context of a governmental framework that did indeed provide opportunities to increase the effectiveness and relevance of city planning.

# Notes

1. Housing and Home Finance Agency, *Beautification Aids for Urban Areas* (Washington, D.C., 1965).

2. Board of Supervisors Resolution No. 486-67, adopted July 31, 1967.

3. San Francisco Department of City Planning, "The Beautification Program for San Francisco," 1967. Adopted by the Board of Supervisors as part of Resolution No. 486-67.

4. Letter of September 24, 1971, from the author to Joseph Caverly, manager of the Recreation and Park Department; also September 1971 letter to the author from James H. Price, HUD area director.

5. Board of Supervisors Resolution 87-72, May 1, 1972.

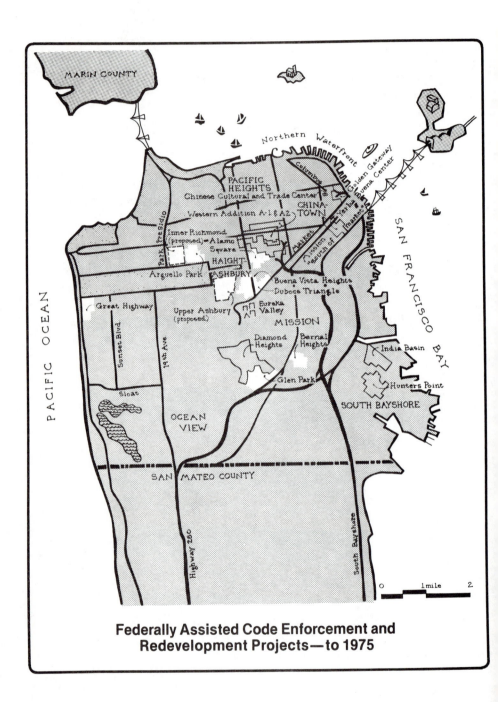

**Federally Assisted Code Enforcement and Redevelopment Projects—to 1975**

# Chapter 5
# Case Study: Planning and Code Enforcement in San Francisco Neighborhoods

The importance of maintaining existing urban environments, particularly residential ones, and of adapting them to current living standards would seem self-evident. Our cities are not going to disappear. They exist, and they house most of our people. And they have proven immensely difficult to change in any drastic way. Most important, the cities that we have, however well or poorly conceived, represent enormous social, economic, and physical investments, and investments in valuable energy resources as well. They cannot be discarded.

Nevertheless, the overall direction of city planning has not usually been toward the preservation and maintenance of what we already have. When public and private energies have not been channeled to provide new development, they have been focused on demolition and rebuilding of the older urban areas that displease us. Urban redevelopment, part of the Housing Act of 1949, was concerned as much with the clearance of slums as it was with the provision of new housing. It was not until 1954 that the idea of housing rehabilitation found its way, modestly, into federal housing legislation, and not until 1965 that it became a significant part of national housing policy.

San Francisco has not escaped the national preoccupation with building and rebuilding. Once most of the vacant land was used up, real estate developers looked for and found investment opportunities that would permit more intense and presumably more profitable uses than had previously existed on individual sites. Zoning laws either permitted the new development or could be changed if necessary. The process of more intense development radically changed the appearance of downtown San Francisco. Prestigious residential areas like Russian Hill, Nob Hill, and Pacific Heights also began to look different, as the two- and three-story buildings gave way to high-rise apartments. By the late 1960s the process had started in some less affluent neighborhoods, albeit at a more modest scale. If perfectly sound buildings disappeared in the process, too bad—progress was progress. It was an era in which growth and new development were welcomed. Usually the change occurred incrementally in both time and space: it was a slow process, a process of small alterations in an area rather than an overnight transformation. People did not necessarily stop to question the value of what was being replaced.

Private redevelopment is gradual, public redevelopment is not. Seeing an opportunity to eliminate dilapidated and substandard housing and equally poor environments, perhaps impatient with the pace of private rebuilding, and certainly captivated by the possibilities of accumulating large sites through its power of eminent domain, San Francisco took advantage of federal legislation and funding and embarked upon seven major redevelopment projects, all completed or underway by the late 1960s: Diamond Heights, Golden Gateway, Hunter's Point, Yerba Buena, Western Addition A-1 and A-2, and India Basin. All but one were primarily clearance and rebuilding projects. Only two did not involve major dislocation of people.

In 1965 at least two more areas were slated for early clearance and redevelopment, Inner Mission and Northern Waterfront. Another six areas were being considered for a combination of clearance and rehabilitation; these were Bayview, Bernal Heights, East Mission, Eureka Valley, Haight-Ashbury, and Ocean View. Altogether there were almost 50,000 housing units in the 15 areas.[1] This was almost 20 per cent of San Francisco's total housing stock. Three more areas, Chinatown, Haight-Fillmore, and South of Market, were being considered for clearance and rebuilding at some later unspecified date. At that time, six areas, with 19,684 units, were undergoing concentrated code enforcement activities. In terms of money, the number of people who would be affected, and the social, economic, visual, and environmental impact, it is clear that total or near-total demolition and rebuilding was the city's major policy in relationship to its older areas. Most other large American cities were pursuing the same policy.

But San Francisco remains a basically sound city. Of approximately 255,000 housing units, the 1960 U.S. Census found 84 per cent standard. Indeed, in five of the seven earliest redevelopment projects referred to above, the census designated fewer than one-fourth of the units as seriously substandard.[2] The challenge was and is to keep the city sound, especially in its residential neighborhoods, without major upheavals in community values. It is a challenge too seldom recognized in American cities, including San Francisco.

During the late 1960s and into the 1970s, the San Francisco Department of City Planning was actively involved in neighborhood planning as well as in designating and planning subsidized code enforcement projects that included modest public improvements. Initially, the code enforcement projects were related primarily to the Federally Assisted Code Enforcement (FACE) program, but eventually they evolved into a local program. A major purpose of these efforts was to help maintain the city's older areas and adapt them to contemporary environmental standards. We will explore the ways in which the department went about its work in relation to both its formal and informal mandates, and we will look at the effectiveness of its efforts.

The primary area of concern of the planning department is the physical development of San Francisco in relation to the people who do and who will interact with it. The department is supposed to prepare a master plan that presents "a broad and general guide and pattern constituting ... recommendations ... for the coordinated and harmonious development, in accordance with the present and future needs, of the city."[3] The department is also charged with implementing its plans. Both maintaining existing neighborhoods and promoting programs directed to that end fall within the mandate.

The San Francisco Housing Code, which was revised in 1962, also charges the director of planning to recommend to the chief administrative officer designation of "conservation areas." A conservation area is defined as "an area of the city and county which is to be protected from blighting influences and maintained in a safe and sound state or, in a declining area, improved and preserved from further deterioration."[4]

The master plan that was in effect in 1966 said little about maintaining existing residential areas. However, a section of the plan addressed urban renewal, which it defined as a program that "uses all available public and private devices for revitalizing the city." It called for the creation of extensive "conservation" areas for the protection and preservation of basically sound areas.[5] There are also many references to proposals for code enforcement and conservation in the *San Francisco Community Renewal Program*. But the reality is that large-scale clearance and redevelopment projects continued to be the order of the times in the mid-1960s.

By 1971, a revised element of the master plan dealing with housing and residential land use proposed, as its first objective, to "maintain and improve the quality and diversity" of existing residential communities.[6] This "plan for residence" had been in preparation since 1968. Five of its policies were aimed directly ("Make extensive use of code enforcement") and indirectly ("Decrease the reliance on property taxes as a . . . revenue source") at achieving the objective. Other elements of the master plan concerned with transportation and urban design would later reflect a similar concern. It is fair to say that in the late 1960s, the city planners were aware of the primacy, among their long-range, citywide responsibilities, of maintaining and adapting the existing environment.

Neighborhood and housing conservation can also be viewed within the planning department's overall strategy of increasing its relevance and effectiveness in the community. The department was trying to respond to issues at three different geographic scales: citywide, neighborhood or district, and individual projects for areas as small as one parcel. Although conservation is a citywide concern, it primarily involves the neighborhood or district scale, where people live and where changes to the physical environment are experienced most intimately.

In addition to their geographic emphasis, the planners considered issues in three different time frames: those that could be addressed only with long-range plans and programs, those that could be successfully addressed in from four to six years (roughly equivalent to an elected official's term of office), and issues that permitted immediate (up to one-year) responses. Within this context, maintaining existing neighborhoods was viewed as a long-range effort, in the sense that, to be meaningful in the life of the city, the effort must be continuous and have long-term consequences. But it was also short-range, in that implementing a program for a specified area is likely to take three or four years, and immediate, in that actions directed toward a specific property occurred fairly swiftly once a program was under way.

To a considerable extent, plans and action programs to maintain and improve older residential areas were viewed by the planning department as a part of its neighborhood planning efforts. The planners were learning some important things about neighborhood planning. Much of it, they discovered, was conservationist in nature. Planning with neighborhood residents was not likely to result in proposals for drastic physical change, particularly if the neighborhoods were reasonably sound in the first place. People are not likely to come up with plans that will result in massive disruptions for themselves. If they want to move, they want to do so at their own pace and on their own terms.[7]

The planners also found that people who engaged in neighborhood planning were often as concerned with preventing things from happening as they were with bringing about something new. It was the threat of something new—an urban renewal project—that inspired the Bernal Heights Association to prepare its own neighborhood plan, one that had nothing at all to do with the removal of people. (Their reactions were described by Robert Cassidy in an article in *Planning* magazine.[8]) In 1967, in the South Bayshore, only after residents were assured that no housing demolition was in store was the planning department able to get on with more constructive planning.

Since the late 1960s, three kinds of neighborhood planning activities had been carried out by the department: comprehensive planning, liaison planning, and planning that took place at a scale somewhere between the first two. The first involved what the department considered a major commitment of time and manpower. For about two years, two, and sometimes three, full-time staff people were assigned to prepare plans for one large area of the city. The type of neighborhood planning that they were engaged in was intended to be comprehensive in scope, similar to, but more detailed than, citywide planning. It took place within the citywide plan framework, but it also influenced citywide planning. Neighborhood residents participated in the planning process, although whether their participation was adequate is a question that would be answered differently by planners and residents in different cases.

The department had nowhere near an adequate staff for its neighborhood planning efforts, but then not all parts of the city required the same degree of attention. The planners chose areas to work in both according to the expressed desires of residents and according to need, as it was perceived by the department. There was a clear need to deal with environmental issues in the South Bayshore, for example (always related to social and economic concerns), and redevelopment efforts had to be placed in a larger physical context. In Chinatown, where the problems included inadequate community facilities and some of the worst housing in the city, citizens had long demanded some kind of neighborhood planning.

The staff began its comprehensive neighborhood planning efforts by first getting to know the neighborhood and then participating in informal discussions, both with individuals and groups. Later, the staff would call a general neighborhood meeting at a site that would be acceptable to all people in the community. Choosing a site became very important in a neighborhood like South Bayshore, for example, because some people would not go to what was considered other people's "turf." Notices of the meetings were distributed in the neighborhood, and announcements were made at meetings of neighborhood organizations. At the first meeting, at which anywhere from 50 to 150 people might show up, the planning director would usually advise the people that his staff was going to be doing planning in the area. He stressed that the planners would be accessible to residents and that they actively sought their involvement. At this first meeting, too, the director would outline what he and his staff saw as some issues to be addressed, but he would stress that he was mostly interested in hearing from the residents about their concerns. Considerable time at the first meeting was usually spent in telling people just what the planning department was and what it could and could not do. These early meetings were often tense, at times like confrontations, as the people aired their suspicions of government officials and questioned their motives.

In the following months the staff developed and revised work programs and got to work on substantive issues. Occasional community-wide meetings were called to discuss such major topics of concern as housing, traffic, transportation, community services, jobs, recreation and open space, and the neighborhood shopping district. (The staff, during this period, was collecting data and researching and analyzing material on these topics; the findings were reported verbally or in small publications.) At the meetings, preliminary ideas for programs were presented and discussed. New concerns kept emerging, and unfamiliar faces were always showing up as others disappeared. Generally though, a core of regulars, from 20 to 50 people, was always there.

With one exception, the department was never organized or associated formally with a particular citizens advisory committee. Top staff had concluded that any one group rarely represents all the varied neighborhood interests, and they were certain that any group that the department organized would be suspect. If people formed their own organization, that would be fine, but the department's approach would continue to be to call neighborhood-wide meetings. The planners did meet with individual groups when they were invited, and they went to all sorts of local meetings. But they presented their work and tried to come to decisions at the general open meetings. For the one area where the planners made an estimate of the number of people who took part in their work—South Bayshore—they concluded that about one per cent of the residents participated.

In Chinatown, the planning department established a formal advisory committee, following a six-week search for residents who represented all interests of that community. It was generally agreed that the group was representative. Eventually, though, its meetings were opened to all comers. Committee membership carried with it no special privileges, except perhaps the expectation that members would work harder than others.

The question of control of any plan and of veto power over its contents always came up. The planners took the position that they worked for the planning commission and were responsible to it. They said that they would try to come up with plans and programs that were responsive to neighborhood needs and acceptable to most people, and that they would support those plans before the commission and elsewhere. They made it clear that there might be disagreements on specific proposals from time to time and that any ensuing battles would and should be fought out publicly.

The plans and programs that resulted from the neighborhood meetings were presented at commission meetings and were followed by public review. The final step in the neighborhood planning process was to submit the plan, including all the revisions, to the commission. The commission usually endorsed the plan with a resolution charging the staff to carry out its recommendations.

At the other end of the scale from comprehensive neighborhood planning was liaison planning, which was supposed to provide at least minimal planning services to all the districts in the city regardless of whether specific planning projects were under way. The idea was to keep neighborhood groups informed, to relay to them the department's point of view on specific issues, to bring neighborhood concerns back

to the department, and generally to promote citizen participation in the planning process. It was a way of establishing ties with communities, and by doing so the department hoped to put itself in a better position to respond to their needs. Planners were assigned to specific neighborhoods, and up to 20 per cent of their time was to be spent in liaison work. If a neighborhood was doing its own planning, with or without consultants, the liaison planner was expected to help and to keep tabs on what was going on. The goal was to cover every area of the city, but that goal had not been realized by the mid-1970s.

Liaison planners were in the thick of immediate neighborhood planning decisions: whether or not to permit hospital expansions, whether to grant permits to wrecking yards in South Bayshore, whether to close a street. When people came before the planning commission to argue a zoning case, they usually knew the planners, and the planners knew them. It was easy for the liaison planners to act as advocates for people they knew. Unfortunately, that intimacy also made it difficult to recommend against those same people when that proved necessary.

Between the full-scale neighborhood planning and the liaison efforts, a third level of planning took place. It is a type of planning best defined by examples. A planner might spend half, or even full time, for instance, developing programs to carry out the plans that had been prepared for a given area. Or a planner might be assigned to assist the two neighborhoods that were part of the federally funded Model Cities program. Detailed planning and design of small public improvement projects, regardless of funding source, might also be carried out within this context.

It is difficult to assess the effectiveness of the neighborhood planning efforts. A tally sheet would have to include things that did not happen (a parking garage under a small Chinatown park) as well as those that did (a moderate-income housing development in Chinatown and mini-parks in the Mission). There were also failures, such as inability to secure a community center in Haight-Ashbury and to get more mini-parks in Chinatown. One certain positive result is that many more people became involved in planning for the future of their neighborhoods, and their voices were beginning to be heard more and more clearly.

Planning associated with concentrated code enforcement was much more focused and tangible than neighborhood planning. But the planning department saw both the Federally Assisted Code Enforcement program (FACE) that was born out of the Housing and Urban Development Act of 1965 and earlier concentrated enforcement programs as important vehicles for preserving neighborhoods. They offered ways to carry out some of the objectives and policies of the master plan that was slowly emerging and, in doing so, to make city planning work. FACE was also seen as a way to help carry out plans prepared at the neighborhood level. It was, then, a form of neighborhood planning in its own right.

FACE was a program that involved the inspection of all the structures in a designated area. Owners whose buildings had violations of the city's housing code were offered low-cost federal loans to do the work that was needed to bring their buildings up to par. For low-income owners there were outright federal grants. Besides the loans and grants, the city was to make environmental improvements such as street repaving, burial of utility wires, tree planting, and traffic circulation and parking changes. Two-thirds of the administrative costs of the program were paid by the federal government, the rest by the city.

Since areas that were showing early signs of deterioration were considered prime targets of the program, FACE could be viewed as preventive medicine. It was a way of stopping the kind of physical deterioration of buildings and their environments that leads to slums and then to slum clearance. Planners saw the potential of the public improvements that accompanied the program. If the small-scale experimental improvements were successful, they could be used elsewhere more broadly: street narrowing and traffic diverters to slow down or keep traffic out of neighborhoods are examples. And in areas where little or no previous planning had taken place, the decision to undertake a code enforcement program and its concomitant detailed agenda of neighborhood improvements represented a form of project planning.

Finally, the planning department saw FACE as an alternative to redevelopment. It was a program that the department could use to advantage in its continuing conflict with the Redevelopment Agency. Redevelopment, and the agency, were anything but popular in most neighborhoods in those days, especially those that needed improvements. Even so, the Redevelopment Agency pretty much ran its own show. Originally viewed by many city planners as another tool to help carry out citywide comprehensive plans, redevelopment was anything but that in the 1960s. San Francisco's agency was endowed with massive amounts of federal funds, a large staff, freedom from most city hall red tape, and prestige among the business community and elected officials. And it usually got what it wanted on matters related to city planning. In 1967, shortly after naming a new planning director, the planning commission voted against his recommendation on a major redevelopment issue, supporting the agency instead. The phrase, "redevelopment tail wagging the planning dog," then popular in planning circles if nowhere else, was born of such experiences.

Successful FACE-type projects, which required minimal dislocation of residents, could provide another flag for people to rally 'round. The prestige and influence of the planning department, positively identified with FACE, might grow in relation to that of the Redevelopment Agency, and the program, once elevated as a major policy tool of the city, might help rein in some of the agency's influence on planning matters.

It should be understood that although code enforcement is directly related to the responsibilities of the planning department and although the planning director is charged with making recommendations as to where and when concentrated programs should take place, neither code enforcement nor FACE was primarily the department's responsibility. Both were the responsibility of the Bureau of Building Inspection, which is part of the Department of Public Works.

The Bureau of Building Inspection is in charge of enforcing those sections of the housing code that pertain to hotels and apartment buildings. During the 1960s, it operated an extensive program to do just that, largely on a "worst-first" basis. The housing code is primarily concerned with basic health and safety matters such as fire, structural, and public health hazards rather than with the more contemporary building standards of the building code. The staff was as much concerned with saving older buildings as with simply enforcing the code. In one area near a hospital, for instance, it encouraged the renovation of older buildings for much needed housing for hospital employees; it was aware that merely enforcing the code might result in large-scale dislocation. Long before the FACE program existed, the city's inspection personnel understood that rehabilitation was an important goal. They interpreted their charge broadly, and nonlegalistically, in a manner totally consistent with the planners' point of view. This attitude may be accounted for in part by the fact that a small group of key staff in the bureau had come from the Health Department and had had what might be termed an American Public Health Association upbringing, embracing the comprehensive environmental view of health that had influenced so many city planners. Indeed, there is some indication that, in the early days of concentrated code enforcement, the bureau was doing as much of the planning related to the location, size, and timing of the program as were the city planners.[9]

By the late 1960s, the bureau and the planning department were working together, with FACE the key program in the fight to preserve existing residential areas. Some 18,000 units in 5,000 buildings in seven neighborhoods had been or were in the process of being brought into conformance with housing code standards. (The neighborhoods were Pacific Heights, West Nob Hill, Visitacion Valley, Buena Vista Heights, Glen Park, and Great Highway.) The Bureau of Building Inspection and the Department of City Planning wanted to build upon and to surpass that record.

The planning director was charged with recommending the areas where concentrated code enforcement was to take place. That kind of recommendation would inevitably involve formal and informal criteria for the selection of appropriate neighborhoods, detailed assessments of likely areas, meetings with community residents to determine the program's acceptability, and a formal recommendation to the CAO, who would forward the proposal to the Board of Supervisors for a final determination.

There was no shortage of criteria. The *San Francisco Community Renewal Program* had listed three major ones for designating concentrated code enforcement areas: a high incidence of housing deficiencies that did not tend to upgrade themselves; a high percentage of families with children; and population pressures bringing overcrowding and illegal conversions.[10] Fourteen areas met those criteria.

There were other, less formalized standards for recommending neighborhoods for FACE. Areas where capital improvements were scheduled were favored, since the federal two-thirds contribution could then be maximized without requiring new local cash for the city's share. Also favored were areas that had a high degree of home ownership. HUD encouraged an interest in areas where code compliance costs would be low and within the capability of most owners to finance on the private market. Field inspections helped determine the appropriateness of areas under consideration. Another significant factor was neighborhood interest in a program. An area that was already in a non-federally aided program had a good chance, especially if enforcement activities had only recently begun. Fairness then suggested that property owners be given an opportunity to avail themselves of the federal low-interest loans.

For the first four FACE areas (Arguello Park, Buena Vista Heights, Glen Park, and Great Highway), the last standard proved very important. Three of the four had started under the earlier program. Only in the Great Highway area is there much indication that the planning department played a significant role in determining the first FACE areas.[11]

As time passed and with the apparent success and acceptance of the program, the criteria changed and the department's role grew. Both the city planners and the building inspectors tried to direct the program to areas where it might help solve already developed environmental problems. They wanted to see if the program could be effective in areas with less stable conditions than in the first four. As a result of their efforts, two out of three FACE areas selected in the second round were areas that had been earmarked for drastic urban renewal programs in the earlier Community Renewal Program. (The two were Alamo Square and Bernal Heights; the third area was Duboce Triangle.) Of eight additional areas that the planning department proposed for FACE in

1971 to carry out its "plan for residence," over half had been considered for urban renewal earlier.

Choosing areas that might be suitable and might meet established criteria was one thing. Getting to the point of final recommendations of specific areas, and seeing them approved and into operation was another. Here the planning department was very much in evidence.

In every case, at least one neighborhood meeting was held prior to a final recommendation. Usually, there were a few individuals or a neighborhood group that understood the FACE program and wanted their area to be considered for it. In most cases those contacts provided the planner's initial entry into a neighborhood.

Bernal Heights is an example. This was a neighborhood in which residents had fought designation as an urban renewal area. A year later, in 1966, the Bernal Heights Association came out with its own plan for improvement. It called for modest public improvements, primarily landscaping, walkways, lighting, open space, and a few traffic changes, certainly nothing that might suggest publicly financed acquisition of private housing. The plan did not include a thorough analysis of housing problems or community facilities or of marginal shopping areas or of the potential for new development. To some planners it seemed a rather lightweight, cosmetic plan. But it was the neighborhood's. Arrangements were made by the staff to have the plan presented to the planning commission.

Earlier in 1967 the FACE program had been explained to the association's board and to its full membership. The association's plan was endorsed by the planning commission in late 1967, with instructions to the staff to devise a means of implementing it. At around the same time, a delegation from the neighborhood toured an early FACE area and inspected a number of houses where work was under way. A relatively new member of the planning department, Richard Gamble, had been active in the association and was trusted by its members. Gamble was now working on the FACE program. In January 1968 the staff recommended that a somewhat modified version of the plan that had been developed by the association be implemented in large measure by use of the FACE program. All this went on *before* a first neighborhood meeting was called for the purpose of designating a specific FACE project.

The Bernal Heights experience was not typical. There was considerably less neighborhood contact prior to a first meeting in the

Alamo Square area, an area that was adjacent to a large, ongoing re-development project in the Western Addition, a clearance project that involved massive relocation of the mostly black residents. But even in Alamo Square, contacts had been made with members of the local Economic Opportunity Council and with members of the Alamo Square Association, so the initial meetings would come as no surprise.

No matter how many neighborhood residents the planners had met with earlier, it was essential to have good attendance at the neighborhood meetings that were called specifically to consider the FACE program. Notices were mailed to all property owners and circulars left at all house and apartment doors to assure that renters were informed. The meeting announcements advised residents that their area was being considered for the program and contained information on the nature of the program. Anywhere from 60 to 200 people attended the meetings, which were all held in the evenings in the neighborhoods.[12]

All the meetings had similar agendas. The planning director started by explaining the FACE program and also explaining the procedure that had to be followed in making a recommendation to the CAO. He would lay out the boundaries of the area that was being considered and describe some of its basic physical, social, and economic characteristics. A short slide presentation would follow, illustrating the kinds of home improvements that might prove necessary and that could be made as part of the program. Costs were given for specific cases. The kinds of public improvements that could be made in a FACE area were also described.

Representatives of the Bureau of Building Inspection would then explain the code enforcement process. They described the individual building inspections that took place after appointments were made with owners, the reports to owners of code-required improvements, and the assistance that was made available to guide owners through the steps from identifying a structural or health problem to an ultimate solution. One of the FACE loan officers was always on hand to explain the federal low-interest (three per cent) loan program, the opportunities for refinancing, the loan limitations, who was and was not eligible for grants, and the like. It was made clear at the meeting that once an area was approved, the Bureau of Building Inspection ran the program, not the Department of City Planning. The bureau would establish field offices in the FACE areas. The planners' role would be confined primarily to working with citizens on the public improvements.

People's concerns became apparent during the question and discussion period that followed every meeting. Initially, there was great skepticism about the program and those guys from city hall. And there was uneasiness over the prospect of outsiders, inspectors, entering a house and looking around. What business did they have doing that! The building inspectors, the enforcers of the code, posed a considerable threat. Their head man, Al Goldberg, often made an observation to the effect that the law was the law and that sooner or later all multi-unit buildings would be inspected and brought up to code anyway.[13] That kind of statement didn't help matters. The city planners, on the other hand, were usually viewed as a no-threat contingent and seemed a more calming influence at the meetings. The planners would invite residents to visit areas where one form or another of code enforcement had taken place, to talk to people, and to see for themselves how well the inspectors behaved. Whether or not people took the invitation, they seemed impressed by the openness of the approach.

There were other questions and concerns too. People wanted to know whether property assessments and taxes would rise as a result of improvements. There was confusion about which standards were going to be enforced, the housing code or the building code, whose higher standards pertained to new construction. Owners wanted to know how to get loans and still bypass the red tape. Others asked about grants. What about hardship cases, such as those involving older people? There was fear over what might happen if the inspectors found illegal units. The answer was that they often could be accommodated legally. Other questions: What might happen to the rents of low- and moderate-income people? Would they be forced to move? Were low-interest loans available to people who had already brought their houses up to code without benefit of the program? The answer to the last, unfortunately, was no.

On the whole the meetings were positive and informative. The threat of renewal, largely an imagined threat as far as the city planners were concerned, seemed to hang over the Alamo Square and Bernal Height communities, although the planners tried to make it clear that this was not an either/or situation. They said they were proposing FACE in those areas to keep them from running further downhill and because they thought they could be rehabilitated. More positively, questions about whether a person should start needed repairs immediately or wait until a program was under way were indications that the program might be accepted.

Late in each meeting questions about how and when decisions were to be made usually came up. How would people be advised? Would a vote be taken? What about a vote then and there? What about more information? How could people let their wishes be known? The planning director's response was that the process used in making a recommendation was far from perfect. He said that he knew that the program would not be successful if a lot of people weren't for it. He did not want a vote at the meeting, he said, because none had been scheduled, because he didn't know how representative the group was, and because people had already started to leave. He added that the staff hoped to hear from people in the weeks ahead and to answer the unanswered questions. The staff would call another meeting if one seemed warranted. People were told approximately when a recommendation was likely, and the director made it clear that he had no intention of going before the Board of Supervisors without significant neighborhood support. He had no desire, as he put it, to be crucified at the board. Besides, a no vote by the board might beget more no votes, and he wanted the program expanded, not stopped. He and the staff had better judge community sentiment correctly.

Those were the considerations used, in conjunction with the selection criteria, to determine the final recommendations. In one case, in the Sunnyside district, an area that was in better physical condition than some of the other possibilities, two residents started a petition against a project following a community meeting. They got enough support to cause the director not to recommend the area. The opposite was true in Bernal Heights, Alamo Square, and Duboce Triangle, where the first neighborhood meetings evoked favorable response. In only one of these areas was it necessary to call a second general meeting before a positive recommendation was made. Later, in other areas, more than one meeting was usually held before the matter went to the board. In only one case, the Haight-Ashbury, was neighborhood testimony anything but overwhelmingly favorable.

With the exception of the Bernal Heights and Alamo Square programs, there had been relatively little participation in neighborhood planning by residents in the soon-to-be (or not-to-be) FACE areas prior to the general meetings called by the planning department. The department had been in contact with a few individuals and one or two organized groups, but their representativeness was unknown, and there had been no specific planning of the kind that might conclude with a plan—nothing that stated clearly "this is what we want" and "here are the ways we expect to get what we want." It is rather ironic that in the South Bayshore, where considerable participatory planning had taken place and where the planners felt FACE would be most appropriate, the Model Cities agency resisted the program time and time again both for fear of finding illegal conversions and for fear of rent increases. The planners had reason to believe that neither would be a problem. They were not problems elsewhere, and preliminary economic studies did not indicate that the situation would be any different here. But the planners never did take their case directly to the neighborhoods involved. In the areas where FACE did move ahead, participation started at the first neighborhood meeting.

Generally, the most direct involvement of residents came in the detailed planning for public improvements within the FACE areas. On the possibility that projects would move ahead, people were encouraged to sign up at the neighborhood meetings for a planning advisory committee. No one was excluded. In Bernal Heights, for instance, 15 people worked with Dick Gamble to decide what street improvements should be made, what trees should be planted and where, what blocks should have overhead wires removed, and where a small sitting and play area was possible. The advisory committee meetings were long and time-consuming. Invariably, both the neighborhood and the planners would want more than was budgeted. Together, they would put pressure on the Department of Public Works. It did them no harm that the Bureau of Building Inspection was a part of Public Works.

In the Alamo Square FACE area participation went far beyond planning for public improvements. The Western Addition Project Area Committee and the Economic Opportunity Council were suspicious of any move by the city that might result in rent increases or the dislocation of residents. Their suspicion was understandable, for people had been displaced in neighboring Western Addition redevelopment areas. For these reasons, the recommendation of the Alamo Square FACE area depended upon the formation of a citizens advisory committee that would work with the program on relocation arrangements, prevention of rent gouging, and appeals by tenants, as well as detailed public improvement planning.[14] The committee was active throughout the FACE project. It had the help of the planning department and later some of its own staff support as well.

The most pervasive questions were precisely those that most concerned the Alamo Square residents: Would people have to move? And would rents increase beyond the ability of the residents to pay? These questions became more pressing as the program expanded into lower income areas where there were more buildings with structural and environmental deficiencies than in the first areas chosen. They were questions that required research.

In 1967 and 1968 the planning department and the Bureau of Building Inspection undertook a "code enforcement feasibility study" of the worst block in the Alamo Square neighborhood. They concluded that considerable dislocation might result from the deconversion of illegal units and from the rent increases that would indeed be occasioned by the costs of code compliance; approximately 19 per cent of the people (22 per cent of the households in the block) might have to move.[15] The study also indicated that dislocation would be even greater if the housing code were enforced on a citywide "worst-first" basis without the low-interest loans that were a feature of the FACE program. These findings were announced at the Alamo Square neighborhood meeting, and the planners said they were quite prepared to exclude the block from the FACE project. But the people of the area, including the tenants of the block in question, decided that they wanted the block included. FACE, to them, may have been the lesser of alternative evils: the possibility of a redevelopment project seemed much worse.

The two agencies released another study in December 1968: *Section 312 Loan Limits*. This study indicated that federal legislation limiting the low-interest loans to moderate-income property owners would preclude expansion of the FACE program into the city's older, more deteriorated neighborhoods. These were the areas that lending institutions were reluctant to make loans in; many knowing people concluded that they had been at least unofficially "redlined." Any available loan funds were for short terms and at high interest rates. If building owners in these areas borrowed at the higher rates, they would be likely to pass the cost along to the residents in the form of higher rents. Dislocation would be a result. Heavy lobbying on the part of San Francisco, and other cities as well, helped change the law to allow a system of priorities which permitted other than moderate-income property owners to take advantage of the federal loans.

The grim specter of greatly increased rents for improved properties in a city with a very low vacancy rate remained. The results of a study of rental behavior in the first four FACE areas that the planning department and the public works department released in December 1971 are significant here. The study, called *Rent and Code Enforcement*, concluded that the program had not resulted in significant rent increases and that the reverse may have been true: the subsidized loan program may have contributed to keeping rents down. Rent increases in all but one of the four districts were below the city average, and they appeared to be more the result of tax increases than of improvement costs. Furthermore, fears of widespread tax reassessments were not substantiated; assessment increases in FACE areas were less than those citywide. Finally, the study showed that loss of tenants because of rent increases appeared low. By late 1971, in fact, displacement of residents for all causes amounted to less than one-half of one per cent. Across the Bay, Berkeley's planning director reported the same phenomenon. There were only modest rent increases in the one FACE area in that city.

The planners had several theories to explain why rents were not increased drastically. These included both the classic unwillingness of some owners to risk loss of "good," long-term tenants and their lack of knowledge of "what the market would bear." It was not uncommon to find neighboring owners with almost identical units charging significantly different rents. The planners also wondered how long the phenomenon might last. They feared that as the potential of the program became more widely known, real estate speculators would seize the opportunity for making a quick profit. But in the early seventies, speculation was still not the rule.

The two agencies involved in code enforcement published a number of other studies and reports. Some were undertaken to spur the federal government to accept the local FACE areas that the planners had picked.

The official federal view was not always favorable. A San Francisco-based representative of HUD is reported by Robert Cassidy to have observed that, "the intent of the program is to catch an area that's just beginning to have problems—and nip the problem in the bud. But the areas they chose were over the hill."[16] Apparently HUD felt that way about all three of the second-stage projects. Yet the code enforcement feasibility study of Bernal Heights indicated that even if per-unit rehabilitation costs were higher than in other FACE areas, renovation would be a sound investment in most cases. The study also indicated that property owners in the neighborhood did qualify for loans.[17] Perhaps most important, the study discussed the many noneconomic factors that were used to determine whether or not an area was suitable for the FACE program. Not the least of these was the residents' attachment for their houses, which could lead them to invest in rehabilitation regardless of what cost-benefit economics suggested.

By 1972, both the city planners and the housing inspectors had reasons to feel that the FACE program was working well. Bureau of Building Inspection data show that some 6,400 dwelling units in over 3,000 buildings had been brought into compliance with the housing code by the end of that year. The work was helped along by 921 federal low-interest loans and 320 federal grants. The professionals no longer had to sell the program. Many—supervisors, planning commissioners, the head of a major civic planning organization, people in the neighborhoods—considered FACE to be the city's most effective and least costly program for restoring and maintaining good neighborhoods. The maintenance of existing neighborhoods had become a cornerstone of the planners' citywide master plan, and FACE was a major program to help achieve that objective.

But for all intents and purposes the FACE program was dead or fast dying in 1972, stopped, along with other housing programs, by the Nixon administration. FACE funds were cut from the federal budget in June, and $70 million for low-interest loans was impounded, supposedly because the program was inflationary, unsuccessful, and wasteful.

As many as 150 cities, including San Francisco, were left in mid-

program. The staff of the Bureau of Building Inspection spent considerable effort trying to secure funds that had been promised, but even so
people who got started late on their homes found themselves without
loans for long periods. In early March, Washington returned two applications, indicating that there were no funds for the program. The city
planners were reluctant to recommend new areas or even to put them
on a waiting list. It would not do to make promises and then not deliver.
That would only lose hard-won credibility.

If HUD officials in Washington were prepared to let their program
go down the drain, those in San Francisco and many other places were
not. By 1974, 83 cities and 14 states were planning or had already begun
their own non-federally assisted property rehabilitation program. Using
a model developed in Norfolk, Virginia, the city planning and code
enforcement staffs drew up a plan for a city-sponsored "Rehabilitation
Assistance Program"—RAP. The new program would come as close as
possible to reproducing the best features of FACE.[18] Although it would
be impossible to reduce interest rates to the level that had been
provided federally, below-market-rate loans were still to be central to
the program. The criteria for choosing RAP areas were derived from the
FACE experience as well as from the objectives and policies set forth in
the residence element of the master plan. These criteria included
meeting the financial needs of neighborhood residents, displacing the
fewest number of tenants on account of rent increases or demolition,
and maintaining racial, ethnic, and economic integration where it
existed. In all areas, the widespread support of residents was to be an
important factor in the selection.

The contribution of the planning department to the RAP program
was considerable. A couple of staff members had particular expertise in
FACE and the housing programs. They were naturals to work with the
Bureau of Building Inspection, city attorneys, banks, elected officials,
and citizen groups in preparing the new program. It took almost a year
to bring the program to a point where it could be placed before the
Board of Supervisors and the mayor. It was finally approved in June
1973.

But it would take almost four years to shift from FACE to RAP.
Among the reasons for the delay was the need for legislation at the state
level, for a local charter amendment, for test cases in the courts, and for
a favorable ruling by the Internal Revenue Service. The first RAP program, Inner Richmond, began in November 1976. Two or three addi-

tional areas were being considered in early 1977. In the meantime, the
FACE program was slowly being completed.

What did the FACE program achieve in San Francisco? If matching
or bettering the basic health and safety standards of the city's housing is
a measure, then some numbers will help to answer the question. By the
end of 1976, seven FACE areas were virtually complete. 7,642 dwelling
units in 3,462 structures had been brought into compliance with the
housing code. Before the program started, of 10,124 dwelling units
inspected in 4,533 buildings, only nine per cent were found to be
without code violations. In 1977, more than 90 per cent of the buildings
that had violations conformed to code requirements.

The 1,077 low-interest loans came to a total of $15,323,000—an
average of $14,227 per building, in most cases just over $5,000 per
dwelling unit. Federal grants were made to 358 property owners (only
37 since 1972), totaling $871,248, or $2,434 per building. It should be
noted that the owners of the buildings in the FACE areas often went
beyond the required improvements, whether or not they received
low-interest loans. Only about one-third of the owners took advantage
of the loans.

The total administrative cost of the program to the middle of 1976
was slightly over $6.8 million, which amounted to about $880 per unit
and almost $2,000 per building. In the last four years of the program,
administrative costs per dwelling unit rose considerably. The Bureau of

Building Inspection estimated the total public cost of the FACE program for the seven areas with over 10,000 dwelling units at about $11 million. By way of contrast, the Redevelopment Agency estimated the public cost of one redevelopment project—the Western Addition A-2 project—at $126,600,000 in 1973.[19]

When they are compared to the estimates of need, the code enforcement production figures are not as encouraging. The 1965 Community Renewal Program had called for concentrated code enforcement for over 30,000 housing units between 1966 and 1972.[20] The total under FACE was less than one-fourth of this figure. The targets called for in the department's first housing recommendations had also not been met. And the program had not expanded beyond the first seven areas. Late in 1972, the planning department estimated that, at the existing pace, it would take 37 years to extend the code enforcement program to the 35 or 40 areas that needed it most. The estimate included some 57,000 dwelling units out of a citywide total of just under 332,000.[21] It did not include any programs in the two Model Cities areas. Such estimates account in part for the staff's chagrin over the demise of FACE and its eagerness to find and work on an alternative program.

The structural soundness and safety of individual buildings are only part of a satisfying environment. Thus, FACE spent approximately $1,700,000 on public improvements: planting street trees and doing other landscaping work, improving streets and walks, creating play areas. The figure does not include the work done by the telephone and electric companies to bury the utility lines. The improvements became more evident as the program progressed. They played little part in the early Great Highway project near the ocean, but the absence of overhead wires and the new street trees are obvious improvements in Glen Park. The most notable improvement in Bernal Heights is a new pedestrian stairway that cuts across the hilly neighborhood and provides three new sitting and play areas.

By the time the program moved to Duboce Triangle, the improvements were more extensive and more substantial. Sidewalks were widened; traffic diverted; parking patterns changed; and devices installed to slow, if not to discourage, auto traffic on residential streets. Many small play areas were created, and these are heavily used. It is hard to see how a federal official could say that this area did not look much different from the way it did before except for "some nice paint jobs," as the HUD official was quoted as saying in the article cited earlier.[22]

It is not always easy to measure objectively what a program of this kind has achieved. No comprehensive studies have been done and none is likely to be forthcoming. It is hard to assess with certainty whether the improvements that were made would have been made without the program. The staff of the Bureau of Building Inspection says that commercial loans are now available in and around the Bernal Heights FACE area, an area where they were not available earlier. According to Bernard Cummings of the bureau, the FACE loans had a lower default rate than the usual loans granted by savings and loan institutions. A federal audit conducted by the General Accounting Office concluded that San Francisco's FACE "considerably upgraded rundown properties and benefited their owners, tenants and neighborhood."[23] On the other hand, the report was critical of the fact that a high proportion (45 per cent) of the loans were made to people with incomes of over $15,000 a year. To some, areas like Bernal Heights are "still Bernal Heights." But to others such as Genette Sonnesyn, who lives in that area, "Wonderful things have happened on Lundy's Lane."[24] To the city planners, *both* assessments, if accurate, meant the program was successful.

In recommending nine areas (including Inner Richmond and Haight-Ashbury) for concentrated code enforcement under FACE and RAP, the planning department was fulfilling one of its responsibilities, as mandated by the city's housing code. To some extent, the department's involvement in the program went beyond a literal interpretation of its formal responsibilities. However, the principle of protecting and preserving basically sound areas is elaborated on in a 1960 amendment to the master plan and is rooted in the original document. The role the department played in explaining the program to neighborhood people and in gaining acceptance for it by the neighborhoods and by the Board of Supervisors can be interpreted as promoting the master plan, a charge given by the charter.

By the early 1970s, maintaining and improving neighborhoods had become the most important objective of the residence element of the master plan, and the planning staff was actively pursuing that objective by proposing a program of assisted code enforcement combined with public improvements. The department also was involved in the detailed planning and design of neighborhood improvements, even though there was no direct legislative mandate for this activity, which is normally assigned to the Department of Public Works. The planning department was intensely interested in the neighborhood maintenance programs, and it possessed considerable expertise in the area. Also, the planning department existed in an organizational framework that permitted such activities.

In regard to the planning department's strategy of working at three geographic scales, it seems clear that neighborhood maintenance was both a neighborhood and a citywide concern. The department's efforts to make more extensive use of concentrated code enforcement combined with public improvements were only modestly successful in relation to estimated need. The program was never large enough. On the other hand, the results of the program emphasized what many residents already knew—that most of their neighborhoods were basically sound and that drastic actions were not required to keep them that way. Concentrated code enforcement helped to turn long-range city policy toward neighborhood maintenance.

It has been noted earlier that the program also represented a type of neighborhood planning in its own right. It is worth observing, however, that at the start of 1977, neither FACE nor RAP had been used in any area where the planning department had been actively engaged in a comprehensive neighborhood planning program, although that situation was scheduled to change. Remarkably, these programs had not been used to help carry out the plan prepared by the staff for the South Bayshore district. It is hard to say why, whether it was due to staff failings, to the ineptness of the Model Cities agency, or to a lack of enthusiasm by neighborhood residents. For whatever reasons, the department was not able to use a favored program in certain areas where its early use would have seemed most likely.

The freedom that was permitted the planning department's staff is noteworthy. Without in any way downplaying the importance of the Bureau of Building Inspection, it can be said that the city planners became the major citywide advocates of concentrated code enforcement. Many of the planners were motivated by their concern for social equity, especially in the area of housing. They were given reasonably free rein, both within the department and in the larger context of the city's governmental framework.

The planning department was free to promote FACE and RAP with individual members of the Board of Supervisors and in the board's public meetings. In the late 1960s, the director had a number of lunchtime lobbying sessions with supervisors. When the public hearings showed overwhelming support for FACE, lobbying became less necessary. Later, it was the younger staff members, together with Bureau of Building Inspection personnel, who worked with individual supervisors in preparing the RAP program.

Throughout, the mayor was supportive, though never highly involved in the code enforcement program. In all likelihood, the planners could have pursued neighborhood maintenance programs equally well if the department had been directly responsible to the chief executive or to the legislature. Their position under a commission did, however, give them the latitude they needed.

The contention here is that in regard to the concentrated code enforcement programs, city planning worked. It worked in the sense of helping people adapt their homes to contemporary standards, without significant hardships. In doing so, it helped the city as a whole—physically, socially, and economically. It worked in the sense of achieving long-range objectives and policies that were a part of the city's master plan. And it worked in that it helped establish citywide neighborhood maintenance policies.

Of course, FACE was a federal program, and the city was in large measure taking advantage of federal largesse. It was also vulnerable to federal whims and fancies. But concentrated code enforcement in San Francisco started before the federal program got under way, without federal help, and local people developed their own program to replace the successful one the feds abandoned. Indeed, there is some indication that the city accomplished more, faster, with its earlier nonassisted code enforcement projects than with FACE. It is also true though that the FACE areas had greater problems and were in part chosen because of their need for subsidized loans.[25]

Although the planning done in the FACE areas proved to be effective as a limited type of neighborhood planning, it was not a substitute for more comprehensive neighborhood planning. Code enforcement and public improvements are not necessarily the most relevant issues in neighborhoods. Where they are, though, appropriate FACE-type planning can be effective.

The history of FACE indicates the importance of a close and sympathetic working relationship with an operating agency, in this case the Bureau of Building Inspection. By comparison, the relationship with the traffic engineers in the Department of Public Works in transportation planning matters has not been so sympathetic. And the kinds of public improvements successfully implemented in FACE areas to divert or to slow traffic have been nowhere near as noteworthy elsewhere.

Maintaining existing residential environments and adapting them to satisfy emerging needs and living standards is by definition a continuous process. When we fail, the consequences can be visible, dramatic, and socially painful. When we succeed, we may not know it. The jury is still out and will continue to be as to the success or failure of San Francisco to maintain its residential neighborhoods. There is no question, however, that city planning helped to focus the issue and to find a solution.

# Notes

1. These figures and proposals derive from Arthur D. Little, *San Francisco Community Renewal Program*, October 1965.

2. See Little, pages 18 and 32, for definitions. Hunter's Point and India Basin have been omitted, the former because so many of its units were temporary "war housing," and the latter because it was primarily an industrial area.

3. Section 3.524 of the San Francisco Charter.

4. Section 203.2 of the San Francisco Housing Code, as amended in January 1962.

5. San Francisco City Planning Commission, *The Master Plan of the City and County of San Francisco*, 1966. Part II is "The City-Wide Urban Renewal Plan."

6. San Francisco Department of City Planning, *The Comprehensive Plan: Residence*, 1971.

7. Examples of neighborhood plans and their basically conservationist nature, are *South Bayshore Study: A Proposed Development Plan*, June 1969; *Bernal Heights Neighborhood Improvement Program*, December 1968; "Haight-Ashbury," July 1973; *Mission Neighborhood Plan*, May 1965; all issued by the San Francisco Department of City Planning. Also see John W. Bourne, Gregory Montes, Burger and Coplans Planning Consultants, *A Plan for the Inner Mission,* Book 2, March 1974; and Planning Association for the Richmond, "Richmond District Improvement Plan," December 1972.

8. Robert Cassidy, "San Francisco Fights to Save FACE," *Planning*, June 1973, pp. 5-7. *Planning* is the magazine of the American Society of Planning Officials.

9. These and other observations about the history and outlook of the Bureau of Building Inspection were gathered in an interview with senior official Bernard Cummings on January 11, 1977, and from letters of October 19 and October 27, 1965, from S. M. Tatarian to James R. McCarthy and December 16, 1965, from Robert Levy to McCarthy.

10. Little, *Community Renewal Program,* p. 26.

11. Letter from the director of the Department of Public Works to the director of the Department of City Planning, October 19, 1965. The conclusion was reinforced during the interview with Bernard Cummings.

12. A letter of March 15, 1968, from the planning director to Thomas Mellon, the chief administrative officer, contains an estimate of the number of people who attended.

13. All buildings, one- and two-unit structures as well as multifamily structures, were included in the FACE program. One- and two-unit buildings were not included under normal code enforcement programs.

14. March 15, 1968, letter to Thomas Mellon.

15. San Francisco Department of City Planning and Department of Public Works, *Code Enforcement Feasibility Study*, 1968, p. 22.

16. Cassidy, "San Francisco Fights to Save FACE," p. 5.

17. San Francisco Department of Public Works, *Code Enforcement Feasibility Study: Bernal Heights*, November 1968.

18. For an accounting of the non-federally assisted property rehabilitation programs, see U.S. Department of Housing and Urban Development, *Examples of Local and State Financing of Property Rehabilitation*, August 1974.

19. San Francisco Department of City Planning, *Residence—Strategy and Programs*, December 1973, p. 56. Other estimates at that time were $8.9 million for the Western Addition A-1 project, $59.3 million for Yerba Buena, $36.1 million for the India Basin Industrial Park, and $53.2 million for Hunter's Point.

20. Little, *Community Renewal Program*, p. 19.

21. San Francisco Department of City Planning Memorandum of September 21, 1972, by Richard Gamble. The estimate of 331,887 total dwelling units in the city as of December 31, 1970, is from San Francisco Department of City Planning, *Changes in the San Francisco Housing Inventory, 1970,* May 1971, p. 6.

22. Cassidy, "San Francisco Fights to Save FACE," p. 5.

23. Letter from Henry Eschwege, U.S. General Accounting Office, to Carla Hills, Secretary, U.S. Department of Housing and Urban Development, March 8, 1976.

24. Cassidy, "San Francisco Fights to Save FACE." The comment about Bernal Heights is attributed to W. L. McCabe of HUD.

25. The first six nonaided areas in the city's program, three of which later became part of FACE, had over 19,500 housing units, according to Little, *Community Renewal Program*, p. 18.

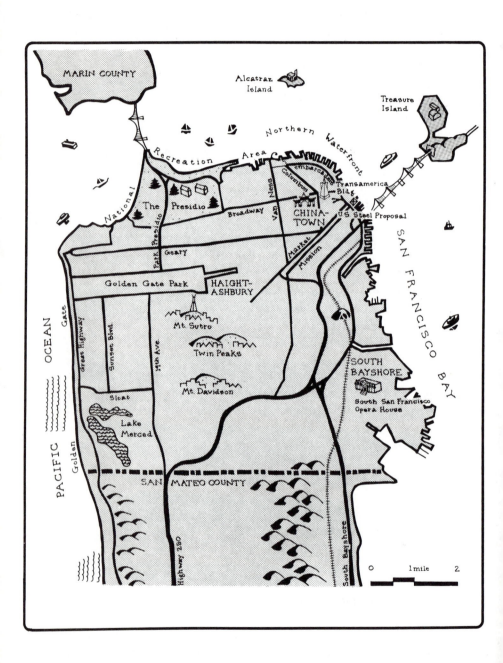

# Chapter 6
# 1969-1972: Making City
# Planning Work

The period from the start of 1969 to the last quarter of 1972 was one of intense activity and productivity for the planning department. It was a period of rapidly growing influence for city planning and for the department, despite serious conflicts with the mayor and disagreements with the planning commission over individual issues. If there was a golden time for city planning during my almost eight years as planning director, this was it.

The issues that had to be considered and resolved during this period seemed larger, more significant, and more precedent setting than those that came up at other times. They included proposals for individual developments like the Transamerica Building and a U.S. Steel office, hotel, and port complex at the waterfront, and proposals for scattered-site, low-income housing projects in middle-class areas. There were conflicts with the Army over its proposal to build housing on vacant land in the Presidio and decisions on whether or not to build ramps from the ends of the unfinished elevated freeway to the ground. They were issues of the sort that were calculated to arouse the passions of San Franciscans, issues that could be perceived as having long-term implications for the city.

Many of the issues arose at a time when they could be viewed in the light of our recently completed citywide and neighborhood plans or of the plans that were then in progress. Most of our planning, I felt, was of a high caliber. Only a staff that had developed into a first-rate professional organization could have done that kind of planning and dealt so well with the kinds of issues that confronted us.

One way of looking at the period is in relation to changing environmental values, to growing trends toward urban conservation and

preservation. Increasingly, the notions of bigness, growth, and untram-
meled development that had prevailed for so long were being challenged. It was a time, too, of personal change for me, as the subtle and
not-so-subtle differences between San Francisco and the cities where I
had spent most of my life began to have their effects. As opposed to most
other big cities in the late 1960s and early 1970s, San Francisco did not
need major physical change; it was well worth saving as it was. San
Francisco's decentralized form of government, with its naive, almost
textbook qualities, was beginning to make some sense to me, too. But
within this context of changing and sometimes competing values,
disagreements and confrontations between myself and the mayor and
planning commission were inevitable.

It was inevitable, too, given my nature and that of the other actors
on the scene and given the magnitude of the issues, that these years
would be marked by high points of immense personal and professional
satisfaction as well as lows. The latter almost always accompanied
defeats like the failure of the planning commission to support me on the
Transamerica and U.S. Steel proposals, defeats that left me wondering
what I was doing in San Francisco. The high points, including our
victory against the U.S. Steel proposal at the Board of Supervisors, our
completion of the plan for residence, and community acceptance of our
urban design plan, symbolized what planning was supposed to be about.

For many city planners, the foundation for their work is the comprehensive or general or master plan. It provides a set of objectives,
policies, maps, and programs, all directed to the vision the community
has of its future. The master plan is supposed to serve as the basis for both
daily and long-range decisions that will influence the physical development of the community and the quality of the urban environment that its
people might enjoy. In theory at least, each public and private action is to
be consistent with the plan. In many ways, the master plan is the beginning of a decision-making process with regard to the physical nature of
the community. That is the classical view of the master plan.

If one takes such a view of what master planning is supposed to be, it would be somewhat misleading to say that we were making comprehensive city planning work. At the outset we did not have a master plan that was adequate to serve as a sound basis for all of our decisions and recommendations, nor did all the programs we were advocating stem from objectives or policies that were embodied in such a document. Further, we were not preparing one, all-inclusive plan that would address the full range of subjects that are normally found in a master plan. Instead we were preparing individual elements, chapters in a way, of what might ultimately become a complete plan. We were publishing and adopting those elements as we went along.

Three of these individual master plan elements were completed by early 1972: housing, urban design, and transportation. They dealt with subjects that were important to San Francisco, and they set a framework for all the planning to follow. In the meantime, we tried to look at the day-to-day issues in the light of the possible long-term consequences of our recommendations. For example, we might ask if it made sense to put more low-income housing near the Western Addition, where there was already plenty. Would it not be more consistent with the recommendations that we were developing in the housing plan to scatter smaller developments throughout the city? The process of deciding immediate matters helped to clarify our values as we developed the policies that would become part of the larger plan. At weekly staff meetings and in-house reviews, the issues that were to come before the commission were discussed, and these discussions also helped us to form policies for the physical development of the city. So too did the give-and-take with citizens at regular meetings. Thus, even before our planning document was published, our public recommendations throughout this period were based on policies that were slowly evolving, as well as on the existing master plan. By the end of 1972, we had produced examples of successful programs, legislation, and day-to-day decisions that were based upon our series of comprehensive plans. It is in that sense that we were making comprehensive planning work.

The sequence of steps—plan preparation, presentation, and adoption—was similar for each element. Initial research was accompanied by preliminary reports. After careful internal review, including discussion with a committee of the planning commission, we published and presented a preliminary plan. We tried to make these presentations special events, with widespread media coverage. There was little public participation in the plans to this point, and some people expressed hostility for that reason. Before the public hearings, we presented the plan to neighborhood groups. We based our revision of the plan on what we heard at the meetings and hearings. By this time there were usually a lot of people advocating the plan. They had become involved. Even if this was not the purists' view of how to involve citizens in a citywide planning process, it did seem to work. A key to it all was in taking the review period seriously and being open to change.

The first and most important of our citywide plans was the plan for residence, which we initially presented in 1970.[1] Most clearly and directly, the plan called for maintaining and preserving existing neighborhoods and housing. It called for de-emphasizing slum clearance and public projects that would result in uprooting people. The criteria it proposed for future projects were intended as brakes to the freewheeling redevelopment process. These criteria emphasized providing, not eliminating, low- and moderate-income housing. The emphasis was on small projects; for instance, small, evenly distributed public housing developments. We proposed to convert some nonresidential land to residential use and to intensify residential densities in a few areas. We also called for a regional housing plan. The publication of the housing plan was accompanied by an extensive set of recommendations for its implementation.

At first, the spokesmen for lower income, minority people expressed anger because we had not consulted them directly in preparing the plans. But when they found that we had addressed their major concerns in the first place and that we were willing to make changes during the review period, most of them became joint advocates with the planning department staff and helped to get the plan adopted by the planning commission. We were helped by an editorial in the *San Francisco Examiner* that said, in effect, that we should limit the amount of housing for low-income people because the more that was provided, the more poor people would come.[2] It was the kind of exlusionary view we could respond to with ease. We had more trouble with the Redevelopment Agency, which didn't like the idea of having limits placed on its future options. Ultimately, though, the commission supported us.

The plan for transportation also was completed and adopted during this period.[3] It asserted the importance of public transportation in such a densely developed city as San Francisco and emphasized the need to limit auto traffic both downtown and in residential neighborhoods. The plan recognized that there might be limits to the amount of traffic that could be handled. In a section on "fundamental assumptions," it spoke of possible limitations of employment and physical growth if desirable environmental standards were to be maintained. The plan's potential longer term implications as a factor in controlling growth in the city were not immediately or universally recognized. Nevertheless, it put to bed, officially, the freeway-oriented transportation planning that came on hard times with the freeway revolt of 1966. After changes were made to the preliminary plan, it too was supported by neighborhood groups.

Not all of our citywide, comprehensive planning efforts were successful. On the grounds that public facilities and services could best be planned by the agencies most responsible for them, we tried to engage in cooperative planning ventures with them. It did not work out. Twice during this period we tried to plan with the police department. But it seemed that every time we were about to come up with a plan the chief would be replaced and the new head man would have a different approach to providing police services. The third time was to prove a winner in terms of completing a plan—maybe it was because the new chief lasted long enough. We had a similar experience with the library people. At just about the time when our collaboration had produced a modest, workmanlike plan and we were prepared to go public with it, the head librarian backed away and sat on the proposal long enough for us to turn to other work. My sense was that the library hierarchy was unsure of itself. It did not like public hearings, especially on anything that might be even remotely controversial, and it did not want to be bound by policies, preferring to deal with individual issues as they came up.

Our failure to produce a school facilities plan was painful. The area was extremely important, especially in a period of court decisions over integration and busing. A friendly school board member, Howard Nemerovski, had requested our help, and we assigned a very capable young staff member to work with school administrators on a plan. After months of work, when we were close to publishing a first joint report, the superintendent of schools and some of his high-ranking aides found reasons to postpone. They were in the midst of a number of controversies, and I suspect that they were fearful of even the possibility of any more. Passions had been aroused by recent court decisions on busing and the mayor's unexpected speech opposing a particular integration plan. The situation was complicated by the resignation of the superintendent. It was not a time that was sympathetic to long-range plans and policies. So an unfinished first draft of a plan for schools went into a file drawer. The mayor once asked me to show him the draft. But either because he never read it or because, having read it, he disagreed with its approach, he never told me what he thought of it. We made other attempts to cooperate with school officials to prepare a plan, but they were never successful.

We completed our plan for the South Bayshore area, presented it one evening in the historic South San Francisco Opera House, and saw it endorsed by the planning commission after receiving major support by the community. In fact, the neighborhood people said it was their plan, not ours. We accomplished some significant rezoning directed to preserving the shoreline for public open space instead of allowing it to be filled in and used for marginal industrial development that could not produce jobs anyway. It was the beginning of a long struggle to create a shoreline park on the Bay, based on a proposal that came jointly from our staff and from South Bayshore residents. Other proposals related to housing, circulation, and local shopping would demand our continuing presence. I had enjoyed immensely being personally involved in the work to date.

Now, however, after having finished the plan and having gained a high degree of community acceptance, I made a major tactical error. Instead of maintaining direct contact with the neighborhood, including calling our own meetings, I chose to work through the newly established Model Cities agency. I reasoned that we should try to strengthen a fledgling, grass-roots agency rather than run our own show. But in doing so we gave up one of our greatest sources of strength—continuous direct contact and influence with residents. Also, I did not foresee the great problems of organization and staffing, and of credibility, that the Model Cities group would have in its own backyard, making it less than dynamic during the years of its existence. It might have been necessary to work through this new, "local" agency. Still, I continue to question my judgment on this one.

The plan for the northern waterfront area was approved after many public hearings. We also accomplished some rezoning to conform with the plan. But at the request of the port commission, the planning commission postponed a recommendation on height controls along one stretch of waterfront next to the Bay Bridge. It would take a major San Francisco donnybrook to resolve the matter.

There was not much fun for me in our work on the plan for this part of the waterfront. The people involved—and they seemed to be legion—were so uncompromising in their viewpoints and so strident in their presentations that reasonableness, satisfaction, or accomplishment seemed impossible. The innumerable public and private meetings at every step along the way went on for hours. They can be characterized best by picturing Robert Katz of Telegraph Hill methodically relating, at each meeting, how we got to a particular point, what had been promised or implied (as he saw it), why most development proposals were for too much or were otherwise unacceptable, what misstatements had been made, why and how the port commission was misdirected and misleading, and what if anything should be done.[4]

One side seemed to want no development and the other no controls. Whenever I thought we had reached some kind of consensus, a new militant group would spring forth, and the meetings and hearings and battles would start anew. Planning, or nonplanning, for the northern waterfront seemed to be a continuous process. It was only when I accepted the possible futility of it all that planning for that area become fun.

Our involvement in Chinatown produced a plan, prepared by our consultants, that addressed the housing and recreation needs of the area. We issued a newsletter in Chinese—I never knew what I was signing—and provided translation services at public meetings, making it much easier for Chinatown residents to participate in the planning. Soon after completion of the plan, we prepared a proposal to redevelop a very small site for low-income housing. Dislocation would be minimal. It was important that we, not the Redevelopment Agency, had taken the lead and had been primarily responsible for the project plan. This was redevelopment that grew directly out of a plan prepared by residents and approved by the planning commission. It was being used here as an implementing tool to carry out a general plan. The planning department, not the Redevelopment Agency, was saying where a project should happen.

One of the top Redevelopment Agency staff members said we would never get approval from the Board of Supervisors, especially since the project would require a $500,000 local cash subsidy. He was wrong. A large number of residents turned out to support the proposal, and the board, responding at least as much to the people as to the department, did not turn us down. We had come some distance from my first appearance in San Francisco, when I was ineffectual in opposing a change in the Golden Gateway project.

It became clear at neighborhood meetings that people dislike rapid change. Over and over again, they expressed anger at new development that was out of keeping with what existed. In response to the concerns that were expressed—more traffic, loss of families, replacement of older homes with unattractive, "plastic," new buildings—we suggested that they, not we, initiate "downzoning" applications. In one or two cases I taunted and challenged the people to action. It was important, I felt, that they do the work necessary to complete an application, that they become involved and committed to a cause. This would not happen if our staff did the work. We would be city hall imposing its will on the people. A small group of residents, including a sculptor I knew well, took our challenge and prepared a rezoning application for about a three-block area. The downzoning would decrease significantly the extent of development that would be permitted. The result, they hoped, would be to preserve older housing. The group collected signatures of neighborhood residents on petitions to go with their application. After the application was filed, we reviewed it in considerable detail. Our recommendation to the planning commission, totally in support of the rezoning, not only was important to its decision but also made the community residents and the planners immediate allies when the matter came before the Board of Supervisors. And as allies, it was then easy to advise the residents and to work with them on the subtle strategies involved in getting a favorable final vote.

The approach worked well and became the forerunner of a number of future downzonings. The result in this case was a four-to-three vote in favor by the planning commission and approval by the Board of Supervisors.[5] Later, while we were working on a neighborhood plan for the Haight-Ashbury area, residents proposed a much larger and more drastic downzoning, most of which we happily accommodated. There would be other occasions on which we could not agree with neighborhood downzoning applications and these, of course, were trying for all concerned. All in all, however, I was more than pleased with the role we were playing in what could be called the politics of city planning.

Inevitably, we were involved in planning projects that did not fall into convenient categories like neighborhood, citywide, comprehensive, or long- or short-range. I referred to them at the time as ad hoc projects because that seemed to be a convenient term. They were increasingly related to the more comprehensive planning activities of the department.

One of our ad hoc projects involved the landmark South San Francisco Opera House in the South Bayshore area. Two of our staff members, Sam Jung and Calvin Malone, seeking a way to save the building, received considerable help from two sympathetic HUD employees, Sam Weinstein and Bob Boalt; and we started working on plans to turn it into a community center. We continued to be involved in the mini-park program, although this was now logically the reponsibility of the Department of Public Works and the Recreation and Park Department. Considerable coordination was called for. The mayor's office, eager to get the money in the first place, seemed less than dynamic in implementing the program, once funding had been assured. But people in the neighborhoods, especially lower income areas like Chinatown and the Mission, wanted the small playing and sitting areas. So we pressed everyone involved and again advocated for the neighborhoods.

On a grander and more classic urban design scale, I continued to act in the role of client on behalf of the city for the redesign of Market Street. We solved the problems of coordination with the principals of the three architectural firms involved—Mario Ciampi, Lawrence Halprin, and John Warnecke—by advising them that at least two of them would have to be present at biweekly joint meetings on design policies. Otherwise no decisions could be made and work would stop. After I canceled one meeting we had no further problems.

It was more difficult to get the Board of Supervisors to agree on the street tree to be used—sycamore—a decision that, technically and legally, it should not have been involved in. We spent hours and thousands of dollars worth of staff time debating the issue. The decision of San Franciscans in the 1968 bond issue vote to spend all that money on Market Street made it fairly easy to pass an ordinance controlling signs along the street. The impetus was the erection of three especially offensive billboards at locations made highly visible by the creation of new plazas. At least one billboard company had overplayed its hand.

There were many other ad hoc projects: a design to beautify Mission Street at the new rapid transit station, a new height limit along the ocean, studies to extend rapid transit south to the airport and north across the Bay to Marin County, and a proposal to redesign the dangerous ocean-front Great Highway as a smaller, less direct parkway that could also provide local play areas. During this period, we were also involved with the approval of at least twelve low-cost housing projects. Most of them were small; most were for the elderly; a few were for families. The policy of distributing public housing throughout the city rather than concentrating it seemed to be taking hold.

Our minor involvement with creation of the Golden Gate National Recreation Area is noteworthy because its success stands in sharp contrast to our attempts to create a shoreline park in the South Bayshore area. In response to a request from the Bureau of Outdoor Recreation, I assigned my administrative assistant to work with a task force on a preliminary plan for national recreation facility along the ocean. It was to have an urban orientation. By 1972 the 35,000-acre GGNRA was assured. Its advocates were largely middle- and upper-income whites. There were few lower-income or minority people living close to it. Try as we might, we could get almost no one interested in working for a shoreline park along the Bay, where lower-income blacks lived. Few middle- or upper-income white conservationists were prepared to work for that park.

The proposed rezoning of a parcel in the Mission or the prospect of a hospital expansion in another neighborhood might be just as significant in the eyes of nearby residents as a large waterfront complex of hotels, offices, and stores. All, including the small zoning cases, were issues in that they constituted development proposals by the owners of agents of private property that found their way before the staff or commission and that required staff recommendation and action. Development proposals emanating from public agencies also had to be dealt with. All of these issues were different from the ad hoc planning projects in that they were initiated and advocated by others, and they were usually confined to a small or finite site, even though they might affect a larger area.

Our approach to handling private development issues, the small as well as the large, was fairly straightforward. It was similar to the approach we took with the International Market Center in 1968. We took the position that, for the kinds of development proposals that had to come to the planning commission for approval, our positive recommendation (if we were prepared to agree to the use at all) would be dependent upon the developer's meeting what we called "urban design terms of reference." These terms amounted to conditions that we felt to be important from a planning standpoint, generally related to function and design, but at times with social overtones as well. Unless the conditions were met, we would recommend against the proposal.

The success of this approach depended on many things, not the least of which was early consultation with developers and their architects. No one wants to change a design once it's completed. We encouraged developers to see us early so that they would be aware of our concerns before the designs went very far. There were other factors that influenced the success of the process: the reasonableness of our analysis and of our conditions; the extent of the developer's influence with the planning commissioners, the supervisors, and the mayor; my own relations with the same people; the developer's perception of our strength; and the interest and support of the public.

I tried to minimize the developers' direct contact with the commissioners and the mayor and often threatened to recommend against any proposal, good ones included, if developers tried to lobby directly with them. One doubts the effectiveness of that ploy. We played the game in as forceful and direct a manner as we could. I paid a lot of attention to individual development issues and let people know, as early as possible, where the planning department would stand and why. Ultimately, it was important that everyone involved have a high regard for the work of our staff and that the developers have a sense that we could make our recommendations stick.

Inevitably, the process led to conflicts. The developers, being people, didn't follow "the rules." They never do. They did talk to and influence the mayor and the commissioners. Even when the developers agreed to our conditions, that didn't guarantee that interested citizens agreed or were pleased. Sometimes there were honest differences of opinion. We won some and lost some, although for the most part I think we won more than we lost.

In the meetings and the conflicts and the wins and losses, I learned and relearned a considerable amount about the nature of the development process. I learned over and over again that most architects felt comfortable wearing two hats—they had no problem telling you what was good design and in the public interest one day, while serving in their civic role, and then contradicting themselves the next, when representing a client. I learned that out-of-town developers and their architects were less sympathetic to local concerns and traditions and rarely more inventive than native folk, that they were less likely to play by local rules, and that they were more likely to bring political pressures to bear for their development proposals. I learned that if a public relations firm or the chamber of commerce were involved with a proposal, there was a good chance it would be bad. To this long-term, fairly liberal Democrat, there was some humor in realizing that very wealthy, moderate Republicans like Mortimer Fleishhacker and Bill Brinton took a lot of convincing on any given issue but that, once convinced, they would hang in there with you to the end, while New Deal-type Democrats tended to waffle pretty quickly on environmental issues. (In reponse to an accusation that a pending rezoning would decrease the value of a particular property and therefore constituted taking it without compensation, Fleishhacker responded that he knew the person involved bought and sold stocks, that there was no assurance that the stock prices would always go up, and that he didn't see why it should be any different with property than with stocks.)

And I learned a little bit about the role of bluff in the life of developers, like the one who assured me he had firm, first-rate financing for his ocean-front development at the same time that I was being called by an old friend in the Midwest inquiring about the wisdom of financing that very same project. It sounded strange to him, my friend said, and he wanted to know if I knew the person who was seeking his help. I learned a lot.

I learned especially that fighting the issues on a case-by-case basis is too risky, too enervating, and too often a losing bargain. If nothing else, the politics involved in any given case could beat the planners more often than not. There had to be a process and plans that had teeth in them.

It is difficult to draw objective conclusions as to our effectiveness in handling these issues. Should we be considered effective if our recommendation was upheld by the planning commission? By the mayor? By the Board of Supervisors? Or is a better measure of effectiveness whether or not a project we advocated actually got built? What if a building we favored got stopped by a lawsuit, which we could not control, or if one we opposed got stopped the same way? What is a major issue? Who decides? If we looked at all possible cases, we would find considerable agreement with staff recommendations, since so many of the cases were simple and clear-cut. Should we use our negative recommendations as a guide, or how often we were upheld? But then what about all the "yes" cases where people did follow the process or were influenced by our input to their work?

By one of these measures, however, we were not very effective. Out of five negative staff recommendations on ten major cases, the commission did not uphold the staff once. (The ten were the Transamerica Building, U.S. Steel, Sutro Tower, Holiday Inn on Van Ness, Haas Russian Hill apartments, Ferryport Plaza, Lake Merced Condominiums, Playland Condominiums, Petri Russian Hill, and Nob Hill apartments at California and Jones; the first five received negative recommendations.) It happens, though, that two of the five, U.S. Steel and Haas, never got built anyway.

Despite the sad tale told by the limited statistics, I think that we were, in general, effective in handling the major development issues. Also, by taking strong and often noisy positions on most issues, we were helping to highlight them in the public eye. People knew what was going on and had a chance to make their positions known.

Of the public development issues, two are worthy of note here. One, a confrontation with the Army over future development in the Presidio, was a conflict between different levels of government. It illustrated an emerging local awareness of federal developments that might affect the city. The other issue was a conflict within the local government itself over the best use of a piece of city-owned property, the so-called Presidio Car Barns (no relative to the Presidio).

The military has owned the 1,700 acre Presidio about as long as San Francisco has existed. By and large, it has taken good care of it. Its stature in the eyes of San Franciscans is not unlike that of Golden Gate Park. It was generally understood that since the Army owned the site and since the federal government was at a higher level than local government, we had no control over what was done with the land.

In the late 1960s and early 1970s the Army had plans to build additional housing in the Presidio. It also negotiated with the San Francisco Board of Education to build two elementary schools. There were other development plans too, none consistent with local ideas, which were largely conservationist in nature. There were strong objections to the housing and to the schools. As public improvements, the schools would have to be referred to the planning commission to determine their conformity to the master plan. The public was concerned that the new construction would be at the expense of open space, views, and trees. It is almost certainly true that widespread antimilitary feelings associated with the Viet Nam conflict played a part in the reactions to the Army's proposals.

The citizens expressed their militancy at the public meetings we held as part of the referral process. Letters and direct communications were exchanged between well-placed San Franciscans and high officials in Washington.[6] In the end, the mayor backed up the position that was taken by the critics. The net result of all the activity was an agreement by the Army not to build any more housing. Even more important was its agreement to refer all future development proposals to the planning department and planning commission for findings as to their conformity with city plans. On November 25, 1970, Board of Supervisors Resolution 690-70 was signed in the mayor's office. I referred to it as the Treaty of the Presidio.

Neither Mayor Alioto nor the planning commission was so helpful in deciding what should be done with the Presidio Car Barns. This city-owned property had for many years been used as a storage yard for diesel and trolley buses. It was located at the intersection of two major streets, diagonally opposite a large Sears store. Apparently, during his first election campaign, the mayor had promised a more intense use of the property, one that would get it on the tax rolls and bring in more revenues. What he had failed to observe was that it was a promise that no one had asked him to make.

Before public property can be sold and developed, it must be found surplus to public needs by the Board of Supervisors. Such a finding starts with a decision by the custodian of the property, the Public Utilities Commission in this case. At first, the general manager of utilities indicated to me that the site should not be abandoned. But the mayor had his way with the general manager, and it was not long before developers turned up with ideas. They started talking about a major shopping center, possibly with offices as well, and considerable space for parking. But the Board of Supervisors still had not ruled that the land was surplus. Any private use would also require a zoning change.

The position of the planning staff was that the land was not surplus to public use. There was a continuing need for transit service facilities. Besides, we said, if the land were declared surplus, the public should dispose of it in a manner that would further public policy. A large shopping center in that location could only take customers away from downtown, from the local commercial strips that are characteristic of

San Francisco, and from a black-sponsored center that was proposed for a nearby redevelopment area. Thus, we opposed using the site as a shopping center. If development were to occur, we favored housing, including a certain percentage for low- and moderate-income people. Unfortunately, the mayor had more influence with the planning commission than I did, and a series of staff recommendations was defeated, even though most people at a public hearing also opposed the commercial center.

By the time the matter came to the Board of Supervisors, there had been so much negative publicity that the supervisors refused to declare the property surplus. In this case, the diffuse nature of San Francisco's government, for all its cumbersome qualities, was not without merit as far as city planning was concerned.

Despite our never-ending problems with Civil Service, we were becoming a top-notch, active staff. The quality of our work was good and getting better. We could hold our own with developers and with bureaucrats. And word was getting around that we had some smarts. There was an overall commonness of purpose, and understanding as to the most important issues and a willingness to take on the controversies. Not that everything was sweetness and light on substantive planning issues. We argued and debated a lot, especially at the Monday morning staff meetings where we reviewed and took positions on upcoming cases. A large measure of credit for our progress, at least in part of the office, belonged to Dean Macris, the assistant director for plans and programs. His enthusiasm and energy were as contagious as his abilities were obvious. He had the magnificent strength of being able to deal successfully with the toughest, most cunning bureaucrats. His Chicago years had been well spent.

Many of us were friends as well as colleagues, and we spent a lot of time together socially. So there was a good spirit, overall, and we could share in each other's joys. We shared in personal grief and losses as well. From 1969 through Jim Paul's death in 1973, four staff members and one commissioner died of cancer. With increasing commitment, personal as well as professional, came greater sadnesses as well as joys.

The city planning constituency that had existed previously became more broadly based and grew in strength during this period.

Neighborhood people had been involved in the plans and programs that we were producing, and they had been listened to. We were reasonably accessible and responsive, and people seemed to feel they had a place to go, a place to be heard. I think that the quality of our work was having its effects. People were beginning to understand that we were fairly independent, that we were likely to advocate what we thought best from a city planning point of view, and that they could get a fair shake from us.

We were becoming somewhat more influential with other departments, too. Most of the other local agencies seemed to recognize that we had some fairly intelligent people on the staff and that it might make some sense for them to work with us. Our familiarity with neighborhood issues may have suggested that we could help other agencies achieve their objectives. Our sense of what was politically possible and our ability to get programs funded also helped our relations. More significant, I suspect, is that the other departments thought of us as having a fairly good rapport with the top decision makers, including the mayor. Whether or not they were correct is less important than the fact that that was their perception. In any case, we became increasingly involved in joint efforts with the Police Department, the Municipal Railroad, the Recreation and Park Department, the Bureau of Building Inspection, and other parts of the Department of Public Works.

In truth, our relations with the Department of Public Works were less than outstanding. The two departments saw things very differently. Public Works was automobile-oriented—with a vengeance. It could find a hundred reasons for freeways, for more traffic lanes, for street widenings, but never one reason for narrowing a street; twenty reasons not to plant street trees, but damned few to help get them. Public Works could be counted on to testify before the planning commission that the development it was considering—any development—would not cause undue congestion. It didn't matter how large the project would be or how small the street was. The idea of public transportation was fine with

Public Works, but not at the expense of autos. Its standard solution to downtown parking problems was more garages. At first, I thought the problem was one of communication, that the Public Works staffers were nice guys and we just didn't know how to talk to them. Planners always think that's the problem. I was wrong. We really did differ, and there was no way we could persuade them of the rightness of our positions.

But they had power. Public Works is an old and large department. Its people know their way around city hall. They let contracts and they build and maintain things; a lot of money flows their way. Other departments are highly dependent upon them. Public Works is under the chief administrative officer and its staff has a better line to him in his role of planning commissioner than the director of planning does. We tried to get through or around them time and again but with only modest success. We were better at stopping them by mobilizing citizen support and by directly contacting sympathetic supervisors. Myron Tatarian, the Public Works director, once confided to me that we had developed the power to stop just about anything his department proposed. When I suggested in turn that he and his staff also had the power to frustrate public policies they disagreed with by simply dragging their feet on projects or by subtly changing their designs, he shrugged but didn't deny it. Subsequent attempts to be more cooperative and "positive" were only mildly successful.

However bad our relations with Public Works might have been, it would be hard to categorize it as an out and out enemy. The chamber of commerce came closer to that definition. I think the only time we ever agreed with the chamber on anything was when we favored a development proposal or when its members knew that some kind of plan or program was inevitable and that ours was the best it was likely to get. Development, development, development—that was the name of the game. That, after all, is why the chamber of commerce exists. It might publicly express a concern for quality development, but every private proposal must have been just fine, because I don't remember the chamber's ever being opposed to one. New offices, high density housing, parking garages, highways, shops, more nonmaritime uses along the waterfront, more tourist attractions—the chamber wanted them all, always. It wanted as few controls and as little city planning input as possible, because that only hindered private development. It was opposed to almost anything that would increase taxes, particularly to services or facilities that were not downtown-oriented. It was not opposed, however, to a whopping public subsidy for a public transportation system—one that would bring more people downtown. When the planning department and the chamber agreed, I would look a second time at our position to see if I was on the wrong side. We did not agree too often.

Good relations based on mutual respect between the planning commission and its staff, particularly the director, are obviously central to the smooth operation of a planning department. The commission does appoint the director, and it alone can fire him. It also sets policy for the staff. Most of the time, we got along just fine. There were periods, however, when our relationship resembled a fast-moving roller coaster, hitting peaks and troughs in rapid succession.

There was little conflict in setting the overall tone and direction of the department. In a rather simplistic but nonetheless real sense, our objectives were similar: to "do right" for the long-range physical development of San Francisco in relation to its people, balanced by concern for immediate needs and equity. The commissioners were as eager as I to keep San Francisco a fine place to live. For the most part, the commissioners were bright, knowledgeable about the city, and prepared to listen and learn. They were available to me and the staff and advocated for us when that proved necessary. All except one or two stayed out of the day-to-day running of the department. In most cases, they gave considerable weight to staff recommendations, and on issues where nothing personal or political was at stake, their debate was often spirited and productive. Most important, they agreed with me more often than not. Mutual respect and affection existed to a high degree.

It was not all business. I gave dinners for the commissioners and enjoyed their hospitality as well. Jim Kearney knew where Julia Porter kept her liquor and long after dinner, when Julia had stopped serving, he would get it and we would drink and sing late into the night. On other occasions Julia would fill me in on the histories of people of note, including fellow commissioners.

I became close friends with Walter Newman and Mortimer Fleishhacker. Newman, as the years passed, gave more and more time to the commission and became increasingly oriented toward conservation. Fleishhacker was the epitome of a planning commissioner, surely the hardest working commissioner I would ever know. He read and commented on everything. He used his personal influence with the Nixon administration to get funding for housing in Chinatown. He served on every manner of committee, no matter where or when it might meet, and his decisions were consistently oriented to people rather than to special interests.

There were conflicts, too, unfortunately. If I ever could be said to have had a honeymoon period with the commissioners, it ended when they approved the Transamerica building over my opposition. Soon after that, with prodding from the mayor, they approved another project I felt to be ill advised, the U.S. Steel building on the waterfront. At an executive session during that period I told the commissioners that if they made many more decisions like those, I would quit. On such major issues I continued to advocate my position, not the commission's, before the Board of Supervisors, and some commissioners were none too pleased with that. The widespread acceptance of the urban design plan when it was published in 1971 brought us back together with a new feeling of common purpose. But that consensus would in time be shattered by fights over other development issues. Our relationship went up and down.

Looking for and finding a pattern to our disagreements can be self-serving and misleading. Nonetheless, some of the occasions for our periodic disenchantments are clear: we drew apart when the commission failed to take our professional advice on precedent-setting matters; when it gave more weight to the views of other professionals than to the expertise of its own staff; when it ignored its own policies, which had come after hard-fought battles, in favor of decisions of the moment; and, most devastating, when the commissioners voted on major issues for solely political reasons.

Sure, all of this can also be summed up by saying, as some did, that I was furious when I didn't get my way on important matters. That would be true. Whatever our differences, though, there were never personal animosities between me and the commissioners—with one exception. And that commissioner antagonized others as well. The exception did, however, make being a planning director less pleasant than it had been before.

One might have thought that the two ex officio members of the commission—the chief administrative officer and the representative of the Public Utilities Commission—would represent two "sure" votes for staff positions. It didn't prove to be so. In the toughest development cases the two were likely to vote in favor of the development. They were often slow to support the staff on public plans and programs. On occasion the Public Utilities representative even voted against recommendations that were directed to helping public transportation. In time it became clear that on any important issue he voted the way the mayor's office wished.

The bubble burst between the mayor and me during the election campaign of 1971. Although it had become clear early on that we were very different kinds of people with very different values, we got along just fine during his first term. At heart the mayor was a laissez-faire development man. His advocacy of most big development proposals allowed for no mistake as to where his sympathies were, and his Darwinian theory of urban growth made me shudder.

One wondered about the mayor's interest in being mayor. Within less than a year of his election he was more than passively engaged in running for vice-president, and in 1970 he made a run for governor. I was not happy with the extent of the interest he displayed in the day-to-day workings of government. However, he did seek my counsel and, I believe, listened to me on most public matters that were related to city planning. Our meetings were frequent and casual. I kept him up to date on projects that were pending, and my staff cooperated with his. I continued to feel little or no compulsion to hide my opinions on planning matters, even when our views were diametrically opposed. I felt that as long as I didn't knock him, there would be no retribution for my difference of opinion.

I was at home on Yom Kippur day, 1971, when I got word that the mayor wanted to talk to me. I telephoned him late that afternoon and learned that he would be shooting a TV ad for his campaign the next morning on a boat in the Bay and that he wanted me in it. He wanted to be talking to me against a background of San Francisco. It was an abrupt request, one that immediately made me uncomfortable. But the mayor expected a quick, clear, affirmative answer, and I said, "Yes."

I was terribly bothered by that phone call and by my reply. I didn't want to campaign for anyone. That was not the job of the director of city planning in San Francisco. In 1966, when Jack Kent was explaining the job and San Francisco's government to me, he had observed that historically the planning director and other top appointed officials survived changes in administration. He said that these positions were not looked at as political. As naive as that may have sounded, I, with perhaps just as much naivete, had come to believe that it was not only true, but proper as well. It is also true that Mayor Alioto would not have been my choice in the forthcoming election and although I would campaign for no one else, neither would I feel comfortable putting my name out publicly for him.

So, after much soul-searching, hemming and hawing, and thinking about the consequences, I called the mayor back and told him that I could not do what he had asked, that I felt it would be improper. I wished him luck. He was his usual courteous, understanding self.

There were no immediate repercussions from either the mayor or his staff. But after his overwhelming re-election, the coolness set in. I got the word from old friends (although perhaps exaggerated) that my name wasn't too well regarded in the mayor's office and that my days were numbered. It was clear that I was on the outs. From that point on, I had fewer meetings with the mayor, and I found them harder to arrange. And the meetings were uncomfortable when we had them. I told one or two friends—old family, well regarded San Franciscans—that I was in trouble with the mayor, but I don't know what, if anything, they may have done on my behalf. I counted the votes on the planning commission and concluded that I would not be fired. I wondered if Mayor Alioto had counted them too. Even though I discussed the matter privately with him in an attempt to clear the air, that incident colored all of our future relationships.

My tumbling stock with the mayor and his staff was balanced to some extent by my rising influence with the Board of Supervisors. The 1969 and 1971 elections confirmed a board that was reasonably sympathetic to city planning. We continued to be responsive to the supervisors and spent time briefing them on what we were doing generally and in relation to specific issues. Information we produced as a result of our research was considered untainted and was sought out. The supervisors could use it.

Individual board members saw us in direct contact with voters much more often than the mayor and as often as planning commissioners. At evening and weekend meetings in neighborhoods, at committee meetings, and at full board meetings, we were there. It was clear that we had direct, honest, and friendly relations with the voters. More often than not, we were joint advocates with citizens for this or that plan, policy, program, or piece of legislation. This was not lost on supervisors, and it was the Board of Supervisors who made policy in San Francisco. After being supported by residents so often, we retained considerable influence with the board on those occasions when we stood alone.

The two major daily papers treated me well. On one occasion, Donald Canter, top urban reporter for the *Examiner*, wanted to know if one of my zoning recommendations—on height controls along the ocean—had been intended to help the landowner, a politically important person who also happened to be on one of the city commissions. I had recommended allowing greater height for a two-block stretch at a major entrance to the city than in surrounding blocks. I told Canter that I tried not to know who owned land in the city for just that reason, so that I couldn't play favorites, and that I did not know in this case. When Canter told me who it was, it turned out I had met the man once at a friend's house. But I didn't know he was a commissioner of anything. In fact, I didn't even know what he did for a living. I had never spoken to him about the zoning matter. I told Canter that the paper could, of course, print what it wished, that I saw little way for me to prove that my recommendation was based solely on my best professional judgment. But I reminded him that he would be fooling around in public with my integrity and credibility if the paper implied any wrongdoing on my part. I said the same thing to his editor when he called and asked if my department or I had done anything to deserve being questioned that way. The news story that came out was free of any innuendo about my motives.

On another occasion, in 1971, I was invited to have lunch at a private club with the editorial board of the *Chronicle*. The first question was what I thought about the mayor. I laughed and responded that I didn't know many people in the room and certainly didn't know anything about their individual relationships with the mayor, so I'd be pretty stupid to answer that question in anything but the vaguest terms. Most of the other questions had to do with the urban design proposals the planning department had just completed, with individual buildings, the waterfront, housing, and transportation. It was a good meeting with a lot of give-and-take. I was being given the opportunity to present the city planning position on a number of issues, and I thought I was being heard.

In a society not particularly oriented to city planning it was important for me to learn that my chosen work had a few strong, steadfast advocates. I was also aware that today's advocates could become tomorrow's opponents as allegiances shifted, often for reasons with little connection to city planning. It was important for the department in general and for me specifically to have our own sources of support beyond the mayor and the commission. We needed to do top-notch professional work of the kind that would be recognized broadly. An agency or an individual with outside stature is a little less susceptible to attack and to hurt than one without.

My views of city planning were undergoing considerable change during this period. I had entered the field almost 20 years earlier with the notion that the point of it all was to build beautiful cities for people to live in and enjoy and to solve as many social problems as possible. Graduate education and big-city planning experience taught me to take a more pragmatic approach. The issues related to race, poverty, housing, and social services were still to be attacked, more strongly than ever, but it was foolhardy to ignore the forces of the market place. It was said that they were inexorable and had to be provided for. Indeed, if city planners could only provide for and help to create order out of what was going to happen anyway, they would have done more than expected. This approach—ascertaining what was likely to happen and providing for it with efficiency—was considered practical and necessary if planners wanted to be effective. Compromise and reasonableness were counted among its strengths.

By the late 1960s, I was beginning to question some of the pragmatism I had been rewarded for in graduate school and in pre-San Francisco jobs, and I was going back to dust off earlier values. Why did the market forces always have to be accommodated? Why was continued physical growth inevitable and good? Why did those needs that were countable—traffic for one—always seem to get a higher priority than those that were less tangible—housing for poor people for instance, or even a magnificent view? Were the social welfare forces that always seemed to want higher densities and lower environmental standards, presumably to keep housing costs down (for poorer people)—were they in reality committed to a permanent underclass? What would pragmatism mean for the future of San Francisco? Would it mean New York?

I was changing. San Francisco and the Bay Area were weaving their web. Certainly, my concerns about the quality of San Francisco's environment were not up to the standards of our most vocal conservationists. I doubt that they ever will be. But then the chamber of commerce types were not too happy either. At times I wondered where the outside power base I sought for the planning department was to be found.

My personal thoughts about the nature of San Francisco's government began to change, too. It was naive, cumbersome—something out of an eighth-grade textbook. But maybe that wasn't so bad after all. In physically small, understandable, still working, and still largely sound San Francisco, with its diverse, accepting, usually tolerant, and always involved and vociferous population, maybe it was good that no one had too much power, including, reluctantly, me.

Stepping back from the years between 1969 and 1972 and viewing them through slightly squinted eyes so that only the major patterns emerge, it is easy to see that the thrust and weight of people's concerns were changing. There were growing concerns about the environment, about conserving what existed that was of value, about the social and physical excesses of large-scale urban redevelopment, about the look of the city, and even about the wisdom of any additional development— and these concerns were coalescing and successfully challenging values customarily associated with civic boosterism and a reliance on technology and building that had been dominant since the late 1940s. Because shifts in values are rarely abrupt or clear-cut, the changes may not have been apparent, even to the principal actors involved. For some, business was going on as usual, even though the nature of the game was changing.

To be sure, there was still a great deal of new construction during this period. Much of it was downtown, but there were also new hotels and office structures and new apartment houses along the waterfront and elsewhere. Many if not most of the new developments were totally consistent with existing laws and policies, and many never represented issues in the sense of being challenged. Increasingly, however, they were contested, and that in itself represented change. When local governmental processes—including public debates before the planning commission and Board of Supervisors—did not result in findings to the liking of a project's opponents, they were quite likely to take their case to the courts and to nonlocal agencies that might have jurisdiction. Even if judges found in favor of a project, the time spent waiting for a decision could take a toll on development.

Other issues were at least as significant as the challenges to private developments: neighborhood-sponsored downzonings, a continued anti-freeway militancy that expanded to include almost any roadway improvement, opposition to a new subway, and an increased interest in the preservation of older buildings. These new issues testified to a rising concern about the quality of urban life. The success of efforts to stop or at least slow down large redevelopment projects such as Yerba Buena was telling us clearly that the dignity of poor people, those who called such areas their home, was as important as a more conventional defini-tion of progress.

Two very different people symbolize the changing times. Alvin Duskin, for a while a dress manufacturer, emerged as a major public force. On three occasions he placed full-page ads in the two dailies to prevent commercial development of Alcatraz Island and to campaign against high-rise development.[7] He spearheaded two referenda that would have placed drastic limitations on the height of all future build-ings in San Francisco. And he scared the pants off the chamber of commerce, forcing it to spend a small fortune in defeating his proposi-tions. Never mind that Alvin Duskin didn't always win his fights. He was having an effect.

Justin Herman, on the other hand, almost always won. If there was a symbol of large, publicly sponsored development projects and of the marriage of public and private development in civic boosterism, it was this brilliant and dynamic director of the San Francisco Redevelopment Agency. Golden Gateway, Western Addition, Diamond Heights, the Chinese Cultural Center (Holiday Inn), Hunter's Point, Butchertown—all were his, and he had plans for more. Never mind that in the early seventies his projects were being thwarted in court battles, and never mind that he and his agency were increasingly responsible for large amounts of well-designed moderate-income housing. With Herman's death in August 1971, an era ended, too.

Changing concerns, priorities, and philosophies of government at both the federal and state levels both reinforced and ran counter to those that were being manifested locally. Toward the end of 1972 some of the changes would begin to have an effect on government and city planning in San Francisco.

Whereas the growing strength of neighborhoods in relation to planning and development issues bespoke decentralization that was consistent with San Francisco's form of government, centralization appeared to be the word of the day in Washington. Congress had for some time bemoaned the tendency toward increasing power in the hands of the executive, while within the executive the operations of government became more and more focused in the office of the President. It is not surprising, then, that the feds, following their own model, looked to deal with strong chief executives in addressing urban problems, regardless of whether or not this was the way local governments chose to do things. They wanted to transact business with one centralized, coordinating authority rather than with the many local agencies that had previously been involved. To help achieve that end in San Francisco the federal government would ultimately fund an Office of Community Development in the mayor's office.[8] It was inevitable that such an office would conflict with the responsibilities and powers of the Department of City Planning.

In a contrary direction, one supposedly aimed at greater local self-determination, the winds from the East brought an increasing likelihood of something called revenue sharing: near-automatic grants to local governments to use largely as they saw fit. Revenue sharing was to take the place of most of the so-called categorical programs in the housing and urban redevelopment fields, some of which had started in the Depression. It seemed ironic to me that just as sensitively designed, small-scaled, and scattered low-income housing projects were gaining ground, just as the moderate-income housing programs were beginning to have impacts, just as the demand for Federally Assisted Code Enforcement was outstripping our ability to produce, and, yes, just as urban redevelopment was starting to be used sensitively to provide housing—just at that time the feds were walking away from those programs. We would have to look for new ones locally.

People in California and throughout the nation were beginning to concentrate their attention on the environment, and that concentration was reflected in San Francisco. In 1970 California passed the Environmental Quality Act, and the state supreme court held that the legislation applied to private as well as public projects and that environmental review would be required for them.[9] In San Francisco, the planning department was charged with preparing environmental impact reports. Moreover, the Board of Supervisors assigned to us the responsibility for making environmental assessments of projects carried out by other public agencies.

For me, and I think for city planning in San Francisco, there were more high points than defeats in the years that began in 1969 and ended in the early fall of 1972.

The disappointment, in 1969, of seeing only one public official show up at our first-class presentation of the South Bayshore plan, held in the South San Francisco Opera House after it was cleaned up by a few dedicated staffers, was more than matched by the overwhelming public response to the publication of the urban design plan in 1971. It was the kind of winner a planner dreams of.

Nothing could counter the personal "low" and feeling of despair that followed my refusal to be part of Mayor Alioto's 1971 campaign. And I was more than a little chagrined over the planning commission's failure to back me when I opposed major building proposals. But my anger was partially assuaged when some of these projects never succeeded in getting off the ground, hampered by law suits and also by lack of support from the Board of Supervisors. In rejecting the U.S. Steel proposal at the waterfront, the supervisors in effect adopted the very restrictive height controls that my staff and I had originally fought for, but which the planning commission had rejected.

Acceptance of our plans for housing and transportation, the saving of the South San Francisco Opera House, the neighborhood downzonings, and community backing of the small Chinatown redevelopment project were particular high points. But they could hardly compare with the satisfaction that came with the final passage of the citywide height and bulk ordinance in August 1972, an event that brings this period to a close. This was citywide legislation geared to carrying out a most significant part of the urban design plan. It was a concluding step in a classic city planning process that includes plan preparation, adoption, and then implementation. It was making city planning work.

There was one ominous and disconcerting note as we moved to the end of 1972. During the early months of that year, more of my time and energies had been spent on the height and bulk ordinance than on other matters. It was essential to get that ordinance passed. I hadn't paid too much attention to what was going on in the mayor's office, especially in relation to shifts in federal policies and programs. When Jack Tolan, the mayor's deputy for development, casually—almost jokingly—wondered about the possibility of having Dean Macris join the mayor's staff, I was sure that my negative response had ended the matter.[10] I was wrong.

I was quite surprised when I received a call from the mayor and heard him ask how I would feel about Dean's joining his staff. He would serve under Tolan as the head of the new Office of Community Development, which would be funded wholly by the feds. My response was strongly negative, and I told the mayor that I had so advised Tolan earlier. I said that Dean was a key member of the staff and that he would be very hard to replace. Intuitively, I knew that power would begin to shift with such a change and that this new office would ultimately come into conflict with the planning department. While I did not advise the mayor of all my reasons, I thought I could stick with my position. For one thing, I felt sure that Dean would not want to make the shift.

I was wrong about that, too. Within a day, I told him about the call and my reaction to it. To my surprise, he said that he was indeed interested in the job and wanted to pursue it. I would not stop that. Throughout the following weeks, I had a sense that something had happened earlier, when I wasn't looking or paying attention, that a script unknown to me had been written and was being played out in some previously prescribed manner.

That Office of Community Development was established in October 1972. As I have noted, it had the strong help of the feds, who didn't know and didn't care about local customs or constitutions. Some of the recommendations of the Charter Revision Committee that had been defeated so handily by the voters in 1969 showed signs of becoming reality.

# Notes

1. San Francisco Department of City Planning, *The Comprehensive Plan: Residence*, 1971. A preliminary version was presented in 1970. The planning commission adopted the final version in April 1971.

2. "A Remarkable SPUR Proposal," *San Francisco Examiner*, September 10, 1970.

3. San Francisco Department of City Planning, *The Comprehensive Plan: Transportation*, April 1972. The preliminary plan, for citizen review, was presented in August 1971.

4. For an example, see San Francisco City Planning Commission minutes of February 13, 1969.

5. The case, ZM 71.3, was approved by the planning commission in March 1971 and by the Board of Supervisors in June.

6. Commissioner Fleishhacker wrote to David Packard, Deputy Secretary of Defense, on December 26, 1969. Packard answered on January 15, 1970, and Fleishhacker wrote again on March 13.

7. The three ads: "As Big A Steal As Manhattan Island," October 9, 1969; "Skyscrapers Are Economically Necessary, But Only If You Own One," October 19, 1970; "Hold the Confetti Even If 'T' Wins—The Builders Still Run This City," October 18, 1971, *San Francisco Chronicle.*

8. The Office of Community Development was established in October 1972 and funded completely by HUD.

9. California Supreme Court, *Friends of Mammoth v. Board of Supervisors of Mono County*, 1972.

10. Letters of May 9 and May 15, 1972, from John Tolan, Jr., to the author, and letter of May 11, 1972, to Tolan.

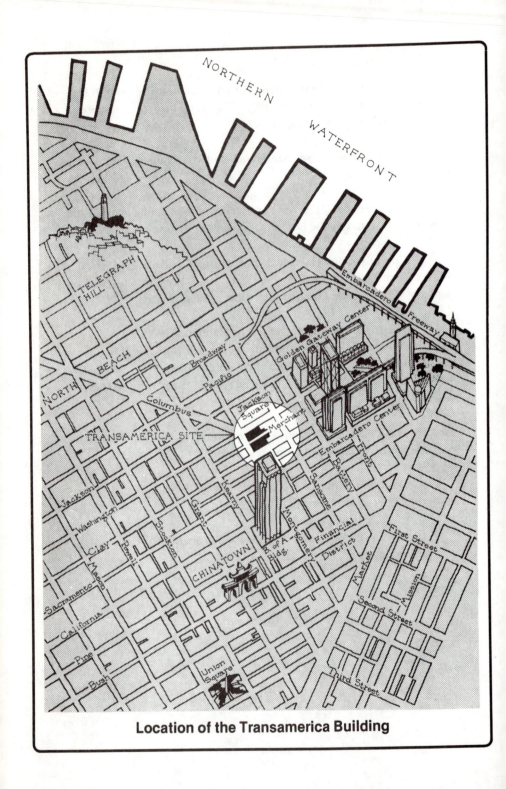

**Location of the Transamerica Building**

# Chapter 7
# Case Study: The Transamerica Building—An Ad Hoc Development Issue and the City Planning Process

On January 6, 1969, Tom Mellon, San Francisco's chief administrative officer, called the planning director and requested him to meet that afternoon with officials of the Transamerica Corporation to see designs for the new headquarters building they were considering.[1] Mellon had already seen a model of the building. The meeting was to take place at the Transamerica offices, which were located in a four-story, turn-of-the-century building in the historic Jackson Square area. The planning director, rather uneasy about being informed in this abrupt way about an apparently well-advanced proposal, adjusted his schedule to go to see the designs. The chief administrative officer was, after all, one of the planning commissioners.

The Transamerica Corporation is a conglomerate whose holdings include Occidental Life Insurance Company of California, United Artists, Budget Rent-A-Car, Lyon Moving and Storage, Transamerica Insurance Group, Transamerica Title Insurance Company, and much else. It was once the holding company for the Bank of America. Between Mellon's morning call and the afternoon meeting, his staff had advised the planning director that there had been one or two meetings some months earlier with architects representing Transamerica but that no serious designs had been put forth and that future meetings were to be held before that occurred. None had been called.

Approaching the old Transamerica building that afternoon, together with several key staff members, the planning director was a bit surprised to see the Public Works director, the city engineer, and the head of the Bureau of Building Inspection heading in the same direction. Since they all worked under the chief administrative officer, it was reasonable to assume he had sent them. The city officials were met by a Mr. Butts of the Transamerica Corporation, who led them to an upper floor meeting room. There they met among others, Edward L. Scarff, Transamerica's president, and Gin D. Wong and Peter Kirby, representing the office of William Pereira, the architect. Introductions accomplished, the group proceeded to a meeting room, where, resting on a table in the center of the room, there was a model of an office building.

The model was in the shape of an elongated pyramid. It was a miniature of a building that would be 55 stories, approximately 1,000 feet, high. By way of contrast, consider that the tallest building in San Francisco at that time was the Bank of America building at 52 stories, 778 feet. The site of the proposed building was the end of Columbus Avenue, one of San Francisco's two diagonal boulevards; the building was to face Montgomery Street, the most prestigious financial address in the city. To the south, across Clay Street, was the financial district. To the north, across Washington Street, was the Jackson Square area with its low brick buildings and narrow streets—and of course the Transamerica headquarters. Beyond that was the Broadway entertainment district. Three blocks to the east were the Clay-Washington ramps to the Embarcadero Freeway and the Golden Gateway Redevelopment Project. To the west lay Chinatown. In short, the site was strategically located at the edge of downtown in an area known as the Portsmouth Corridor. It was an extremely visible location.

Scarff told the city officials that the Transamerica board of directors had just chosen that particular building for the new headquarters. It seems the directors had rejected four other designs, and now they wanted to get the required approvals for this one. There seemed to be no question in their minds as to the propriety of their proposal; their main objective was to get on with the job as quickly and efficiently as possible.

The planning director advised the Transamerica representatives of four probable concerns that would have to be addressed. First, to discourage traffic problems and congestion, the planning code (zoning) required special approval as a conditional use for any structure in that location whose parking space amounted to more than seven per cent of the total floor space of the building. This building appeared to fall into that category.

Second, Transamerica was proposing to build over an alley called Merchant Street, and the propriety of giving up the city's air rights to this public right-of-way would have to come before the planning commission for a finding of conformity with the city's master plan. Third, on June 29,1967, the planning commission had declared its intention to exercise its powers of discretionary review over any building that was proposed for the Portsmouth Corridor to assure its compatibility with the surrounding structures and land uses; and the corporation had been advised of this policy. The planning director found both the shape and great height of the proposal to be incompatible with the surrounding area.

Finally, the planners advised the Transamerica officials that the planning department had a standard policy for cases in which a proposed use or building was not a matter of right, where instead the owner-developer sought something out of the ordinary from the city, such as the use of air rights or a conditional use permit. If the planning department were prepared to consider such a matter in the first place, the planners explained, it was in the public interest that the development achieve urban design standards as defined by the city agency responsible for such matters. The same would hold true for development proposals at particularly sensitive locations. Developers and their architects were therefore invited to work with the city planning staff early in the design stages so that "urban design terms of reference"

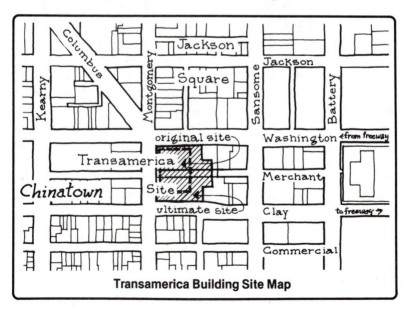

**Transamerica Building Site Map**

could be established for any given site. If the architects and the city planners were in agreement, they could go before the planning commission and other official bodies as joint advocates instead of as adversaries. The planners reminded the Transamerica representatives that their architect was aware of the policy. In 1968 Peter Kirby had been associated with the architectural firm that had prepared designs for a controversial International Market Center at the foot of Telegraph Hill. That building did not get built.

The meeting ended indecisively. While it seemed clear that Transamerica wanted to move ahead as quickly as possible, no one said in so many words that the design chosen was already cast in concrete. There appeared to be some possibility of change, although the Transamerica representatives probably had a different view of what change might mean than the planners did. The planners hoped that Transamerica would choose to follow the consultation procedure they had outlined and that the building would not be announced publicly until additional meetings had been held. If the corporation wanted specific information about making official application for its building, that information would be forthcoming on request, just as it would for any other applicant.

The Transamerica building is typical of the type of ad hoc development proposal—a building or a complex of buildings proposed for a limited site—that can become a major issue in American cities, with a direct relationship to city planning. San Francisco offers many examples of such proposals: a proposal for a high-rise apartment development on the waterfront, an office-hotel-shopping-port proposal next to the Bay Bridge, another high-rise apartment building on Russian Hill, the Bank of America building. In New York City, the World Trade Center or the major developments over the Grand Central and Pennsylvania railroad stations might be examples. A Chicago example might involve the demolition of the Stock Exchange. In other cities, the issue might center on a redevelopment project, a subdivision, or a proposal to construct a public building in a park. Neither the public nor city officials always see such proposals as controversial when they are first put forth. For some, it is not until after they are up—when someone says, "How did that happen?"—that these buildings become issues. Some are never thought of as problems at all. But when such building proposals are issues, before, during, or after the fact, the effectiveness of city planning and of city planners is often judged by the outcome. How well or poorly these issues are dealt with by city planners and the city planning process established by local government is therefore of some importance.

Buildings like Transamerica often become issues because they attract attention. They may be unforeseen or a departure from what has existed in the past or different from other buildings in their vicinity. Often they become issues because they break an unwritten rule of a community, such as "Don't build tall buildings on the waterfront." They are usually large and visible. They may offend someone or do damage to a neighbor, at least in the neighbor's eyes. When the proposals are large, there is often a good deal of money involved, and money attracts attention. Corporate egos also seek, and get, attention, and the same holds true for their architects. But perhaps the most important, at least as far as city planning is concerned, is that realization of the proposal may depend upon the developers' getting something from the city, something they do not have, something without which a proposal may not move forward. The "something" may be a subsidy, a change in a law (such as zoning), permission to buy or use public land, or special approval for something out of the ordinary. In any case, official and often public attention is called to such proposals because the getting or giving of that something requires public scrutiny as part of an established process of government, the city planning process.

The Transamerica proposal provides an opportunity to examine an ad hoc development issue within the larger framework of the substance and process of city planning as determined by local government. The case permits an assessment of the effectiveness of that process in dealing with this kind of issue. To do so, a number of questions require answers and explanations: How did the planning department respond to the issue? Was it related to the concerns of other city agencies? Who were the most relevant actors? How was the issue resolved? Did precedent play a role in the resolution? Could it have been resolved in some other way and what might it have taken to do so? What were its consequences for the development of the city, for the people who live and work there, for city planning? Before we attempt to answer these questions, it is important to define the issue in relation to city planning in San Francisco and to explain how the matter became an issue in the first place.

It should be kept in mind that cases of this type can only serve as the basis for limited generalizations; every case is at least a little bit different from the next. However, the Transamerica case is similar to a number of others in San Francisco in the way it became an issue in the first place, in the nature of the substantive matters that were at stake, and in the official and unofficial procedures by which it was resolved. The Fontana Towers on the waterfront and the proposal for the International Market Center at the foot of Telegraph Hill are two of the many such cases that came before the Transamerica proposal. A proposal by United States Steel, a Holiday Inn, and a high-rise apartment building on Russian Hill are three that followed. The Transamerica case stands out from the others mainly because it was the subject of so many articles and so much national publicity. There are similarities (and differences) between this case and dozens of others in other cities.

Whether or not to vacate Merchant Street and to give up the air rights over the street and whether or not to permit extra off-street parking there were issues with which the planning department had to deal. They are directly related to the formal responsibilities of the department as these are defined by the San Francisco charter.[2] A procedure has been established to deal with these kinds of issues: referral to the master plan in the case of the street vacation and conditional use zoning in the case of the parking. The parking question was considered minor by everyone involved, both because the site was close to freeway entry and exit ramps and because the Transamerica Corporation was assumed to be flexible on this matter.

The matter of the planning commission's consideration of this or any other building proposal under what is termed the power or right of discretionary review is a bit less clear, but it is no less real in relation to the formal responsibilities of the city planning department. Fundamentally, the power of discretionary review allows the planning commission to exercise its discretion concerning any permit application when the general welfare requires review.[3] It says, in effect, that the terms of the city's zoning ordinance are to be considered *minimum* requirements and permits the commission to determine whether the broader guidelines of the ordinance are complied with in specific cases. This means that in specific cases and for sound reasons the commission may place more stringent requirements on a project than the zoning otherwise calls for. San Francisco is unique among California cities and perhaps in the nation in its use of the discretionary review power. The fact that the planning commission had announced its intention to use this power meant that a public hearing would be required for the Transamerica building. After a hearing, the commission would have the option of permitting the building, denying it, or permitting it with conditions. Its negative finding could be overruled, on appeal, by a vote of four of the five members of the Board of Permit Appeals.[4]

Decisions on vacating the street and on the discretionary review would have to be based in major part on some substantive city planning concerns, including in this case something called "urban design" or "urban aesthetics." Urban design has been a significant city planning concern since the "City Beautiful" movement of the early 1900s. In the post-World War II years, some planning professionals and academicians tended to frown on urban design as an elitist concern that was irrelevant to critical urban issues. The people of San Francisco, however, often have been concerned about the design characteristics of their city. In 1969 this concern was growing. San Franciscans did not have an urban design plan at the time—a plan that might have provided policies, guidelines, and answers to questions of how a particular building should relate to the design of the city as a whole—but its planners had made known their general design concerns about this Portsmouth Corridor area.

City policy, exemplified in a recent major rezoning of the downtown area, was to direct significant new office development southward, away from the Portsmouth Corridor. The corridor was to be a transition area between the intense downtown and the Jackson Square and North Beach areas with their many small, fine-scaled, and often historic buildings. The intent of city policy was to minimize development pressures on these areas. A 65-foot height limit was in effect in large sections of both of these areas and in the Portsmouth Corridor. This limit was intended to provide a transition to the unlimited heights that were then permitted in the downtown. The issue of height also arose in relation to nearby Telegraph, Russian, and Nob Hills. It had been long-standing city policy that these hills should remain distinct features of the skyline, separate from the man-made hill of downtown. In sum, the location and height of the proposed Transamerica building were major issues, the former because city policy was to direct major new development away from this area, and the latter because of urban design considerations that dictated the desirability of keeping new development at a scale compatible with its surroundings and of maintaining the city's visible topographic forms.

The shape of the proposed building was of major concern to the city planners, although the issue here did not relate to a previously articulated policy or principle. They viewed San Francisco as a fine-scaled city, primarily composed of small, rectangular buildings on small, rectangular lots, tightly developed and with few stand-out, "look-at-me" buildings. Except for major public structures, it was the *whole* that was important to them rather than any outstanding, individual piece. The shape would have been of much less concern to the city planners had the building been located in the middle of the downtown area where it would have been less visible. A nonpublic, extremely high, pyramidal structure at the end of the Columbus Avenue vista, directly adjacent to low, brick, small buildings was not their idea of a building that fit in at this location.

The planning process itself could be viewed as an issue in the Transamerica case. Assuming that both parties have legitimate concerns in relation to a building proposal, it is important that the developer and his architect and the planners employed by the city communicate their intentions and concerns to one another as early as possible, preferably even before design work starts. The purpose is to let the developer know, as precisely as possible at any stage, what the public interest is concerning the project. The developer lets the city know his special needs and, in turn, knows what he might or might not do without a conflict. Experience had shown the city planners that, at least regarding building design issues, conflicts where investments of time, money, and egos are involved do not produce considered decisions. Rather, when such conflicts took place, it was usually the combatant with the most effective political resources who won. The planners felt it was important to have an established process to minimize conflict and had set up an informal design review procedure for these kinds of proposals. To some extent, the stature, or effectiveness of the commission and staff were related to it.

The review process had been in operation for over a year and most developers and their architects had chosen to follow it. During that period the few who had ignored the process had fared badly in the ensuing conflict. The planners didn't know whether the Transamerica Corporation, even at this late date, would choose to participate or whether it would choose to bypass the established procedure. Would the corporation try to go over their heads, to the mayor or to the Board of Supervisors or to individual planning commissioners? If Transamerica did successfully bypass the planning department, there was a bigger danger to face: that others would also choose to go that route. How would that, the planners wondered, affect the stature of city planning in San Francisco.

These, then, were the major issues presented by Transamerica's proposal as seen by city planners: the street vacation and discretionary review issues, the issue of urban design, and the issues relating to the planning process and the stature of city planning. It is hard to know how these issues were defined by all the others involved, except perhaps by interpreting their subsequent actions. Certainly, speed was of the essence for the Transamerica Corporation. A state law permitting insurance companies that established headquarters buildings in California to deduct their property taxes from their premium taxes was to expire at the end of the year. California companies that owned headquarters buildings before January 1, 1970, or had them under construction by that date, could continue the practice. Transamerica owned more than one insurance company, and, depending on which company it registered the building under, it could deduct $500,000 to $1 million a year from its taxes.[5]

Any assessment of the Transamerica case should begin with the 1967 approval by the planning commission of the zoning proposals for the whole downtown area. At that time, there was strong sentiment on the part of downtown property owners in favor of including the Portsmouth Corridor in the most intense "Downtown Office District" classification rather than in a less intense classification as had been proposed by the staff. The planning director said then that he was willing to recommend the zoning change so long as the planning commission would establish a policy of discretionary review in the corridor. The commission agreed—in the words of its resolution, "looking toward maximum flexibility for new development in these blocks consistent with good design and studied relationships to other properties."[6]

At the time of the commission's action, Thomas Feeney, who was the attorney _____ ___ least three of the lots that later were included in the Transamerica site, w__ ____ by Commission President William Brinton whether he had any objection to __ discretionary review policy. Feeney, according to the minutes of the June 29 __ting, replied in the negative and indicated that he was "of the opinion that h__ clients should work with the commission in an effort to achieve the best development of their properties in any case."

Transamerica was aware of the discretionary review policy at least from the time the downtown zoning proposals came before the Board of Supervisors in September 1967. On September 12, the planning department wrote to Transamerica to confirm the commission's decision and enclosed a copy of the resolution establishing the discretionary review policy. In response, John Beckett, chairman of Transamerica, sent a letter the next day endorsing the commission's proposals, especially as they related to preservation of Jackson Square and North Beach. Beckett also noted that "as the financial community expands, it appears only logical that the expansion will follow the now established eastward trend toward the Golden Gateway and the Embarcadero Center." The Transamerica site was northward, not eastward.

On September 6, 1968, a representative of the Pereira firm came to the planning department to disclose to the staff concerned with zoning and downtown development that Transamerica was acquiring property in the Portsmouth Corridor. He indicated that he recognized the importance of working with the department in the development of such a large building (he mentioned 30 stories). As he described the designs that were being considered, he seemed to pass quickly over a pyramid form, treating it almost as a joke. He was advised that the department would like to have further meetings in which "urban design terms of reference" for the site could be considered prior to the commission's discretionary review. As has been noted, no such meetings were held.

Transamerica's unwillingness to follow the design review process set up by the city planning staff is one reason why the building became an issue. Another related explanation may be found in the sense of stature or power held by both the corporation and its architect. It did not necessarily ascribe high value to the opinions or expertise of a bureaucracy's city planners. Other explanations may be found in the zoning that would permit the building in the first place and in the failure of the planning staff to prepare and disseminate specific design criteria for this site and for the corridor as a whole immediately upon passage of the new ordinance. A reasonable conclusion would be that the issue could have been, and in fact was, foreseen and that the planners failed to take the steps necessary to prevent the controversy. In its defense, the department would hold that it could not prepare realistic guidelines without first knowing who owned what land and that the planners' meeting with Transamerica's architects was geared precisely to the end of avoiding conflict. In any case, the proposed

Transamerica building was now an issue that would require the city planners' attention.

On January 7, 1969, the day after the planning director saw the Transamerica proposal for the first time, he met with Mayor Alioto to request his intervention, if that proved necessary, in persuading the Transamerica Corporation to change its design approach. The mayor had previously been helpful in getting the backers of another major development to change their designs to meet the planners' objections. Such was not to be the case this time. The mayor appeared to be already familiar with the proposal. In this meeting he sounded rather like an advocate for Transamerica. He made no commitment to support the city staff if there should be a fight. The director left the meeting with a sinking feeling that the issue was already decided, but he knew that the cards would have to be played out.

It took about six months for the matter to be heard and acted upon by the planning commission. During this period, staff of the planning department would attempt to convince the Transamerica Corporation to respond to the planners' concerns and redesign the building. Failing that, the planners would seek to gain support for their position from the general public and from public officials.

Immediately after seeing the mayor, the planning director met with key staff members to advise them of his concern, to direct that urban design terms of reference for the site be prepared as soon as possible, and to remind them of the importance of encouraging other departments to be firm in dealing with the issue. The closing of Merchant Street would, after all, affect the Fire Department, the Division of Traffic Engineering, and the Bureau of Building Inspection (which would be concerned with the safety of a building over a public right-of-way).

During January, the planning staff attempted to keep the mayor from publicly advocating the project. The director made efforts, through the mayor's staff, to suggest that the mayor might not be on the right side of the issue and that nothing would be gained by public advocacy. It was suggested, too, that the planning commission should have the opportunity to come to its decision without appearing to be directed by the mayor. The director also advised the planning commissioners of the developing problem. He told them that gaining public support was likely to be an uphill struggle. For one thing, the top editorial personnel of the two daily newspapers were for the Transamerica proposal. Before the next month was out, Herb Caen, San Francisco's style-setting columnist, was to write about the building in positive terms.[7]

The meetings that took place between the planners and Transamerica representatives were of little substance. A conflict was in the making and the potential combatants were keeping their own counsel rather than dealing directly with the differences between them.

On January 27 and 28, Transamerica presented the designs for the new building at two lunch meetings. A flurry of newspaper publicity accompanied the announcement.[8] The second lunch was attended by city officials, most of whom had little to say about the building except for asking a few technical questions. Mortimer Fleishhacker, the new president of the commission, foresaw problems with Transamerica's proposal and sent a letter to Scarff on February 5 requesting a meeting of Transamerica officials with the planning staff. The meeting was held on February 14, but no higher level Transamerica or Pereira representatives attended. The planners told the developers what the major problems of the proposal were and said that if changes were not made, the planning department would oppose it. When it became apparent that Pereira's office was not going to work with the planners, the draft urban design terms of reference were put on paper and sent to Pereira's representative, Peter Kirby, on February 24. The terms set a maximum height of 400 feet, or about 28 stories, and they called for intensive, pedestrian-oriented uses at the lower levels, an architectural scale that would be harmonious with buildings in the adjacent historic area, and a rectangular shape.

In late February the planning director met with the director of the San Francisco Planning and Urban Renewal Association (SPUR), a prestigious general membership organization that was concerned with city planning. With a group of interested SPUR members, mostly architects and planners, they discussed possible strategies for opposing the building.

The planners attempted to meet with Beckett, on the theory that the chief executive of a large corporation is likely to be more flexible and easier to negotiate with than people lower on the corporate ladder. The attempts were unsuccessful. Later, a note from Edward Scarff, dated April 17, made it clear that he was to be in charge.

At a March 11 meeting attended by Scarff and Pereira, the director was asked if he would approve the building if its height were reduced. He said he would not so long as it was basically the same building. In turn, he asked Scarff and Pereira if they were going to change the building in major ways, redesigning it in accord with the department's concerns. They said no, and the director told them he would recommend against the proposal. On that same day Transamerica applied for a site permit for the building. It turned out that the application was incorrectly filed because Transamerica did not yet own the air rights over Merchant Street and because there was a conflict with the building code.

As time passed, some changes were indeed made in the building's design, albeit none that satisfied the planners' objections. The height was lowered. But the site got larger and larger as Transamerica purchased more property. Eventually, the developers were no longer asking for an air rights vacation over Merchant Street. The street was no longer to pass through the building. Instead, they wanted a total vacation and purchase of the street as it passed through their property. They wanted the street to be closed so that they could build on the land it occupied.

Total vacation of the western end of Merchant Street was not a minor matter to the city planners. The narrow (only 31 feet) one-way street might not be needed for general traffic circulation, but it provided service access to the abutting properties, which included restaurants, offices, showrooms, and wholesalers. Creating a dead end would mean that vehicles would no longer be able to proceed down the street after servicing those properties. Trucks would block each other; to get out, they would have to back into a major street. The prospect of traffic jams on Merchant Street might well encourage truckers to provide service from abutting, faster moving traffic streets rather than from Merchant Street as was intended. This would lead to traffic conflicts on streets that were meant only to handle normal traffic, not deliveries. A closing would interfere with fire department vehicles and impede access to fire escapes. Finally, the city planners were aware that streets, in addition to providing light and air, played a major role in determining the scale of the city. Small blocks, simply because of their size, hindered the largest developments and were consistent with fine-scaled San Francisco. For all of these reasons, the city planners were opposed to the street closing.

A few meetings were held with the architects during March and

April, but they were not considering any major changes. While the planners were concerned with the overall concept of the building, the architects seemed interested mainly in details. At one of the meetings, in his office, Pereira seemed concerned mostly with the problem of designing the windows on the sloping facade.

The planning staff met with a couple of neighborhood groups to solicit their support at the inevitable public hearings. The planners also met with any number of architects, most of whom objected to the building's design. After a meeting with columnist Herb Caen, his tone changed from approbation to neutrality, even mild disapproval.[9]

Many of the discussions with the mayor between January and June included an exchange of views about the Transamerica building, which the mayor likened to the Eiffel Tower. The planning director was trying to minimize the mayor's involvement.

During this period it appeared likely that the planning commission would support the negative recommendation that was expected from the department. Only Commissioner Mellon, the chief administrative officer, appeared to be a certain vote in favor of the building. The votes of Jim Kearney and Walter Newman, who were tagged the labor and downtown business representatives, were harder to predict. But Fleishhacker, William Brinton, Julia Porter, and Jim Carr seemed strongly opposed. Carr, the general manager of the Public Utilities Commission, said that he disliked the building and would instruct his alternate to vote against it. (Carr rarely came to the commission meetings himself.) It seemed reasonable to anticipate a four-to-three or five-to-two vote in support of the staff recommendation. There were frequent discussions with commissioners to get and keep their support.

The planners held a number of meetings with owners of property that had direct access from Merchant Street in order to make them fully aware of their access rights and of the difficulties that would result if one end of the street were to be blocked by a building. It was difficult to imagine the city vacating and selling any part of the right-of-way without their agreement. The meetings disclosed that Transamerica representatives were also speaking to the owners and were busy buying or leasing key parcels.

On May 5 the planning department sent a letter to Transamerica outlining the hearing procedure that would be followed. Meetings at Pereira's office on May 12 and 14 were without major substance. After one of these meetings Pereira called the director to ask whether making major changes to the first two floors of the building—the planners had called for such changes—would produce a positive staff recommendation. The answer was that by themselves they would not.

The street vacation issue was placed on the planning commission's calendar for June 12 and was then taken off at Transamerica's request. Revised plans were submitted for a site permit application on June 19. On June 23, the planning director sent a memo to the commission outlining the issues related to the street closing matter. Both the street closing and discretionary review of the building were considered and decided by the commission on June 26, at a regularly scheduled public meeting.

On the morning of June 26, the planning director received a copy of a letter the mayor had just sent to the commission, giving his opinion that the building should be approved.[10] Since Mayor Alioto had never before communicated his views to the commission in this way, the letter came as a complete surprise to the staff. Later, some of the commissioners and one of the mayor's assistants confided that the mayor and possibly his deputy for development, John Tolan, had called selected commissioners to relay the mayor's wish that they vote for the building. This was another first.

The hearing, by San Francisco standards, was small and relatively quiet. The planning commission minutes show that there were fewer than 50 people in the room. Seven people, three of them affiliated with Transamerica, spoke for the street closing, and ten spoke against. The staff recommended that the commission find the closing not in conformity with the master plan for reasons of access, congestion, and fire safety. The staff recommendation on the street vacation issue was overruled by a four-to-three vote. The three supporting votes came from Fleishhacker, Brinton, and Newman. The vote was five to two against the staff recommendation of disapproval of the building based on discretionary review. In late August, the street closing matter came before the Board of Supervisors at a meeting that was much better attended and where more people spoke in opposition. Either more people were becoming concerned or they felt that the board was a more effective place to make their wishes known. Even so, the vote was nine to one in favor of vacating and selling the street.

Other departments besides city planning had a direct stake in the outcome of Transamerica's proposal. Public Works and Fire were usually opposed to street closings, and at first they were concerned about the safety hazards and congestion that could result from closing Merchant Street. Later, though, they found these to be no great problems. It will be recalled that the Department of Public Works and the Bureau of Building Inspection are responsible to the chief administrative officer, who appeared to favor the building from the start. The Bureau of Building Inspection was primarily concerned with building safety, and that concern may well have been responsible for changes in the structure—most notably eliminating the street passage through the building in favor of a street closing.

The city attorney and the Real Estate Department played little or no part in the initial public decisions to vacate the street and to grant a building permit, although these offices were to prove significant later. At another level of local government, the Board of Supervisors was not involved with the issue until after the planning commission took action. The mayor's office obviously played a major role. It was Mayor Alioto who proved to be the most significant public actor in obtaining the building's ultimate acceptance.

Transamerica's role, like that of the planning department, went well beyond those official acts and technical-professional assessments and proposals that are necessary to get a building designed and under construction. An article by Transamerica's public relations manager, John Krizek—"How to Build a Pyramid"—in the December 1970 issue of *Public Relations Journal* not only describes the "kit of PR tools [that helped] win San Francisco's approval of a new high-rise office building," but clarifies the roles of other actors. It is clear that the corporation knew the building would create controversy. Its corporate relations staff was planning the announcement of the new building even before the board of directors had made a final decision to go ahead. The mayor and the chief administrative officer were the first city officials to see the building. The first press conference to announce the building was coordinated with a chamber of commerce banquet so that the chamber could share in the announcement. A special lunch was held for all publishers and general managers of the city's newspapers and television stations, and another lunch was held for labor leaders. Private briefings were held for supervisors. Corporation representatives went to neighborhood meetings held in opposition to the building. (They went

"surreptitiously" and "incognito," according to Krizek's article.) The corporation conducted its own letter-writing campaign in favor of the building to offset the letters from opponents. Krizek's article implies that it was at the corporation's instigation that "a few hippie-looking young men brandishing an 'Artists for the Pyramid' sign" passed out "a leaflet of their own, which included a cartoon showing two ancient Egyptians in a raging argument over the construction of pyramids."

It is doubtful that the chamber of commerce needed any convincing from Transamerica to support the building. It was enough for the chamber to note the revenue it would raise and the number of new construction jobs it would provide. Labor and the chamber were on the same side in this development issue, as in most others, although labor interests were less vociferous than usual in this case.

The role played by the Telegraph Hill Dwellers, a prestigious organization of the neighbors to the immediate north of the proposed building, was not as strong as expected. Perhaps the "incognito" efforts of Transamerica's public relations staff had been effective. More likely, though, the Telegraph Hill residents were piqued at the planning commission for allowing the most intense downtown zone to penetrate this close to them in the first place. As one influential member of the organization confided to the planning director, the members were a bit fearful of a totally negative public image. They did not want to appear to be against everything.

SPUR was also not a particularly active campaigner against the building. Instead, the most active opposition came from a new group, The Environmental Workshop, composed of young environmentalists and urban designers. In 1969 they put out a brochure—*San Francisco and the Transamerica Pyramid*—that described, with cartoons, the urban design issues at stake and, with photographs, showed what the building would look like in that setting. They got petitions signed, picketed Transamerica's headquarters, and tried their utmost to line up public support for their position and to encourage public officials to express their opposition to the project as well. They were not very successful. It is probably accurate to say that at that time not very many San Franciscans were concerned about this particular matter. Individual architects were concerned, but they were generally ineffective in expressing their opposition; ethical considerations prevented them from criticizing the building, except in the privacy of the planning director's office.

Support for the planning department's position came from an unexpected and unsolicited source—private economic consultants. Three or four consultants from Chicago and New York had heard of the pyramid and stopped in to express their dismay at the prospect of such an uneconomical building. Aside from noting the obviously low ratio of usable floor space to total floor space, especially on the most desirable upper floors, they pointed out that drapes, hanging vertically from the ceiling, would be quite some distance from the sloping walls by the time they reached the floor, thereby creating more uneconomical space. They were urged to voice their concerns to the corporation.

While these consultants might have been aware of the tax break Transamerica would receive at the state level, they were probably unaware of a similar tax advantage then being created at the federal level, an advantage that could help offset the uneconomical design. As would later be reported by Donald Canter in the *San Francisco Examiner*, "Transamerica ... had initiated the writing of a special provision into the federal tax reform bill aimed at giving the company a tax break for its planned ... headquarters building. ... Transamerica was one of 14 companies ... that would benefit from special legislation written into the tax measure on their behalf. ... One of those special provisions, [Senator Edward] Kennedy said, would allow Transamerica rapid depreciation of a new nonresidential building."[11] According to the news story, Transamerica's corporate relations manager said that the assumption that the nonresidential building referred to was the San Francisco pyramid was correct.

Krizek's article documents some of Transamerica's efforts to influence the news media on behalf of its building. It is fair to say that the efforts were successful. The major dailies advocated the building from the start. A clear indication of this was a letter to the editor by a former reporter, lamenting the passing of old San Francisco; the *Chronicle* reprinted it as a lead editorial—leaving out the part that damned the Transamerica pyramid.[12] No criticism of the building appeared in print locally.

Precedent favored granting permission for the building, although it certainly did not require it. Few major buildings, once proposed, had been stopped in San Francisco, and fewer still halted for reasons of urban design. The Fontana Towers, built on the city's waterfront some years earlier, had broken an unwritten San Francisco rule that buildings on the waterfront should be low and non-view blocking. Laws had since been passed to reestablish the precedent and prevent similar occurrences, but the Fontana was permitted. As a generally frowned upon building its example might have, but did not, provide a precedent to refuse the pyramid.

There was also a precedent attached to the selling of a street. In the 1960s, San Franciscans attached little value to streets either as open space or as factors that determine the scale of development. If streets weren't needed for traffic or for access, they could be disposed of. However, the Real Estate Department, with approval of the city attorney, did attach value to streets. When a street was to be sold, the Real Estate Department generally charged *one-half* the market value established by property appraisals. Why only one-half? The rationale of the real estate and legal experts was that since the owner had some rights to the street originally, he should not have to pay the full market value, that in fact he had rights to half the value of the street even though it might have been held in fee by the city. This precedent made the purchase of streets attractive to developers in general and to the Transamerica Corporation for the purchase of Merchant Street in particular. No one can know if the corporation would have asked for the street vacation and purchase if the price had been twice the $535,000 it agreed to pay. A taxpayer's suit would decide the correct price in the courts after the street had been closed and sold.[13]

It is useful to look briefly at the resolution of the Transamerica issue in two ways: in terms of substance, and in relation to the city planning process. Substantively, the issue was resolved quite clearly. The street was closed. The building exists. The city planners lost. Transamerica and the mayor won. In regard to the city planning process, the unofficial design review procedure established by the planning staff was bypassed. When any matter of significance came up, Transamerica simply ignored it. On the other hand, the official, legally prescribed process was followed, and this process in itself slowed and might have stopped the building. Some of Transamerica's early applications for site permits, excavation permits, and the street closing apparently did not meet the precise requirements of the law, and they had to be retracted and resubmitted. Since time was critical for the developer, a string of these delays could have affected the resolution of the issue. Transamerica might not have insisted on the original design without the tax advantages that would disappear if construction did not start by the end of 1969.

In the end, the official process was followed, and it provided a number of opportunities to approve or disapprove the building. The public had a chance to express its point of view. If the public had cared enough, it could have influenced the outcome, perhaps to the extent of overcoming the influence of the mayor and chief administrative officer. But the public was not sufficiently aroused. Either people did not know about the proposal and its implications, or they did not feel the issue was of major concern, or, alternatively, they may have known about the proposal and favored it. It seems reasonable to conclude that at that particular time in San Francisco not enough people considered one oddly shaped building in a questionable location enough of an issue to merit greater involvement.

If the city planners' assessment of the proposed Transamerica building was correct, then its effects on the city and immediate area will be negative. The planners most involved in the case continue to believe their recommendations were sound. While it is not likely that one building is strong enough to set the character of a city or to make or break it in terms of city design and development, each building adds or detracts. The Portsmouth Corridor, with a strangely shaped Holiday Inn, an almost black Alcoa building—an anomaly in light-colored San Francisco—and finally the pyramid, has developed into an architectural sample box of unrelated shapes, sizes, and colors. The city has always welcomed variety, but in the past it has been expressed within a generally unified overall structure and scale.

San Francisco has not been undone by the Transamerica building, but the resolution of the issue and its immediate consequences were disheartening to the planning department. Some developers and architects concluded, correctly, that they could bypass the process established by the planning staff to develop urban design guidelines for particularly sensitive projects. Instead, developers could go to the mayor, or to some of the commissioners, or perhaps to the chief administrative officer and get early backing. While there is nothing new about this practice, it invariably leaves the city planning staff on the losing side, and it had not been common for two years in San Francisco. The informal but effective design review process had been weakened considerably.

In the longer run, the resolution of the issue may have been responsible for a heightened awareness of urban design and downtown growth issues. In 1970, the proponents of the U.S. Steel development on the waterfront used the same high-powered tactics as Transamerica. The planning commission approved that proposal, too, but in the face of strong citizen opposition, the Board of Supervisors voted to reject the proposal and to support the recommendation of the planning staff.[14] Also, the anti-high-rise initiatives that surfaced in 1971 and 1972 may in part have been outgrowths of the Transamerica issue.

An immediate consequence of the Transamerica issue was the split that developed between the planning commission and its staff. Heretofore, they had agreed on most major issues, but for a period of at least two years after, they agreed less often, and at times the staff itself was unable to support the commission's actions before the Board of Supervisors. There were also times when the staff actively argued against the commission at the board. This breach lasted until a citywide urban design plan was produced in 1971.

Perhaps more significant was the split that occured within the commission and betweeen at least one of its members and the mayor. Commissioner Brinton was incensed that Mayor Alioto had written to the commissioners in favor of the building. To him, the mayor's letter constituted unwarranted interference in the commission's business, and he said so many times. When his term expired in 1970, he was not reappointed, primarily because of his outspoken criticism of the mayor. Ultimately, Brinton was to become a major force in the fight against the massive, downtown Yerba Buena redevelopment project, a favorite of San Francisco's business interests and of the mayor.

The Transamerica case teaches us a number of lessons. Some fall into the category of political judgment or strategy. Under this heading, one might question the planning director's wisdom in waiting so long before publicly airing his concerns about the proposal. By going directly to the public through the media immediately after he learned of the proposal and before Transamerica could gain the initiative, he might have aroused enough public opinion to ultimately defeat it. But, as fruitful as this area of inquiry might be, of primary interest here is what the case implies for the city planning process.

First, the case underlines the importance of having a plan that addresses, as specifically as possible, the kinds of issues that the community will face. San Francisco had no such plan to provide guidelines for relating individual buildings to the design of the city as a whole, although one was in preparation. Without such an explicit plan, the planners were, to a considerable extent, "winging it." It would also have been desirable for the plan to have been endorsed at the highest policy-making level of the government.

Even without a plan, zoning could have prohibited the building. It is unimaginable that an 853-foot building in the Portsmouth Corridor would have been permitted if there had been height limitations. On the theory that if anything bad can happen, it will, the planners should have proposed a reasonable height restriction for the area at the time of the downtown rezoning. They had not done so. Instead, the planning commission relied on its discretionary review powers to guard against undesirable development. Its vote on the Transamerica building would indicate that it did not consider the pyramid to fall into that category. Nevertheless, the case underlines the desirability of using zoning as a part of the city planning process to achieve what the community wishes and to prohibit what it does not.

Transamerica's successful avoidance of the design review process only confirmed what the planners already knew—the importance of making the design review process a legal requirement. Developers and architects will not voluntarily become involved in a procedure that limits their options unless they can see a clear connection between doing so and succeeding with their project. The more significant the project and the higher the status of those involved, the more likely it is that someone will try, successfully, to skirt any voluntary process. Transamerica still might have bypassed a more formal procedure and used political clout to win acceptance for its building, but it would have been harder to do so.

The case, like many others, further confirms what many have said: that political pressures will be at least as important and probably more important than technical or urban design criteria in deciding development issues. The more discretion there is in the review process, the less likely that the decisions will be made using the city planners' criteria.

The case further suggests that the planners could have asserted their claims better if they had prepared design guidelines for the area and the site much faster than they did. Such guidelines, especially if they have been considered by planning commissioners or legislative bodies, put the interested parties on notice. If precise ownership patterns are unknown or in flux, then more general or preliminary guidelines might be in order, but the planners will at least have established their presence in the development process.

The case also raises some questions about the master plan referral process. In San Francisco, a master plan referral must be decided at a regular public meeting of the commission. It does not, however, require a public hearing, since a factual finding of whether or not the matter at hand conforms to the master plan is all that is required. In practice, referrals are often decided after considerable public testimony, but the discussion may have nothing to do with the master plan. Quite often, master plans contain no direct policies or guidelines that address the issue at hand anyway. There was very little in the San Francisco master plan that was in effect at the time that could be cited as being directly applicable to the vacation of Merchant Street.

If clear policies and directives were set forth in a master plan, issues such as this one might arise less frequently and, when they did, decisions could be made more easily. Not only should there be no need for a public hearing for most cases, there should also be no need for commission action. Except when appeals or a proposed change in policy are being requested, the staff of the planning department could handle referrals administratively. Public hearings would be required to consider changes in policy, which would be the same as changes in the master plan. It would be reasonable to require more than a simple majority of the legislative body to overrule a finding of nonconformance by the planners, similar to the practice in zoning cases. In fact, master plan referrals, as a means of controlling the uses of *public* property and development, are somewhat analogous to zoning as it is related to the use and development of *private* property. The approach is similar to that under which some state-created regional agencies operate. For example, the San Francisco Bay Conservation and Development Commission and the state legislature adopted a Bay Plan that guides BCDC in its granting of shoreline permits. BCDC has control, via the permit system, of public as well as private projects.[15] The process will only work well, however, when there is something reasonably specific for it to apply to and when it has some teeth.

It is difficult to draw conclusions about the best location for city planning within the governmental framework based on the experience of one case. Nevertheless, the Transamerica example does raise some questions in this regard. San Francisco locates city planning under a commission appointed by the mayor instead of making it a part of the mayor's office, where, according to the opinion of many, it would be most effective. Is it likely that city planning would have been more effective in the Transamerica case if the Department of City Planning had been a part of the mayor's office? Given the political structure of large cities and the forces that usually elect their chief executives, how reasonable is it to expect the mayor to be opposed to major downtown buildings of any kind? If it is also true, that, historically, downtown business interests have had a great stake in electing mayors and that those mayors have in turn found business support to their advantage, then it is also unlikely that mayors will oppose downtown office buildings, on any grounds. If a city requires that recommendations be made on development matters by professionally trained city planners, and if those recommendations are to be made in public, is a mayor's office the best place from which to make them? Isn't it likely that even if the mayor and planner agree on one or more cases, sooner or later there will be major disagreement? And won't it be difficult to ensure the survival of impartial professional recommendations—if the community does indeed want such recommendations? The answers to these questions suggest that for handling cases like Transamerica, city planning would not have been any more effective if it were located under the chief executive instead of under a planning commission or the legislative body. Indeed, either of the last two would seem preferable.

The Transamerica case cannot be counted a success for city planning in San Francisco. Those most responsible for doing city planning and for making recommendations about the physical development of the city were not supported. Professionally, they had not prepared for the case as well as they might. Politically, they were less than effective.

Regardless of the outcome of the Transamerica proposal, the case points to the difficulty that city planning has in dealing with such ad hoc development matters when they become major issues. Conflict situations, especially those centered on large building development issues, make good copy for the press, but they do not necessarily produce considered decisions. The outcome of such conflicts is usually decided in favor of the parties with the most power, fiscal or political. Even if city planners win their share of such battles, and sometimes they do, it is as often by luck as by planning. More discretion in the hands of the

professionals will not necessarily help, because in the toughest cases, especially when the professionals are opposed to the project, they are likely to be overruled in the political arena. Many would say properly so. For city planning to be most effective on these kinds of issues it is important to minimize the frequency of Transamerica conflicts. To do that requires relevant, clear, well-aired, and thorough plans in the first place, followed by implementing legislation, and a governmental process that maximizes the possibility of considered decisions.

# An Epilogue

In May 1972, the Supreme Court of California upheld a lower court's finding, in response to the taxpayer's suit (*Harman v. City and County of San Francisco*), to the effect that San Francisco's policy of charging half the market value of any public right-of-way it was selling was unlawful and that 90 per cent of the full market value would have to be charged. Transamerica was ordered to pay an additional $535,000 for the portion of Merchant Street it had purchased earlier. An unexpected consequence of the issue, then, was to change city policy and to make it more costly, and perhaps less likely, for city streets to be vacated for private use. But it is doubtful that the extra cost, if known beforehand, would have stopped Transamerica from going ahead with its building.

Communication, however, might have prevented the Transamerica building.

On September 19, 1969, well after the planning commission and Board of Supervisors had approved the building and long after I had any desire to meet Transamerica's chairman, John Beckett, we met. The meeting, requested by Beckett through Mortimer Fleishhacker, president of the planning commission, took place in Beckett's office. The essence of it was that Transamerica wanted to build its pyramid 10 stories higher than had been requested and approved. Beckett knew that this would require a new hearing before the commission. But, he said, a taller, more slender building would be more handsome, more deserving of our support. My position was that the best that could be said would be that the building would be less ugly, that I would not change my position, and that I wondered why Beckett cared what I thought, since he had the commission "wired" in any case. Beckett responded that it was important to have the planning director in favor of the building, that it would look better, especially in the public eye. He didn't want another fight. He also observed that well before the initial approval of the building his staff had advised him that if Transamerica came in with a building that was 10 stories lower than the initial conception, I might approve it. I told Beckett he had been misinformed and proceeded to list my reasons for opposing the building, concluding that I would never recommend in favor of it. Beckett had not known my views and said that it was too bad we hadn't met earlier. He said he wanted to give San Francisco "a valentine."

The meeting continued, and after some time Fleishhacker and I, wondering what further purpose would be served, started to excuse ourselves. Beckett, however, had something else on his mind. What if Transamerica came in with a different building of more modest height? I responded that two of the five original designs had looked quite good, and although they were higher than desirable, over 30 floors, I would probably recommend their approval if they were designed sensitively in relation to the site and its surroundings. The problem of speed, really Transamerica's need to have at least a hole in the ground by the first of the year to realize its tax advantages, could be handled, I felt, by everyone working overtime. Beckett seemed interested. The meeting ended cordially. Beckett said that he would think about this new alternative and get back to me early the following week. I recall that as we were leaving, Beckett said something to the effect that it was unfortunate that we had not met earlier.

Early the following week Beckett called. He felt it was too late now to turn around. Too much was involved, the matter had gone too far.

Transamerica officially asked for the greater height on November 13, 1969. The staff recommended against the building. The planning commission voted four to three for it. Excavation started in December 1969. The building was first occupied in the summer of 1972.

# Notes

1. The source of this date, as of many others in this chapter, is the author's appointment calendar for 1969.

2. Mandatory referrals come under section 3.527 of the San Francisco Charter, zoning under sections 7.500 to 7.503. See chapter 2 for a description of mandated responsibilities of the planning department.

3. The power of discretionary review is derived from part III, section 26 of the San Francisco Municipal Code and from the San Francisco Charter. For a description of the discretionary review power

see Patrick J. O'Hern, "Reclaiming the Urban Environment: The San Francisco Urban Design Plan," *Ecology Law Quarterly*, vol. 3 (1973).

4. San Francisco Charter, section 3.651.

5. The law is part of the California Revenue and Taxation Code, part 7, chapter 3, article 4, paragraph 12241. Also see Donald Canter, "Insurance Buildings Rush for Tax Savings," *San Francisco Examiner*, December 15, 1969.

6. San Francisco City Planning Commission Resolution 6112, June 29, 1967.

7. Herb Caen, "Good-Good-Good," *San Francisco Chronicle*, February 2, 1969.

8. "Spire Makes It the Tallest," *San Francisco Examiner*, January 27, 1969; "A Pyramid for San Francisco: Plans for City's Tallest Building," *San Francisco Chronicle*, January 28, 1969.

9. *San Francisco Chronicle*, April 4 and April 27, 1969.

10. A copy of this letter is also in the planning commission minutes of June 26, 1969.

11. Donald Canter, "Tax Bill Contains Break for Transamerica," *San Francisco Examiner*, December 10, 1969.

12. The letter from L.S. Thompson appeared in the *San Francisco Chronicle* on April 4, 1969, the editorial on April 7. Also see "San Francisco's Renaissance," lead editorial in *San Francisco Chronicle*, January 29, 1969; and "Pyramidal Anchor," editorial in *San Francisco Examiner*, same date.

13. *Harman v. City and County of San Francisco*, 7 Cal. 3d 150, 101 Cal. Rptr. 880, 496 P. 2d 1248.

14. For a sense of the developing tenor of the times, see *San Francisco Chronicle* articles by Scott Blakey ("Tower Plan Restudied,"

July 28, 1970) and Jerry Burns ("A Height Formula for Waterfront," November 11, 1970; "San Francisco Supervisors Block the U.S. Steel Tower," February 13, 1971). Also see "Skylines v. Skyscrapers," *Time*, March 8, 1971.

15. Paul Sedway and Thomas Cooke, *Land and the Environment: Planning in California Today* (Los Altos, California: William Kaufmann, Inc., 1975), p. 74.

# Chapter 8
# Case Study: The Urban Design Plan

San Francisco is generally accepted as one of the more handsome American cities. Views, hills, fog, water, charm, urbanity, diversity, intimacy, activity, Victorians, cable cars, Chinatown, Golden Gate Bridge, Fisherman's Wharf, Golden Gate Park—all evoke images of a special urban place. And San Franciscans seem to be aware of their immediate physical environment and of their good fortune. If long association or experience have no effect, then visitors remind them that their city is different.

By the late 1960s, there was a growing list of conflicts over individual building projects that represented, to some, threats to valued physical traditions. The Fontana Towers, a high-rise apartment complex in a very visible location, had broken a long-standing tradition of building only low buildings along the waterfront. The possibility that another project, the International Market Center, would dwarf Coit Tower on Telegraph Hill and block views of the Bay raised an enormous controversy. The "freeway revolt" in 1966 had been as much a reaction to the ugliness of the existing freeways and the disruption they caused as to their questionable functional value in intensely developed urban areas.

The visual quality of some of the redevelopment projects that were proposed had aroused public opinion, and so had the design of the rapid transit stations downtown. In the neighborhoods, complaints were beginning to be heard about the "plastic" apartment buildings that were replacing the Victorians and about the way that the new buildings ignored long-established setback traditions. The issues that were at stake were underlined in the late sixties by the imaginative conversion into a shopping complex of the old Ghirardelli chocolate factory, which was next to the Fontana Towers.

The conflicts were the result of strong pressures for development and change, pressures that were likely to accelerate. Most of the city's land was already built upon; new development invariably meant replacing small buildings with large ones that would often alter the character of existing areas. The size, the nature, and the rapidity of new development threatened to harm the very qualities that made the city attractive to so many people. In short, the physical image of the city was changing rapidly, and the change produced public conflicts over individual development proposals.

On such occasions, regardless of whether the proposal was large (like the Transamerica building) or small, there was no citywide plan against which it could be measured and decided. More important, there was no design plan to serve as a guide for such development in the first place. San Francisco, considered by its own residents to be a very special place, was without a public statement of what the city should look like.

The urban design plan represents a successful effort in comprehensive plan preparation.[1] The plan, and its preparation, may be viewed as a response to issues that fall within the framework of urban design. If the Transamerica building represents a failure for city planning in San Francisco, then the urban design plan represents a city planning success. The Transamerica issue, decided during the period that the urban design plan was being prepared, underlined the importance of having some kind of plan that addresses the issues that a community is likely to face. The city planning process begins (if there is a specific point of beginning) with a comprehensive or master plan. A purpose of this case study is to illustrate that first step.

In June 1967, Robert Weaver, Secretary of the U.S. Department of Housing and Urban Development, is reported to have said in San Francisco that, "This city and every city long ago should have documented for itself and its citizenry a clear and unequivocal physical design for how the city should look and live and feel and breathe."[2] It is doubtful that many San Franciscans perceived the need so clearly.

More likely, they were concerned with individual development proposals and realities that offended them and that they might contest. A new building that might block familiar views and create only shadow where sunlight was normal, vacation of a street in favor of development, loss of Victorians (that often housed low-income minorities), widened or one-way streets that divided neighborhoods, increased traffic and decreased safety, development on land that people associated with open space, billboards, insensitive remodeling, loss of a landmark— these are but a few of the kinds of cases that might bring protests or law suits. On one occasion neighbors observed that construction of an addition to the San Francisco Art Institute might be slightly higher than legally permitted. Their protests brought construction to a halt and, after a long public hearing, the institute was required to remove some already poured concrete and part of one floor from the structure.[3]

Putting all the individual concerns together, one might well deduce the existence of an issue: how to maintain the physical attractiveness, charm, and pleasantness of San Francisco in the face of mounting pressures for drastic change. Put another way, the problem was to moderate and direct growth and change in a desirable and pleasing way. The design of the city had become an issue both because of the controversies over individual developments and because it was a concern that had not been dealt with effectively at a citywide level at a time when many residents found rapid physical change threatening.

There were some pressures and some support for urban design planning at a citywide scale. A joint committee of architects, planners, and landscape architects was pressing for such a plan. The planning commission, sensitive to criticism that it was overly concerned with two-dimensional land-use matters, was sympathetic, and the staff of the planning department long had seen a need for a plan and was interested in preparing one. In 1967, Mayor Shelley and the Board of Supervisors had responded favorably to requests by the planning department to hire new staff members with urban design expertise.

Before moving on to an accounting of the way in which the planning department dealt with the issue, it is useful to consider, however briefly, the relationship of urban design to city planning as a whole and to the governmental process associated with city planning. To some, urban design, city planning, land-use planning, urban physical planning, and urban environmental planning are all pretty much the same thing. Professional city planners as well as the lay public often use the terms interchangeably, and if the public's contact with city planning is limited to matters of design or transportation or housing, then it might well think of those single activities as constituting city planning. But to the planners involved in preparing the urban design plan, the activities are quite different. Urban design, to them, is a part of city planning.

City planning may be defined as "a continuing and deliberate effort to arrange the physical fabric of an urban settlement in such a way as to meet the social, economic, and political needs of people, within the constraints of the natural environment."[4] It is the determination of what goes where, why, how, and when in urban environments in relation to the people who live in and use those environments and to the environment itself. That definition, in no way unique, but considered by some in the field to be too limited in scope, is consistent with the thrust of city planning that is found in San Francisco's charter—a basic concern with the physical development of the city.

Urban design has been viewed as a subfield of city planning, dealing primarily with the sensuous, aesthetic, and visual qualities of the urban environment. It is concerned with the "visual and other sensory relationships between people and their environments, with their feeling of time and place, and their sense of well-being."[5] That is how the city planners in San Francisco viewed urban design in relation to their more encompassing city planning mandate. It was a definition that included most of the design-related issues expressed by the people of the city.

As early as Daniel Burnham's 1905 plan for San Francisco, urban design considerations had been a part of the city's planning efforts.[6] Visionary in its system of parkways, diagonal streets, quiet plazas, and open space, the Burnham plan was considered too ambitious for a city intent on rebuilding after the earthquake and fire of 1906. Urban design considerations had also played a part in the enactment of the special height districts that had existed in San Francisco since 1927. The master plan that was in effect in the late 1960s contained some design-related policies. Recent zoning efforts in and around downtown also had addressed some design issues, and plans completed after 1965 for at least two different city districts dealt with urban design as a subject matter. Nevertheless, urban design considerations were rarely made explicit in the plans that were adopted, and they did not exist at a citywide, comprehensive level.

It is not always understood by those concerned with the visual and sensory relationships between people and their environment, especially by those offended by the design qualities of new development, that city planning departments are rarely responsible for the direct design of anything. City planners in public planning departments are not normally responsible for the design of private or public objects, from buildings, to signs, to parks. Designers working for private or public clients, other than planning departments, design such objects. Similarly, physical development projects that involve a definite area, client, building program, and completion date are usually designed by architects in private employ rather than by people working in city planning departments.[7] Employees of redevelopment agencies sometimes come close to having direct design responsibilities for projects, but they, of course, are seldom combined with the staffs of city planning departments. The designers in a city planning department may be part of a team with responsibility for the design of a public system, such as roads, parks, or lighting, but they will rarely have direct design control or overall responsibility for it.

On the other hand, city planners are often responsible for preparing general plans for road, transit, open space, walkway, and even lighting systems. Here there is often overlap in regard to who designs what, but the final design authority usually rests with an operating agency.

The public planner/designer is likely to have most direct influence at the level of city or area design involving the general spatial arrangement of objects over an extended area. There are usually many clients to satisfy. It is also likely that the public planner/designer will have only partial control and that he will be involved with a design that is never complete. Since public planners may influence and regulate whatever is built but rarely design it themselves, the importance of setting a framework for legislation and influence becomes clear, if the public wishes to recognize and deal with urban design issues.

In 1967, the staff of the planning department decided to undertake a citywide urban design study and plan that would, "become a major part of the city's comprehensive plan."[8] Other approaches had been considered. For instance, a comprehensive revision of the city's master plan might have included urban design considerations. But the likelihood of getting funds for such a large undertaking, estimated at well over $1 million, was less than remote. Alternatively, urban design factors could have been included in an element-by-element revision of the master plan (as part of the individual elements that dealt with housing, transportation, commerce and industry, public facilities and services, open space, and so on). Aside from the funding difficulties associated with this approach, the planners saw the possibility of considerable redundancy, since a single design consideration, such as views, might relate to any number of separate plan elements. Further, this approach might bury urban design as a subject within other areas of concern.

Other approaches included separate design studies and plans for small areas most susceptible to rapid change and conflicts, design plans for larger districts that could serve as examples for the rest of the city, and plans for the design, use, and expansion of public lands and buildings, including new publicly sponsored projects. The initial work outline of the planning department, embodied in a document called "Purpose of the Urban Design Plan and Study," embraced the most central features of these other approaches within the proposal for a comprehensive citywide urban design study and plan.

Whether or not the proposal would be carried out depended in large measure on the planners' ability to obtain funds. In 1967, there was no chance of the mayor or Board of Supervisors approving the $200,000 to $300,000 that the study would cost. Besides, a previous planning effort, the Community Renewal Program, had left them with a bad taste as far as major city planning studies were concerned.[9] Federal support seemed a possibility although the HUD officials, too, felt burned by the Community Renewal Program. On the other hand, HUD Secretary Weaver had spoken to the need for the kind of planning that was being proposed.

Early meetings with local HUD officials were promising if not definitive. They seemed to recognize that new people were on the scene, and they did not want to punish them for earlier problems. The federal officials were more encouraging about a comprehensive urban design study than about a second possibility, the "South of Market (Street) Study" that had been proposed by the planning department at the same time as the urban design plan. That proposal envisioned a comprehensive plan undertaking, including participation of residents, for a large area south of downtown. It was a district with myriad physical, social, and economic problems but also of much potential. It was home to a large number of low-income minorities. For many years, the area had been eyed for downtown and industrial expansion.

The federal officials came to understand that San Francisco as a county, was eligible for "701" planning funds, although San Francisco as a city (over the 25,000 population limit) was not.

Acting on the possibility of the 701 funds to cover two-thirds of the planning effort, the city planners prepared more detailed study outlines and cost estimates. They knew they would want to study and to analyze the city's natural and man-made physical elements, including topography, views, landmarks, building height, land coverage, open space, and transportation systems. The planners were prepared to work at citywide, district, and neighborhood scales to produce a design plan with accompanying objectives, policies, and principles and to investigate all relevant means of carrying it out.

HUD also required a "social plan reconnaissance survey." One of its purposes was to define what a social plan for San Francisco might attempt to accomplish. The planners were more concerned that it provide sociological input into the design plan they hoped to produce. The total effort was estimated to take two years and to cost about $270,000, of which $180,000 was to come from HUD. The planners would have to come up with $90,000 of local funds.

The planning staff felt that there was no possibility of getting $90,000 from local coffers. Instead, they proposed to assign existing staff to the extent of $70,000 and to seek $20,000 from the mayor and Board of Supervisors. It proved difficult to obtain even this amount from the board. It was necessary for some of the planning commissioners to speak with some of the supervisors to get support. (For instance, Commissioner Julia Porter spoke to Supervisors Peter Tamaras and John Ertola.) In pursuing the matter before the board, the planning director stressed that the plan would provide a framework for private development that would help to eliminate the costly and divisive conflicts that were becoming characteristic of major building proposals. The board approved the $20,000 budget request in early 1968.

Getting a small amount of money from the Board of Supervisors was difficult, but doable. Getting absolutely nothing from the state was almost disastrous. Although funding for the plan was assured by HUD's verbal approval, and although no state funds were involved, federal monies had to be channeled through a state agency. On March 22, 1968, the Planning Advisory Committee of the state office of planning denied the application for reasons that were never made entirely clear. However, there was some indication that the city's own Redevelopment Agency might have been involved in influencing the turndown. (A note in the planning director's files records a discussion with Jack Tolan of the mayor's office that took place on March 25, 1968. Apparently, Justin Herman, the director of the Redevelopment Agency, had said to Tolan, "You can get in trouble with those things." It was also reported that a representative of the state office of planning had spoken with the Redevelopment Agency director about the proposal.)

It took three months of telegrams, saber rattling, and explanatory and face-saving letters to get the matter back on track. With no significant changes from the original, the application was approved on June 21. It was not until the end of 1968, however, that contracts could be signed and work could commence. Approximately one year had passed between the decision to attempt to undertake an urban design plan and the signal to start.

From the outset it was intended by the city planners that a citizens advisory committee—the Urban Design Advisory Committee—be formed to help guide the study and to review and criticize work as it progressed.[10] The intent was to represent a wide range of interests in a workable group of about 20 people with a good knowledge of the city—architects, landscape architects, neighborhood representatives, economists, racial minorities, conservationists, business interests, members of civic organizations, women, top government officials, planning commissioners. Some department heads were included for their knowledge and because they would be instrumental in carrying out the recommendations. If they participated in preparing the plan, the reasoning went, they would be more disposed to carry it out. The same reasoning was behind the decision to select two to three supervisors and a representative of the mayor. It was hoped, too, that the committee would become a force for carrying out the study's proposals.

The advisory committee had a hard time getting started, even after its first meeting, which was called in December by the planning commission. Few supervisors or department heads were present at the early meetings, and their absence was notable. Some committee members, especially the nonprofessionals, weren't sure what they were to do. Understandably, a few wanted to define their charge in the broadest terms, to encompass traffic, housing, education, and other issues. Some wanted to take positions on such current issues as the Transamerica building. They had to be dissuaded by the planning staff, who convinced them that sort of thing was not what they were there for—it was to work on a *plan*.

The staff had made an effort to choose people who might be expected to know the city. It became evident that few did. When they were asked to draw the city or to locate problem areas on a map, they displayed greatest familiarity with the northeast—downtown, Telegraph Hill, Nob Hill, Russian Hill, Fisherman's Wharf, Pacific Heights—the areas most commonly associated with San Francisco. Aside from the districts where they lived, they tended not to know other parts of the city very well. An all-day field trip was arranged in order for them to become more familiar with all of the city and for committee members and staff to get to know each other better.

At one point early on the committee was given a design exercise. Large sheets of paper were tacked on the walls of the meeting room. The committee members were divided into two groups. One was given the assignment of designing an entirely new city in the wake of a devastating earthquake. The second group was to assume that the city had been bought—lock, stock, and barrel—by Howard Hughes, who had hired this group to change it as it saw fit. Money was no object. To the planners, the conclusions and designs of the two teams were less significant than the fact that the committee members were beginning to think about the city in different ways and learning to communicate their concerns and desires.

Planners and committee members alike soon became aware that the committee, chosen by the planning department staff for the most part, was not representative of San Francisco's major interest groups. There were only two black members and one of these, a representative from the Economic Opportunity Council, dropped out in favor of another member of his organization, who was white. One of the two Chinese members, a high school student, became so involved with school activities that he, too, dropped out. There were no Chicano members and only three women. The poor were underrepresented. Unfortunately, the attempts that were made to broaden the committee were never too successful. The staff hoped to compensate for the deficiencies by direct contacts with diverse community groups. Such contact would come through detailed community studies, the ongoing neighborhood planning program, the interviews that were to be conducted as part of the overall study, and the responses to preliminary reports that would be distributed in the community. Nevertheless, from a look at committee membership alone, one might well conclude that the urban design study was in the hands of a somewhat elitist group.

Once it got under way, the committee met regularly, usually monthly. Eventually, it became influential in determining the outcome of the study. Members helped to enunciate the policies and principles that were to find their way into the plan, and they learned to differentiate between citywide matters that were legitimate concerns of the committee and specific neighborhood issues that were not. In addition, the committee's participation kept the planners' language in line, assuring that they communicated in terms that could be understood. And the mere existence of the committee prodded the planners into meeting deadlines for the simple reason that they had to have something to present at meetings.

There were no major conflicts between committee members, although there were differences of opinion. As might be expected, the chamber of commerce representative tended to resent ideas that might be restrictive of development. The conservation-oriented bloc on the committee may have kept him from pressing his concerns more strongly. On the other hand, the architects played roles that were quite different from those they played when they were representing clients at the planning department. Here they did seem to be wearing public as opposed to private hats. They offered and supported proposals to restrict building height, color, shape, and bulk, as well as the disposition of public property for development purposes. It was as if the architects welcomed a strong, conservative plan, recognizing that the normal development forces at work would force them to settle for less than totally desirable projects when they were representing private clients.

During the early period of the study, the planning staff prepared detailed study outlines and work programs, considered consultants to be hired, started hiring special staff for the project (mostly educated as architects and urban designers), and began work they knew would be required. Between December 1968 and October 1970, eight preliminary reports and three special studies were produced and presented to the committee. From 400 to 500 copies of each report were distributed to elected officials, city departments, design professionals, and neighborhood and business organizations. The point of heavy reliance on preliminary reports was to encourage public response. That response could help later in fashioning a final plan. The preliminary reports allowed the staff to assemble the work in an organized fashion and make it available to the participants. They also provided a means of recording the details of the study, which would be helpful for future use in San

Francisco's planning program. The reports allowed staff planners who were not directly involved with the urban design study to keep abreast of its progress. Reports were completed at an uneven pace, varying from one every six months near the beginning to two in one month at the end.

The first report, *Preliminary Report No. 1: Background*, which appeared in March 1969, was intended to advise people what the city planners were up to. (Like the other seven, it is summarized in the urban design plan.) It presented information on the city's climate, natural features, and man-made environment. It included a map of the boundaries of some 82 city neighborhoods. This map indicated that there was considerable overlap among many of the neighborhood associations, and it gave some idea of their relative importance. Committee members were surprised at how much public property there was in San Francisco; the map showed that much of it existed in the form of public rights-of-way.

The publication provided some lessons that would help the city planners in later reports. For instance, some of the maps were almost impossible to read. And the fact that a glossary of urban design terms had to be included indicated that the planners were using words that were not in general use. Clearly, a change in their language was necessary.

The second report—*Preliminary Report No. 2: Existing Plans and Policies*—came out in July 1969. It was an analysis of the urban design content of the many plans and studies and ordinances that had been produced by public and private agencies. It was an attempt to make explicit the urban design policies that were only implied in the existing plans. The report pointed out that, until recently, natural and topographical features had, more than anything else, shaped San Francisco's form and character. Their influence had diminished with the increase in the scale of man-made structures, made possible by technological and economic inventions. The most important design decision had been the imposition of a gridiron street system over the hills, thereby emphasizing the importance of streets and of public views.

The preliminary report noted that two concerns were predominant in most plans: enhancement of the natural topography, and preservation of the special physical character of the city. Yet, the report concluded, except for a general height and form envelope that was implicit in existing zoning laws, no citywide design elements had been articulated. Further, there was a general preoccupation with the area in and around the downtown and too little attention to design in the rest of the city.

During the early months of the urban design study, considerable time was spent in preparing detailed work outlines, starting field surveys, and learning how to work with each other. Four consultants were hired and so were a number of new staff members. Seven people who were new to the department worked on the first three preliminary reports (two had left after the first year). The new staffers were mostly young city planners, architects, and landscape architects recently graduated from various master's degree programs. Some were still students at the University of California's College of Environmental Design in Berkeley.

As the study proceeded, the members of the committee expressed some uneasiness as to what it was to achieve. They were not reassured by the staff's inability to be specific about the plans and the process of achieving them. Partly in response to the committee's concerns, but also to guide the work to follow, the staff worked with the committee to develop a series of goals, objectives, and policies. These appeared in December 1969 as *Preliminary Report No. 3: Goals, Objectives, and Policies.*

Major objectives and policies were not clearly articulated at this point. It was, in fact, a dull, rather unimaginative report, not the kind that would excite anyone. But still, some general guidelines were elucidated. New development, the report stated, should be compatible with the old, and it should also be in accord with natural land forms. The report noted that there was a relationship between physical safety and the design of the city. It also noted the desirability of achieving a community where people knew with ease where they were and how to get where they were going, in short where orientation was not a problem. One general objective was to maintain the city's physical and social variety. Several items were marked as being especially important: a well-designed street system; open spaces; topography; historic buildings and landmarks; distinctive neighborhoods; appropriate height, bulk, and color of new buildings; public views; the waterfront; and hilltops.

A simple one-page questionnaire asking for comments and suggestions was distributed along with the report. Response was light. Indeed, in its first year the study received little attention. In part this was due to a lack of publicity. Although committee meetings were open, they were not announced to the public. Reporters attended on occasion, but they reported little, probably because there were no new major proposals forthcoming and no major disagreements among committee members.

Outside of the meetings, neither committee members nor staff did much to publicize their work. Everyone seemed to be feeling out his way and not too rapidly at that. The work at this point was like a very large pot of stew slowly simmering on a back burner, continually being changed by new additions.

The apparent lack of public interest in the study did not mean that urban design had ceased to be an issue. In fact, during this period, there was quite a lot of interest in specific design-oriented issues. There was public debate, for instance, over the plan for the northern waterfront area where height, views, and open space were major considerations. Public versus private use was an issue here, as it was where the future of Alcatraz Island was concerned, another issue that was being decided at this time. The public was making its voice heard over the Army's plans for more housing (and possibly fewer trees) in the Presidio, and the Transamerica controversy was just heating up. In response to public interest, the Board of Supervisors, in early 1970, approved the department's proposal for a 40-foot height limit along most of the ocean front.

The planning director was generally unconcerned with the lack of public attention to the study—he rather liked it that way until he knew there would be a product worthy of notice. Nonetheless, he was concerned at times that the study was not proceeding as well as might be expected. There were any number of meetings with assistant director Macris and chief urban designer and project manager Richard Hedman to resolve differences and get pointed in one direction. Although the director knew Hedman to be a first-rate urban designer, and valued his abilities highly, they did not always communicate too well. But he was willing to wait before pushing any panic buttons. Hedman and he had been in these positions before and knew that quite a bit of muddling around was often necessary before ideas jelled. As time passed, the director gave more and more of his time to the undertaking, as much out of personal interest as out of concern for the outcome.

Although only three preliminary reports had been completed by the end of 1969, detailed research by staff and consultants was under way. Much of it was presented in January 1970 in *Preliminary Report No. 4: Existing Form and Image*, to which consultants Marshall Kaplan,

Gans, and Kahn; Okamoto/Liskamm; and Donald Appleyard contrib-uted. This was a 207-page, four-part report. The first part, "Quality of the Environment," evaluated every block in the city, rating the environ-mental strengths and deficiencies of each according to a scoring system that was developed to achieve consistency and objectivity. Nine factors were considered, including quality of maintenance, views, distance from public open space, presence of trees and other natural features, and the amount of local traffic. This analysis was to help determine what areas of the city needed environmental improvements.

The part of the report called "Internal Pattern and Image" re-corded for the city as a whole and for each of its districts the elements that allow pedestrians to perceive the organization of the city, to orient themselves. These include landmarks, views, centers of activity, and movement patterns. The study listed design problems and opportu-nities in each district.

A study of the "Road Environment," prepared by consultant Donald Appleyard working with the planning department staff, exam-ined the city as it is seen by drivers on arterial roadways in both short- and long-range views. The visual quality of each section of roadway was evaluated in terms of its maintenance, order, and clarity.

Finally, an "External Form and Image" study used photography to analyze the broad panoramic views of the city. The strong form-giving elements—shoreline, hills, prominent tree stands—were identified, as were disrupting influences. Two working reports were prepared by the consultant for this study.

In sum, the fourth preliminary report represented a detailed de-scription and analysis of San Francisco's natural and man-made physical form elements. It borrowed heavily from the ideas and methods of Kevin Lynch, but it also developed its own survey and analysis tech-niques.[11] By the time the report was published in January 1970, much of its content had been presented to the committee. Still, the members had a hard time digesting it and some of them wondered aloud what to do with it. If the staff at that point was none too sure, no one let on.

Of the special reports and studies that were prepared, the *Street Livability Study* is the most significant. It was written by Donald Appleyard, working with the department's staff, and appeared in June 1970. Appleyard studied three separate city blocks with light, moder-ate, and heavy traffic conditions, in order to determine the effects of traffic volume upon the residents' attitudes and living patterns. The report concluded that as traffic increased, the livability of the street, as defined by the residents, decreased. "Livability," in this case, included such factors as length of residence, satisfaction with the area, degree of neighborliness, where people spent time in their homes (in relation to the street), and residents' perceptions of features in the street environment. The report may not have told anything new to many city planners and residents, for they had long since come to the same conclusions. But it gave them ammunition to press for a reduction and slowing of neighborhood traffic. It should not be surprising that the city's traffic engineers were none too happy with the report.

The *Street Livability Study* says something about the relative effectiveness of consultants. Generally speaking, the two consultants who were hired directly as individuals and who worked either with a few of their own employees or directly with department staff members were more effective than the two firms that were hired. The problems did not necessarily lie with the firms selected. But the staff had less contact with them, especially with the principals involved. This meant that the department had to be more specific about what the consultants were expected to produce than was necessary with individual consultants. It was not, unfortunately, always possible to be so specific. Also, the firms were less aware when shifts in emphasis took place and therefore less able to adapt their work. Thus, it was more difficult to integrate their efforts into the preliminary reports. The cause of the difficulty may well be that the planning department was not accustomed to working with consultants in an efficient and productive way.

Presentation in July of *Preliminary Report No. 5: Urban Design Principles*, by Tom Aidala, the consultant who prepared it with the staff, marked a turning point in the study. This report used words and sketches to present "certain fundamental rules that govern the measurable and critical urban design relationships among elements in the city's environment." It organized these rules, or principles, into three sections: streets and the qualities of pavement, sidewalks, and furnishings ("Extremely wide streets in residential areas devote excessive space to the automobile at the expense of pedestrians, and encourage speeding, creating a safety hazard as well"); relationship of the streets to building facades ("Blank walls are dead places on the street and should be avoided," and "Intricate entries, traditional in San Francisco, add to the visually habitable space of the street"); and the relationships among

External details in building facades, entries, stairways, retaining walls, and other features provide visual interest and enrichment and are consistent with the historic scale and texture of San Francisco.

Visually strong buildings which contrast severely with their surroundings impair the character of the area.

*Above and opposite:* Examples of urban design principles related to conservation and city pattern. (From the *Urban Design Plan*.)

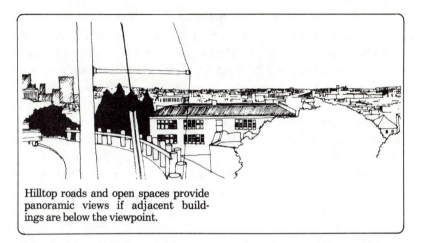

Hilltop roads and open spaces provide panoramic views if adjacent buildings are below the viewpoint.

street patterns, building masses, and topography ("High buildings in a valley obscure the distinction between hills," and "Tall buildings on slopes of hills severely restrict views from above").

The reaction of the committee and of the planning commission was enthusiastic. "The only thing that's missing," said one committee member, "is a principle about overhead wires." A slide presentation of the report at the annual meeting of the San Francisco Planning and Renewal Association met with similar approval. People were responding to these proposals exactly as the staff hoped they would, accepting them as "design truths" about the city.

By the summer of 1970, the planning director sensed that the department had a winner in the making. He could not anticipate the details of a final plan or the form it would take, but he felt sure that it would represent top-notch professional work. The urban design staff was beginning to work as a team. Slowly, the director began to let some of the planning commissioners know that they could expect something good. The Transamerica controversy had soured relations with some of the commissioners. So, also, had the commission's approval, over the planning director's objection, of zoning changes that would have permitted a large U.S. Steel-sponsored development at the waterfront. In a meeting with Julia Porter, a key commissioner, and one with whom his current relations were at an all-time low, the director communicated his expectation that the new plan would help avoid future problems of the sort they had been having; he asked for her help so that the work would not pass without notice or effect. She agreed most readily.

Work continued, and in September, the sixth report, the *Social Reconnaissance Survey*, was ready. It contained the results of interviews with residents in 13 neighborhoods, all with different social characteristics. They had been asked about their satisfaction with the neighborhood, their access to community facilities, the features they desired in the local environment, the trends that they perceived, and the public improvements that they thought should be made. The consultant interpreted the results of the survey in relation to the courses of action that were possible and ranked priorities for various types of neighborhoods. Some of the results provided checks against the environmental surveys. Traffic, distance from open space, and public and private maintenance were seen by the respondents as major problems.

It had always been expected that the studies that would be undertaken would include both large sections of the city and small areas of no more than a few blocks. Seven of these small studies were completed and presented in sketch form in working reports—grouped under the title "Workbook: District and Neighborhood Designs." In the black Divisadero Street area, for example, the staff and an economic consultant known as PACT (Plan of Action for Challenging Times) worked together with a merchants' association on methods for improving a four-block section of the street. Two studies discussed public improvements that might be carried out as part of the Federally Assisted Code Enforcement program. One of these studies presented alternative proposals for air rights development over a rail yard. The studies were valuable in familiarizing staff with the local issues, and the amount of this kind of work increased throughout 1970.

In October, the department released its last two preliminary reports. *Preliminary Report No. 7: Implementation Approaches* described a framework and various means for implementing the proposals being developed. As Peter Svirsky put it in an article in *Planning* magazine in January 1973, the "report took stock of the various city powers in urban design questions, both direct city actions and controls over private development. In the case of each power, the process of public involvement was reviewed and the relevant parties and their decisions identified. This . . . report helped to gear the study to practical actions by which the plan could later be carried out."[12]

*Preliminary Report No. 8: Citywide Urban Design Plans* was the last of the preliminary reports. It described the major components of a final plan: the principles, policies, maps, and guidelines relating to open space and landscaping, arterial streets, and street environment in residential areas; the public values inherent in the retention of street space; and height and bulk of buildings. The response to a questionnaire distributed with the report was light, but it did indicate that the policies and guidelines were reasonable and that, if anything, more restrictions than those suggested would be in order.

Toward the end of 1970, about two years after work on the study had started, most of the scheduled research and analysis had been completed and final plan proposals were under way. In anticipation of events to follow, it is worth reviewing the roles, to this point, of significant actors in the planning process.

Without question, the city planners had played the dominant role in the study. It had been their idea in the first place and they had controlled the work. They also had a major say in choosing the committee, which was their brainchild to begin with. But bringing the work to its present stage had not been all tea and crumpets. When one considers that at least 15 professional staff members and a number of consultants had at one time or another spent large amounts of time on the project, it is not surprising that there were disagreements. The subjects of these disagreements ranged from personal style to matters of substance, methods, and relevance. The fact that scarce staff resources were being channeled into the urban design project aroused some animosity among staff members who were not involved.

Disagreements about design were decided at staff meetings, usually with some sort of compromise, but by executive decision when necessary. If bad feelings remained, they seemed minor compared to an overall sense of purpose and expectation that grew as time passed.

The Citizens Advisory Committee had played an important and active role in guiding the work, especially in acting as a sounding board

for the ideas of the planners. For the most part, however, the involvement of the committee ended when the meetings ended. The members
came to meetings and they did their homework. But then they went
their separate, busy ways. To the planning director, the committee still
appeared to be more a gathering of individuals than an organized group
with a well-defined role. There was no evidence to suggest that it would
become a long-term force for advocating the proposals embodied in the
study.

In general, it continued to be true that the architects on the
committee favored strong public initiatives on the kinds of urban
design questions being discussed. They favored decisive public actions
and controls. Their views carried weight with other members and were
encouraging to the staff, which might well look to the architects for
future support. On the whole, most citizen-members took what might
be termed urban preservation positions. On one or two occasions they
expressed strong misgivings to the director about actions that the
planning commission had taken in favor of specific developments. The
committee took no strong positions on racial or minority issues.

Citizen interest was matched by noninvolvement of officials. The
department heads who were invited rarely appeared themselves, and
rarely sent representatives, and the representatives sent by elected
officials were generally silent. Perhaps they viewed their function on
the committee as primarily information gathering.

To this point, the supervisors had expressed no interest in the
study they had helped fund. They and their administrative assistants had
been given copies of all preliminary reports, but they had not commented on them. Similarly, the mayor indicated no particular interest in
or knowledge of the study, and at meetings with the planning director,
he was usually preoccupied with more pressing issues. But the director
did advise him that the work was progressing and assumed that his
representative on the committee did likewise. During 1970 the mayor
was considering a race for the governorship, and some of his attention
may have been diverted from city affairs.

The planning commissioners were also not actively involved in the
early months of the study, although they did pay more attention as time
passed. On December 1, 1970, for example, Commissioner Porter took
time to write a memo reviewing the last preliminary report, commenting on those ideas that she found particularly appealing and one or two
that she did not. In late 1970, members of a planning commission

committee concerned with plan implementation took a strong stand against street vacations and supported restrictive legislation. They also supported an experimental program that was designed to modify residential streets in order to eliminate nonlocal traffic. However, the committee favored a "go slow, wait and see" approach to legislation that would restrict the future height and bulk of buildings. Future events would help to change this position.

Although reporters from the two major dailies had attended some committee meetings, there had been few news stories on the work that had been done to date. The *Street Livability Study* had received a fair amount of coverage, but on the whole there was probably little more public awareness of the study in late 1970 than there had been a year earlier. Nevertheless, public interest in urban design issues continued to grow. In October 1970, the month in which the last two preliminary reports were released, there was a march along the waterfront to protest the U.S. Steel proposal, and on the nineteenth, Alvin Duskin took out another full-page ad in the *San Francisco Chronicle* to object to high-rise development. "Skyscrapers Are Economically Necessary," read the banner, "But Only If You Own One." In November, the Board of Supervisors passed a policy resolution prepared by the planning staff calling for removal of the truncated overhead Embarcadero Freeway and requiring that any new freeway connection to the Golden Gate Bridge be below ground.[13] Later, the supervisors rejected the U.S. Steel proposal in favor of the much lower height limits that originally had been proposed by the planning staff.

The urban design plan that emerged in 1971 provided a definition of design quality for San Francisco. In it was a set of objectives, principles, and policies (including mapped plans) that dealt with the physical and sensory relationships between San Franciscans and their environment.

The "City Pattern" section emphasized the characteristics that give people an image of the city and its neighborhoods. It talked about the relationships of buildings to land and topography, the street system as an orienting and unifying element, landscaping and lighting, open space, and views. The section on "Conservation" was concerned both with preserving unique natural areas, with maintaining the character of distinctive areas, with preserving historic buildings, and with preserv-

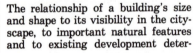

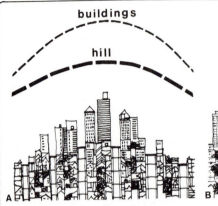

The relationship of a building's size and shape to its visibility in the cityscape, to important natural features and to existing development deter-

mines whether it will have a pleasing or a disruptive effect on the image and character of the city.

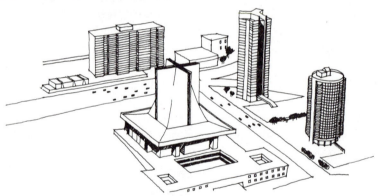

The use of unusual shapes for tall office, hotel or apartment buildings detracts from the clarity of urban form by competing for attention with build-

ings of greater public significance. The juxtaposition of several such unusual shapes may create visual disorder.

**Examples of urban design principles related to new development.**
(From the *Urban Design Plan*.)

ing streets as valuable public open space. The "Major New Development" section included guidelines for the height, bulk, shape, orientation, and color of new buildings. It included policies to discourage accumulation of large parcels unless their development would fit in with the character of the rest of the city. The last section, "Neighborhood Improvement," dealt with all sorts of improvements that would increase neighborhood livability, including ways to limit traffic in residential areas.

All told, the plan proposed four objectives, 86 principles, and 45 policies for the design of San Francisco. It did not include any illustrative plans that would give an architectural expression of what the city might look like at some future date or from which models could be made. The planners concluded that such efforts are usually counterproductive when the main concern is getting a plan adopted and carried out. They felt that models and site plans represented only one physical expression out of the thousands that are possible and desirable, and that too often planners had a vested interest in a particular design. Besides, such models and drawings often made people hostile and suspicious, and they suggested massive, and often arbitrary, public projects that are preceded by condemnation of someone's private property. Too often, the planners felt, the models drew attention from the basic principles and policies that are central to any citywide plan element.

A great deal of thought went into presentation of the study. What was to be presented of all the research, background studies, and rationale for the plan? And how was the plan to be made known to as many people as possible? Merely publishing an attractive study would have used up the short supply of printing funds and would have left the planners one step and months of discussion shy of a final plan that could be adopted. It was unlikely that available funds would have permitted publication of more than 5,000 copies of a quality publication. The staff wanted to present a document that would be adoptable as a part of the master plan. Too many changes in the draft plan would be time-consuming and costly, yet there had to be public review and comment, and that was sure to bring changes.

The decision in the end was to publish a plan in adoptable form, rather than a study with pieces of a plan in it. It had to be attractive and easy to understand, yet in a form and language that could be adopted as a part of the master plan. Background material would have to go in a

Parks on hillsides can be developed for sitting areas with views, and for unusual recreational facilities that take advantage of the hill, such as a long slide for children.

In areas where houses have no front yards, a sense of nature can be provided by planting in the sidewalk area.

**Examples of urban design principles related to neighborhood environment.**
(From the *Urban Design Plan.*)

short section that could introduce or conclude the plan. Peter Svirsky, the best writer in the department and a lawyer with a dozen years of planning experience was to edit the final text. He had participated in the work. A decision was also made to present the plan to civic leaders with some splash via a multiscreen slide show. The show would take place at a central location that would then be opened for continuous public viewing. Dick Hedman was to orchestrate that presentation. These decisions were being made as 1970 came to a close. It would take five months to carry them out.

During the period immediately prior to publication of the plan, the high-rise issue was heating up.[14] By getting nearly 30,000 signatures, Alvin Duskin had managed to get his first initiative to limit the height of buildings on the ballot in the fall of 1971. The issue that people would be voting on was whether all future buildings should be limited to six stories, or 72 feet. Partially in response to Duskin's proposal, but also as a consequence of recent fights over major development projects, studies were being proposed by the San Francisco Planning and Urban Renewal Association and others to assess the costs and benefits of high-rise construction or, as some put it, to determine the effects of "Manhattanization." On May 18, the Planning and Development Committee of the Board of Supervisors held a hearing on the Duskin initiative and the desirability of studies related to the height issue. In his testimony, the planning director used the opportunity to let people know that the urban design plan, which would be released in two days, would address the issue.

On May 20, 1971, the urban design plan was presented to an invited audience that included the mayor, members of the planning commission, the advisory committee, department heads, and officers of neighborhood associations throughout the city. The supervisors were invited, but only two or three bothered to attend. The four-projector, three-screen presentation was an immediate success. Press coverage was excellent, and by Sunday, after three more presentations, standing-room audiences cheered at the conclusion of each showing. Some people came a second time. An estimated 1,300 people attended the initial four presentations. Copies of the plan were given out free at the showings.

In June and July, public presentations of the plan were made to neighborhood and citywide organizations. The response was good, whether the presentation was to a large neighborhood audience in the

Sunset district or to a downtown luncheon meeting of the prestigious Blyth-Zellerback Committee, arranged by Commissioner Fleishhacker. There was an equally favorable response from over 100 people and organizations who provided written comments or who spoke at the three public hearings held in July or August. Although many minor changes would be made as a result of the hearings, the testimony was not so much concerned with the substance of the plan as it was with implementation. Many people seemed to be saying, "Well of course, but what are you going to do about it? What are you, the commission and staff, going to do to make the plan a reality?" There was a ring of challenge to their words.

The city planners had given a great deal of thought to the question of implementation. The last section of the urban design plan publication, called "Implementing the Plan," contained a checklist of the major actions that would have to be carried out, primarily by public agencies. An answer to the question of where to start was suggested by the progress of Duskin's height initiative. Peter Svirsky suggested immediate action to control, citywide, the height and bulk of buildings. The idea was for the staff to make a formal proposal, to which the commission would agree formally, to hold hearings on zoning proposals that would reflect the plan's height and bulk guidelines. The staff would then be given about six months to prepare specific zoning standards and maps. This proposed action, if taken (by adoption of a simple resolution by the commission), would have the effect of putting the height and bulk guidelines of the plan into immediate force as interim legal standards.

Seven months earlier the planning commissioners had favored a "go slow" policy for legislation to control building height and bulk. In August, possibly due to the favorable reception of the urban design plan, they were much more positive. Fleishhacker accepted the idea immediately. Commission President Walter Newman was inclined to approval, but he wanted time to consider the idea, and he wanted to know how other commissioners felt. Only Julia Porter expressed strong misgivings. She was concerned about the rapidity of the proposed action, but she was willing to go along with the rest of the commissioners, and they seemed ready to accept the idea.

At what seemed to the planning director to be the last minute, Newman said that such a major action as interim citywide height and bulk controls should not be taken without the knowledge and approval

of Mayor Alioto. The director, who was then on good terms with Alioto, was nevertheless fearful that the mayor would not approve the action. He, however, was in no position to oppose a meeting. Newman arranged it for the morning of August 26, the same day that the commission was scheduled to take action on the plan and to pass its resolution on the interim controls.

Alioto expressed all sorts of reservation about the proposal. He questioned its legality and the need for such speed. He was worried about the response of labor leaders and about the major developments that might be stopped. Finally, he questioned the need for such an action in the first place. The response was that the action had been found in accord with the law, that it was a step toward implementation of a plan that the mayor himself had praised, that it would provide a meaningful response to the Duskin initiative, that little or no effect on jobs and labor was anticipated, and that it might help stop confrontations over major building proposals. The director added that a long public discussion before interim controls were established would invite a rash of building applications, and if these were filed before the commission acted, the purpose of the legislation would be negated. The discussion went back and forth for about two hours, with no firm decision. Shortly after noon, with the mayor hurrying off to a meeting, Newman asked to see him alone for a minute. He emerged to advise the director that if they informed two labor leaders and got no opposition from them, the mayor would approve the action.

Newman spoke to one of the labor representatives; the director talked to the other, by phone. They had never spoken before. After the director briefly explained the impending action and assured him that the effect on jobs would be minimal, the labor leader asked what would happen, by way of example, to one or two specific properties on Mission Street. He seemed satisfied with the answers.

That afternoon, almost three years after the urban design study started and four years after the staff started developing the idea, the planning commission adopted the urban design plan as part of the city's master plan. In a separate action that was not anticipated by the public, the commissioners took the first step toward implementing the plan by putting in force interim controls on the height and bulk of buildings.

Passage of the urban design plan did not in itself solve any of San Francisco's design-related issues or conflicts. A plan can respond to issues but it cannot solve them any more than house plans provide shelter or full-employment policies provide jobs. Solutions come from the decisions and actions that stem from the documents. The plan addressed issues of height and views, but its adoption by the planning commission did not create low buildings or preserve views. On the other hand, the interim controls did limit height, at least temporarily, and they were possible only because there was a plan to work from. The plan provided a basis for choosing among the various alternatives in a given situation and a framework for considering the probable consequences of any action. That is what city planning is supposed to do; it is the city planning process at work.

It is not our purpose here to provide a critique of the plan or to assess its effectiveness in solving immediate and long-range issues and in directing San Francisco's development to desired ends. We can, however, describe briefly some of the uses to which the plan has been put.

The legislative actions taken by the Board of Supervisors to carry out the urban design plan have been notable. We will see that permanent legislation to replace the interim height and bulk standards was passed with dispatch. In 1972 legislation was passed to establish the old, small-scaled, largely brick Jackson Square area immediately adjacent to downtown as an historic district in conformance with the plan. By 1973 there was an ordinance to assure that overhead building projections into public rights-of-way would produce bona fide bay windows consistent with San Francisco traditions and not simple floor-area bonuses for developers. The interim residential zoning controls passed in late 1973 drew heavily from the urban design plan in regard to front and rear yard building setbacks and off-street parking requirements.

Public design review of private building projects falls within the realm of public regulation of private property. The California Environmental Quality Act of 1970 led to the requirement of environmental impact reports for all significant private and public projects. This meant that proposed projects would have to be checked against the environmental plans of local communities; in the case of San Francisco, the urban design plan. By 1975, the planning department's project review section was using the urban design plan as a design manual for review of some 100 projects each year.[15] In all these cases the planners were in a strategic position to help implement their plan.

By 1977, the plan had been less successful in influencing direct public actions than in regulating private development. The mid-1970s were not noted for significant activities in the way of public improvement projects of any kind in San Francisco. Redevelopment had slowed, as had urban beautification, code enforcement, and rehabilitation programs. There were no major road projects. In the face of mounting costs, fewer major public building projects were undertaken. In the mid-1970s the plan's influence seems to have been limited to a few small neighborhood projects, designed in accordance with the protected residential areas concept to limit and control auto traffic and provide small, landscaped play and sitting areas. The largest of the projects, which was under construction control of the the Department of Public Works, took some two years to get started after it was approved and its funding assured. By that time new participants with different views helped bring substantial reduction in the project's scope. In regard to the plan's influence or noninfluence on public projects, it will be recalled that the heads of the major operating departments, though invited, did not participate significantly in the plan's preparation. They were not committed to the results of that work.[16] On a more positive note, various neighborhood groups have drawn heavily on the plan in doing their own plans. In 1977, designers of a major new sewer construction project indicated that they were sensitive to the urban design policies and principles that were incorporated in the plan. The plan also served as a major input to other master plan elements, most notably in the areas of transportation, recreation and open space, and conservation. Both the background studies and the plan itself are reflected in later work.

The urban design plan came at a time when there was a rediscovery in California of comprehensive planning as a basis for decisions about development and preservation. In 1968, when work on the urban design study started, state laws had prescribed three elements for local master plans. By late 1971, nine elements had been mandated. It is unlikely that San Francisco would have prepared an urban design plan to address concerns held to be important locally had the planners not started the work when they did.

The plan is significant as an educational document; it was widely distributed and apparently widely read. Following its adoption it was quoted in detail by citizens at public meetings to support or to oppose all sorts of planning proposals and new projects. It proved to be a worthwhile aid to citizens in helping to determine the kind of community they wanted.

A problem with all of this lay in the propensity to view the urban design plan as synonymous with the master plan. People forgot, or never knew, that city planning was more than urban design, that an element dealing with housing had been passed and was at least as important, and that elements covering such matters as transportation, open space, public facilities and services, commerce and industry, seismic safety, and changes to citywide land-use plans would be forthcoming. The city planners were aware that such misunderstandings have often led to charges that city planning is an elitist concern. But, on the whole, in late 1971, the planners might be excused the feeling of satisfaction that comes with widespread acceptance of their work.

This account of the preparation and adoption of the urban design plan gives rise to a number of observations and questions: What if urban design had not been the public issue that it was? Would that mean that no urban design plan should have been undertaken, or if attempted, might not have been successful? Did the location of the planning department under a semi-autonomous commission have a significant bearing on the preparation of the plan and on its nature? Would a plan be more oriented toward public works and projects if it were prepared in a mayor's office, or under the legislative body? Would the plan have been significantly different if prepared in conjunction with other elements, or with greater citizen participation? In what ways could the planning department have attracted greater participation by representatives of other departments, and would such participation have insured greater commitment to a final plan? Could the advisory committee have played a stronger role in the process?

As interesting as a pursuit of these questions may be, we are more concerned here in pinpointing the reasons for the plan's successful completion, widespread acceptance, adoption, and early uses. Such an assessment was made by Peter Svirsky in the article quoted earlier, and it will be expanded upon here.[17]

From the beginning, the planners had some general idea of what they wanted to end up with. This may sound obvious, but it is not always true. Knowing what you want means having a work program and budget and trying to stay with them. It would have been easy to run out of time, money, and staff and have no place to go.

Both the plan and proposals for implementation were based on a detailed, step-by-step study done in a professional manner. Study methods were documented and recorded. The preliminary reports were impressive in their detail and thus helped to add legitimacy to the final product. The quiet, unpublicized, back-burner nature of some of the early studies and research was probably important: there were minimal external pressures to produce one thing or another and the planners were permitted to feel their way.

If a good professional job has been done all along, community people are likely to respect the work. They will be more prepared to act on it if there are no major gaps in information and knowledge. Professional competence did not go unnoticed by the community. The department was also aided by the fact that its staff had experience in both policy planning and practical zoning administration. This range permitted considerable interchange of knowledge and experience and resulted in many proposals that could be implemented in straightforward ways.

The urban design plan was prepared with the intention that its policies would be carried out. It included a list of measures to be taken to implement the policies, and one preliminary report was devoted entirely to implementation. Throughout the study period, two questions were asked over and over again: "How would you carry it out?" and "How realistic is the proposal in terms of its being implemented?" This does not mean that no proposal could or should be made without a surefire way of carrying it out. It does mean thinking continually about means of achieving desired ends.

It was important to focus on the plan as a policy document. Specific project designs might have diverted attention from the debate about visual aspects of the environment. Even detailed examples of ways to divert or slow neighborhood traffic were placed in a policy context. As controversies over such matters as the Duskin initiative and individual building proposals continued, the plan was quoted, misquoted, and ridiculed. But it was also given symbolic importance by many and, most important, it was *used* as a basis for one or another position. The public was aware of the policy-setting role of the plan and indicated an expectation that it would be implemented.

Timeliness, public awareness, and understanding of the political climate, and a recognition of opportunities and willingness to use them—all were important to the plan's adoption and to early measures toward implementation. The planners were aware of the nature of the times, and they were convinced that urban design was an issue in 1967. Their plan emerged as public concern peaked. This does not mean that plan preparation would have been a meaningless effort had the timing been less fortunate and awareness less developed. Other times (and other places) with less, or more, public awareness and with different participants would have dictated other approaches to the design of the city. In this case, a responsive and a soundly based set of policies was at hand, to be adopted and implemented when the time was right. What if there had been no plan at this time? The city planners were ready.

Timing was important to the reception of the urban design plan and to its early adoption. There is no assurance that in the future, planners, commissioners, elected officials, or community residents will look as kindly on this plan as those who were present during its early years. But it now exists and must be dealt with. and there is every indication that the plan will indeed be used as a guide for a great variety of design decisions about the city's future.

# Notes

1. The "urban design plan" became the urban design element of the San Francisco master plan upon adoption by the city planning commission on August 26, 1971. The plan was published by the San Francisco Department of City Planning in May 1971. The complete title is *The Urban Design Plan for the Comprehensive Plan of San Francisco.*

2. San Francisco Department of City Planning, "Descriptive Summary of the Proposed Urban Design Study and Plan for the City and County of San Francisco," February 26, 1968, p. 1.

3. San Francisco City Planning Commission minutes of August 22, 1968, Conditional Use 68.20, Resolution 6255.

4. Student Land-Use Group, University of California, Berkeley, "Position Paper on Land Use," May 6, 1976.

5. *Urban Design Plan*, p. 3. See also Kevin Lynch, "City Design and City Appearance," in W. J. Goodman and Eric C. Freund, eds., *Principles and Practice of Urban Planning* (Washington, D.C.: International City Managers Association, 1968, pp. 249-76.)

6. Daniel H. Burnham, *Report on a Plan for San Francisco* (San Francisco: Sunset Press, 1905).

7. See Lynch, "City Design and City Appearance," p. 249, for a discussion of the kinds of design that are a part of city development.

8. San Francisco Department of City Planning, "Descriptive Summary of the Proposed Urban Design Study and Plan for the City and County of San Francisco," February 26, 1968, p. 3.

9. Arthur D. Little, *San Francisco Community Renewal Program,* October 1965.

10. Letter from San Francisco City Planning Commission President William Brinton to David Mayes, a landscape architect on the committee.

11. Kevin Lynch, *The Image of the City* (Cambridge: Technology Press and Harvard University Press, 1960).

12. "San Francisco Limits the Buildings to See the Sky," *Planning*, January 1973, p. 10. Peter Svirsky is a lawyer and planner who was on the staff of the San Francisco Department of City Planning.

13. San Francisco Board of Supervisors Resolution 673-70, November 9, 1970. See also Jerry Burns, "Tough City Stand on a Freeway," *San Francisco Chronicle*, November 10, 1970.

14. Svirsky, "San Francisco Limits the Buildings," pp. 10-11. Also see Patrick J. Hern, "Reclaiming the Urban Environment: the San Francisco Urban Design Plan," *Ecology Law Quarterly*, vol. 3, 1973, p. 539. For a partisan description of major planning controversies, see Bruce Brugmann and Greggar Sletteland, eds., *The Ultimate Highrise: San Francisco's Mad Rush Toward the Sky* (San Francisco: San Francisco Bay Guardian Books, 1971).

15. Dean L. Macris, "Design Review Process,"memo to San Francisco City Planning Commission, March 13, 1975. Macris was then city planning director.

16. To some extent, the relative success of the legislative efforts to carry out the urban design plan as opposed to the limited success of programs and actions requiring more direct public action was determined by the nature of the plan and the people who prepared it. In this regard, the urban design plan can be contrasted with the Boston General Plan of 1965, an urban design-inspired plan. The Boston plan has a strong orientation toward public projects and improvements. It places some dependency upon a "capital web" to shape the city and to influence future development. It was prepared in an era of large and expensive federally funded redevelopment projects by the staff of the Boston Redevelopment Authority. Direct public design or control of projects could thus be anticipated. The San Francisco plan was oriented

more to citywide policies and principles than to the design specifics of public works. It was concerned with the process of all development and with moderating private development, which the planners could not design themselves. An orientation toward influence and legislation, matters that could be controlled by the San Francisco planners, is therefore understandable. To contrast the Boston and San Francisco plans, see Boston Redevelopment Authority, *1965/1975 General Plan for the City of Boston and the Regional Core*, March 1965.

17. Svirsky, "San Francisco Limits the Buildings."

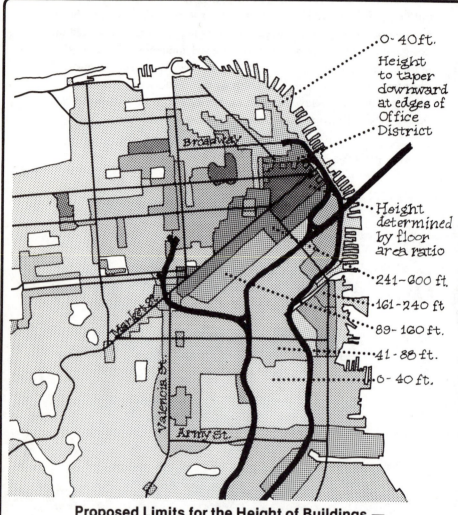

**Proposed Limits for the Height of Buildings —
From the *Urban Design Plan***

NOTE: These proposed policies became much more
specific in terms of location and height as they became
requirements of the height and bulk ordinance. For example, the downtown area with no specific height limit in the
urban design plan became smaller and was given a maximum height of 700 feet.

# Chapter 9
# Case Study: The Height and
# Bulk Ordinance

On August 26, 1971, the San Francisco City Planning Commission adopted the urban design plan as an element of the master plan. It also passed a resolution to hold future hearings on zoning proposals that would reflect the plan's guidelines for limiting the height and bulk of the city's buildings. That resolution had the effect of turning these guidelines into interim law, pending more precise standards. Acting on the suggestion of the planning staff, the commission directed that a draft of a comprehensive, citywide height and bulk ordinance be completed in six months.

This sequence of events is consistent with the way that city planning is "supposed" to work. It is a classical approach to city planning, which envisions a plan for the future physical development of a city, to be followed by an array of programs, specific public actions, and legislation, including zoning, that is geared to achievement of the plan. The zoning laws are supposed to ensure that private development and use of property are at least consistent with the plan.

Things do not always work the way they are supposed to, at least not as far as zoning is concerned. Zoning ordinances often are passed without reference to any explicit plan for the physical development of a community. They have regularly been passed well before any plan has even been thought of. The ordinances may, of course, be helping to carry out some set of unstated physical or social objectives; for instance, they may restrict the community to certain types of people. But that is neither city planning nor plan implementation in the sense we are speaking of here. Even when a city has a master plan, there may be no zoning geared to its achievement, simply because not enough people are interested or because they are opposed to what has been proposed. Sometimes the prospect of zoning legislation evokes more response than the prospect of a commission adopting a new policy, especially if the former is perceived as changing people's property rights. People show up at zoning hearings who never come to plan presentations, with the result that it is more difficult to pass zoning laws.

There are other reasons that citywide zoning ordinances are not always consistent with, related to, or even prepared to carry out city plans. Ordinances may be adopted piecemeal, by geographic area (a specific part of a town), or by subject matter (pornographic book stores) to respond to specific issues in specific areas. Before 1972 San Francisco had as many as 20 special height districts spotted around town.

Further, in many cities, zoning ordinances differ from plans because the two are prepared and administered by different people, not always with the same interests or points of view. Often the length of time required to enact an ordinance is so great that when it is passed, in a form and substance significantly different from when it started, it is no longer relevant to the city planning issues that were being addressed originally. And so much inconsistent development may have taken place during the long period before enactment that the law, once passed, is meaningless. In San Francisco a comprehensive zoning revision that reached the first draft stage in 1948 was not passed until late 1959 and then only after many rounds of changes. For these reasons if for no others, many city planners have wanted little to do with zoning, concluding that it is negative, ineffective at best, and, considering what it is likely to achieve, incredibly time- and energy-consuming.

The staff of the planning department was mindful of the pitfalls, hurdles, and potentially fruitless conclusion of a major zoning effort. The planners also were a bit enervated from the effort of preparing and presenting the urban design plan. Nevertheless, they undertook preparation of a citywide height and bulk ordinance with some relish. The timing seemed right, and it would be a major step toward carrying out the plan. The effort was certain to involve most of those skills and community forces that together constitute the city planning process in a major city: extensive professional work at the staff level; use and testing of the legislative process of government as it is related to city planning; public and not-so-public participation of citizens and interest groups; the politics of city planning; and, timing, or fortune.

The Transamerica case provided an opportunity to examine an ad hoc development issue in relation to the substance of city planning as well as to test the effectiveness of the city planning process in dealing with an individual development issue. The height and bulk ordinance gives us an opportunity to look at the preparation of zoning legislation as a tool to help carry out a city plan, the purpose of zoning as viewed by city planners. It also permits an assessment of the effectiveness of the city planning process in relation to legislation that affects all development, not just an individual development proposal such as Transamerica.

In exploring the case we will be concerned with answers to a number of questions: How did the planning department respond to the task of preparing an ordinance to deal with the height and bulk of buildings? To what extent was the work related to the urban design plan? What, if any, role did the official governmental process associated with city planning play in determining the outcome of the issue? Who were the most relevant actors and what roles did they play? How was the matter resolved? Did the classic notion of a plan followed by zoning to help carry it out work in practice? Is the city in a better position to deal with individual development proposals than it was previously? It is not always easy to separate such matters as professional work, the process of government, and the role of key actors in the politics of government. But we will try to do so to the extent that it seems useful, starting with the response of the department's staff to the task of answering the commission's request for a citywide height and bulk ordinance.

The buildup of the effort was gradual and deliberate, even though time was short and an immense amount of work would be required before a draft height and bulk ordinance, together with zoning maps, could be placed before the commission. Key staffers needed vacations. Others wanted to see the outcome of the soon-to-be-voted-upon initiative to limit all city buildings to 72 feet, or six stories, before starting full steam on their own ordinance. Almost 30,000 people had signed petitions to get the initiative on the ballot. If this measure passed, then the planners' effort might be wasted. Also, some major building proposals that did not conform to the interim controls had to be heard by the commission, and these began to consume considerable staff time.

Work on the ordinance would be handled differently from that for the urban design plan. The plan had been in the hands of a team of urban designers aided by other staff members and consultants. The zoning staff had made significant contributions, primarily in relation to implementation measures. This time, however, the assignments would be reversed. The zoning people, headed by Peter Svirsky, would direct the team preparing the ordinance. The zoning team would be aided by the urban designers who had worked on the plan.

The height and bulk guidelines established in the urban design plan provided the starting point and constant reference points for the ordinance. Without them and all the work that had preceded them, it is doubtful that an ordinance could have gotten started. These guidelines related building size to topographic form, activity centers, view protection, and the established scale of structures in each part of the city. Overwhelmingly, the plan called for the height of buildings to be low throughout the city, no higher than 40 feet, reflecting the existing pattern.

There were to be exceptions, however. The guidelines called for tall buildings, unlimited in height, to be clustered in and around downtown, in a hill form, to reflect but be separate from the natural topography of the city. Tall buildings were also called for on some of the hilltops, on Nob and Russian hills for instance, to emphasize hill forms and to safeguard views. Buildings up to 240 feet tall would be allowed at a few highly accessible centers of activity, such as rapid transit stations in busy commercial areas. The guidelines associated height with efficiency of commercial activity (primarily downtown) and also with a desire to avoid commercial encroachment upon other areas.

Buildings of smaller scale were to be located at the base of hills and in the valleys between them. Where existing hilltop development was low, or where hills were capped with open spaces, new buildings would also remain low to preserve the natural slope of the hill and to maintain public views. Building heights were to taper down to the shoreline of the bay and ocean. The guidelines for height were expressed in ranges that would be appropriate for each area. The bulk guidelines were related to the prevailing scale of development in each area to avoid an overwhelming or dominating appearance in new construction. Wherever greater height was to be permitted, the guidelines clearly sought to achieve slender buildings.

The planners would have to go beyond the guidelines, however.

They would need more detailed studies, and they would have to consider refinements and take new factors into account. For example, the boundaries of existing zoning land-use districts established by earlier commissions and ordinances would have to be considered. The use districts were not to be changed. Height and bulk districts would follow the use district boundaries where this made sense but that would not always be the case. Consequently, a separate set of overlay zoning maps for height and bulk was dictated. Existing buildings whose height violated a norm or was contrary to plan proposals were located and mapped lot by lot; the maps would help the planners to determine final height limitations and to know what exceptions would result from proposals being considered. Development projects already approved but not yet under construction were also mapped. The planners did not want to be accused of trying arbitrarily to stop construction that had already been approved, and they wanted to be aware of the possible consequences of their actions upon imminent projects. Plans that had been approved by the Redevelopment Agency were reviewed to see which development was fixed by agency contracts and which was not and could therefore be controlled by a new ordinance. Ultimately, there would be extended negotiations with the agency over a number of sites.

Both the department's neighborhood plans and master plan elements already approved or in preparation also had to be reviewed to assure that the zoning proposals would accord with them. As much of all this information as possible was put on detailed maps in order to call attention to possible inconsistencies and problems, and to serve as a basis for future decisions. Decisions on all these matters, including what new studies to undertake, were made in the director's office.

Staff planners involved in neighborhood planning were asked to inquire in their neighborhoods as to whether or not special sentiments existed in regard to building height. Over the years, testimony at zoning hearings had been another source of information as to neighborhood feelings. If particular points of view existed and were known, they were noted, but this did not mean such sentiments automatically would be reflected in the draft proposals.

Staff people were constantly admonished not to second-guess what would be accepted by neighborhoods or the public at large and not to take positions either more or less restrictive than they thought correct in anticipation of changes that might be voted after full public debate.

This meant that a good case had to be made before changes in the basic nature of the guidelines in the plan would be made. As Peter Svirsky pointed out in his article on the ordinance, refinements to the guidelines usually lowered the height to be permitted.[1]

In both the urban design plan and the interim controls, the height guidelines were in the form of ranges. Within these ranges, considerable private and public discretion would be possible. Now the staff was to propose that the height limits be precisely defined in 27 separate height districts. The numerical limits to height and the break points between districts would be based on existing building heights, breaks in height set for various construction materials in the San Francisco Building Code, historical precedent, and the criteria established by the urban design plan.

For example, a special height district with a limit of 105 feet had existed for many years in one area of Pacific Heights. No one was quite sure where that precise figure had come from, but buildings had been built to that height. There would be no proposal forthcoming to change the limit. In parts of the downtown and on Nob Hill, no height limits were outlined in the urban design plan. Now, height limits would be proposed for both areas, graduating upward from about 300 feet at the edges of the main downtown office area to a maximum of 700 feet for a small seven-block section at the center and emphasizing the contours of Nob Hill in the same manner but at a lower scale. This would mean that buildings the height of the Bank of America (778 feet) and Transamerica (853 feet) structures would no longer be permitted, especially in their off-center locations. Downtown, detailed studies of the areas around plazas were undertaken to assure that new buildings would not block out the sun.

The planners felt themselves to be especially vulnerable in regard to the bulk guidelines set forth in the plan. Originally, these guidelines had been based on careful inspection and measurement of all major large buildings and on the design judgments of the staff and of the architects on the Urban Design Citizens Advisory Committee. They had spotted buildings that looked excessively bulky in the San Francisco cityscape and noted at what height their bulk became noticeable in relation to surrounding buildings. Alternative methods of measuring bulk had been tested, but even more than with height, the judgment of the design professionals was central to any proposed limitations. What concerned the planners most was the relatively severe floor size limits that could result from their proposals and the objections that might come from developers of big office and apartment buildings. Some office developers were looking to buildings with large floors, in some cases more than an acre (about 43,000 square feet). The city planners were thinking in terms of from 20,000 to 30,000 square feet per floor.

Help came from the local American Institute of Architects committee that the city planners were working with. Some of the architects had commented that their role in the design of the big new office buildings had been replaced in large measure by the computer, usually in the hands of developers and their non-designer agents, which could be used to determine efficient column sizes and spacings, elevator and utility locations, and just about everything else about a building except skin treatment and detailed interior design. One of those architects, from a prestigious office, had ready access to a computer and could test the economic viability of the controls being considered by the department. His conclusion was that, while the proposals that the planners had come up with would not always maximize profits to builders, they would permit economical buildings. Armed with that information and with assurances of public support by the architect, the planning director and his staff prepared to draw up the restrictive limits. Nevertheless, they expected to do battle with real estate and building interests when the proposals became public.

Most public lands, federal and state as well as local, are zoned "public use" in San Francisco's zoning ordinance, partly because the city does not have jurisdiction over properties controlled by higher levels of government and partly because zoning traditionally has been used to control the use of private but not public land. In spite of this, the planners decided to have a shot at placing some controls on the considerable amount of public property in San Francisco. It was decided to designate much of the vacant land owned by governmental agencies as "open space" with *no* height permitted except under very special circumstances. This way the land would be safeguarded against development.

Specific height and bulk limits were proposed for other federal and state properties. These proposals required lengthy negotiations with representatives of any number of agencies. The intent was clear: even if San Francisco had no legal jurisdiction over lands held by other levels of government, and even if the planning department was not always successful in establishing zoning controls over lands in the domain of other city departments, as long as the other departments recognized and agreed in public to the restrictions that were proposed, they would be setting a precedent for accepting some local city planning jurisdiction in the future.

The staff also had to attend to the matter of drafting text provisions for the new ordinance, including detailed instructions for measuring height. Measurement would be particularly difficult on sloping sites, and in some cases, height would have to be stepped down (or up) across a steeply sloping site so that buildings of reasonable height at one edge of a site would not be too high at the other extremity. There would also have to be specifications for all the rooftop features that would be exempt from height limits; mechanical equipment, for instance, and chimneys in industrial areas. The controls related to bulk were difficult to draft. They had to be tested repeatedly with drawings and field surveys to determine whether they would achieve the desired ends.

An early decision was made to write height and bulk controls that were precise and nondiscretionary, in part to minimize the possibility of appeals to the Board of Permit Appeals. Historically, the decisions of that body had favored development interests when they conflicted with city planning requirements. The board had been known to hear and decide cases that the city attorney held were beyond its jurisdiction. Among other things, the final ordinance would specifically prohibit the consideration of any variances from the limits established by the height and bulk districts; any change in those limits would be a legislative measure requiring action by the city planning commission and Board of Supervisors. (The wording of that final ordinance, section 305 [a] of the city planning code is specific: "No variance shall be granted in whole or in part which would have an effect substantially equivalent to a reclassification of property; or which would permit . . . any height or bulk of a building or structure . . . not expressly permitted by the provisions of this code for the district or districts in which the property in question is located.")

The text of the ordinance would have to be almost perfect when it was first presented so that the controls would be easily understood and so that public attention could focus on the general nature of the height and bulk proposals rather than on the details of the drafting. The Duskin height initiative forces had made a drafting error in preparing their legislation, inadvertently raising height limits in single family areas from 35 and 40 feet to 72 feet. They were furious when the department's

A long or wide building becomes excessively bulky in apperance when its height significantly exceeds that of buildings in the surrounding area.

Bulky buildings that intrude upon or block important views of the Bay, Ocean or other significant citywide focal points are particularly disruptive.

Examples of bulk principles of the *Urban Design Plan* that were incorporated into the height and bulk ordinance.

planners made this error public, but it was too late for them to make a correction. It is not known just how the error and attention called to it affected the vote in the November initiative.

How much discretion would be placed in the hands of the planners (including the commission) in administering the ordinance? The question arose many times during the early months of preparation. During the 1960s and early 1970s, American cities relied increasingly on one or another form of discretion in the hands of city planning bodies in administering zoning laws. This was done, in part, to contend with special situations, to permit flexibility, and to achieve better designs than would be possible if strict zoning regulations were applied. Planning agencies might be accused of being arbitrary in turning down some projects but in special circumstances they were able to grant exceptions through conditional use or parallel procedures. The planned unit development and bonus provisions of some ordinances fall into this category, including those in common use in New York City.[2]

However, experience in San Francisco had shown the dangers of holding out the possibility of increased height and more intense development. There had been too many confrontations on building projects. The city planners thought that it was better to require rezoning actions for any height change. Cases that arose soon after the interim controls had been put into effect seemed to verify this conclusion.

An application for a large Holiday Inn near Russian Hill, a building whose height and bulk far exceeded the guidelines of the urban design plan, had been submitted prior to the planning commission's adoption of the interim controls. Thus, the controls had no legal effect on the application, since it was on file prior to the commission's resolution. The building was vigorously opposed by public and planners alike, and the latter recommended that the commission turn down the proposal under its power of discretionary review (which is discussed in chapter 7). But the commissioners were under significant pressure from the developers, and on September 16, 1971, they approved the building.[3] One immediate result of this action was the resignation of ten members of the Urban Design Citizens Advisory Committee, an action provoked by the San Francisco Planning and Urban Renewal Association. Almost immediately, SPUR filed a law suit—unsuccessfully—to stop construction.

Another case was centered on Russian Hill itself, an area for which the staff had suggested a special district with some discretion to permit a limited number of taller buildings. A Kansas City developer, William C. Haas, proposed a project—"Haas Towers"—that would exceed the height and bulk guidelines of the urban design plan. Ultimately, after a long, well-attended, and spirited public hearing, and over the strong objections of both residents and the staff, this project, too, was approved by a split vote of the planning commission.[4] Such cases would have an effect on the final proposals for Russian Hill, but more important, they convinced the planners that they and the commission should be given very little discretion regarding the administration of any height limits.

If imperfect drafting of an ordinance hurt the Duskin height limit initiative, approval of the Holiday Inn and Russian Hill proposals boosted its chances. So did the fact that other high buildings, most of them downtown, had been rushed through by developers to avoid the initiative. Some people were upset because such buildings had been approved (and had received publicity) after the plan had been adopted (even though most of them met the new height guidelines), and thus the whole plan was looked at with some skepticism. Grandfather provisions in zoning are hard to explain to a questioning public that easily forgets that previously there were no controls at all. Although the planners doubted that Duskin's initiative would pass when it was first put on the ballot—it made little sense to them, especially when compared to their own approach—they began to have second thoughts, as new large buildings were approved despite public outcry against them.

The planners might have been growing more concerned about the possible passage of Proposition T, the Duskin initiative. But the chamber of commerce seemed worried to death. It was reported to have spent some $500,000 opposing the measure. This amount included the cost of professionally prepared surveys designed to determine the extent of public support and call attention to the negative consequences of such a vote.[5] In order to lower its own profile, the chamber is reported to have formed a citizens' committee to fight the initiative. Jo Henderson, a member of the earlier design plan committee was asked to serve as cochairman. At one point, perhaps sensing a need to be for something that was better than Duskin's Proposition T, rather than to be merely in opposition, the chamber endorsed the idea of height controls as approached by the planning department.[6] The planners would not quickly forget these positive words, nor would they permit the chamber to forget. In the meantime, the chamber could relax. On November 2, 1971, Proposition T made a respectable showing at the polls but lost with only 30 per cent of the vote.

One week later, on November 9, the planning director was visited by Walter Haas, Jr., president of the locally based Levi Strauss Company and no relation to the Kansas City developer referred to earlier. Haas, who was accompanied by his public affairs director, noted that he had just spent a considerable sum helping the chamber defeat Proposition T. He went on to say that he felt this was a wasteful way to be spending money and that the approach of the planning department made a lot more sense. He wanted to know what he could do to help. Elated, the director asked only that Haas spread the good word among his downtown business associates and possibly arrange a lunch with them, the director, and key members of the planning commission. Haas agreed, though no lunch was ever actually requested. The planning director sensed that he may have missed the boat in not asking for more, but he was feeling better all the time about the prospects of an ordinance.

With the Duskin defeat, the pace of the work in the planning department quickened. More staff time was spent on the proposed ordinance. Between early November and mid-February the director's appointment calendar shows at least 20 meetings on this matter with staff members and commissioners. Usually these meetings took the form of progress reports and discussions of policy questions raised by Peter Svirsky. Often they became long working sessions in the director's office, where detailed decisions were made, sometimes lot by lot, on the nature of the proposals that were recommended.

With the new year, the chamber of commerce and downtown business and development interests seemed to discover that the planning department really was working on an ordinance and that it would soon be made public. Like most people, they did not know what would be in it or how it would affect them. They wanted to participate. Up to this point, the staff had worked only with the American Institute of Architects committee. At a January 12 meeting with Ed Lawson of the chamber, the staff explained that the ordinance would follow the urban design plan, which Lawson had helped prepare as a member of the earlier committee, and that the strict time schedule would not allow full-scale public participation in its preparation. However, there would be plenty of time for public debate when a draft was made public. Lawson was not terribly pleased with this approach, and soon after the director began to hear rumblings from some of the commissioners about the need for participation.

On January 20, the planning director, Svirsky, and three commissioners met at lunch with representatives of downtown interests. They said they wanted to participate in developing the controls and that they had a technical advisory committee to help. Richard Loughlin, representing some of the downtown interests, indicated that they would act together. He was concerned that the staff was using only aesthetics and not economics as a standard for an ordinance. William Dauer of the chamber was concerned that the staff and commission had too much discretion; he wanted developers to know clearly what they could and could not do. Commissioner Fleishhacker was rather testy in defense of the staff. Commissioner Newman, trying to smooth the waters, noted that there would be fixed limits. He said that he thought that all firmly committed downtown projects would fit within the forthcoming ordinance. The director reviewed the department's legal obligations, stated the need for speed, and suggested another meeting in his office at which he could review in greater detail what they were doing. He suggested that the group should put its concerns on paper. He also said that he would under no circumstances show the group the draft maps of the proposed districts, since that would constitute improper premature disclosure. The maps and ordinance would have to be released to the entire public at one time.

On the same afternoon, at a meeting of the planning commission, Commissioner John Ritchie, who had been present earlier, accused the staff and particularly the director of trying to act as dictators on development issues and of exercising too much control over major projects. On the previous Thursday, Ritchie had voted, against the staff's recommendation, to approve the large apartments on Russian Hill. His was a key vote. On Tuesday, that vote had been criticized by columnist Herb Caen in the *Chronicle*. One newspaper, the *Examiner*, would soon echo Richie's cry editorially, and the director would have meetings with editorial writers to try to undo the damage.[7] It was important that there be no major fights before the anticipated publication of the draft ordinance on February 17, less than a month away.

Some staff efforts had already focused on upcoming public hearings. A citywide rezoning such as this required that notices be mailed to all property owners, some 150,000, and that a full-page legal advertisement be placed in one of the newspapers. The $14,000 it would take to do this required a special appropriation from the Board of Supervisors, and the staff wondered how its request would be received. But the supervisors responded favorably and even expressed some impatience.

As February 17 approached, the planners met with the commissioners to advise them of what was coming, including the hearings that were to follow. The planners impressed upon the commissioners the importance of their passing a resolution to have the new proposals supplant the former interim controls. The time to debate the validity of these proposals, the staff held, was during the public hearing process. The commission agreed and on February 17, after the staff presented the proposed permanent height and bulk controls, the commission took the next step. The first of four public hearings would start one month later.[8]

The response to the notices sent to property owners and citizen organizations was light. So was the response to the newspaper advertisement. Those who did call or visit the department offices were more concerned with the meaning of the notice than with the substance of the controls. Evening meetings were held with neighborhood organizations before the hearings, but these too concentrated on straightforward information about what was at hand more than on substance. However, the staff was beginning to get a sense of some neighborhood discontent with the proposals. Many people were unaware that height controls did not already exist, and some felt that the controls being proposed were too lenient. The director had lunch meetings with two or three groups like the Democratic Forum and SPUR to talk about the urban design plan and to invite their active support for the new ordinance. Commissioner Fleishhacker arranged a private meeting with Emmett Solomon, president of Crocker Bank, so that the staff could explain the proposed law and ask for support. Downtown interests were remarkably quiet at this time.

During this period, it became known that Duskin was preparing for a second height limit initiative. The planning director tried to convince him to postpone the attempt until the November election, reasoning that the department's own ordinance would be barely through the planning commission by the June election and certainly would not have reached the Board of Supervisors. If Duskin's second initiative failed in June, as the planners felt was likely, then political pressure for city action to deal with the department's proposal would be gone. The threat of a citywide vote to endorse Duskin's proposal if the Board of Supervisors didn't act on the planning department's ordinance would no longer exist. On the other hand, if the city failed to act by the end of the summer, then Duskin could still push for a November vote and use the city's inaction to support his position. Duskin did not see things that way and mentioned something to the effect that he had his own constituency to consider.

Some 3,000 people attended the four evening hearings, and nearly 200 spoke. The testimony was spirited. The sentiment for greater control was overwhelming. Duskin's second height limit campaign had been mounted by this time, proposing limits of 40 feet in most areas of the city and 160 feet downtown. Backers of the initiative found the hearings an inviting forum in which to get press publicity.

Peter Svirsky described one of the hearings in vivid terms:

"When the initiative was not being discussed, the speakers did a remarkable job of sticking to the planning issues. Inevitably, there were some requests that the height limits be used for a great variety of purposes to which they might not easily be adapted: strict limitation of traffic, control of residential density, preservation of historic buildings, stimulation of socially oriented housing, maintenance of a population balance between homeowners and renters, discouragement of absentee landlords, and setting of an envelope for maximum city growth. The staff and the commissioners also found themselves explaining repeatedly that citywide height limits did not already exist and that the present scale of buildings had not been dictated by legal restrictions. However, the speakers were not interested in comparisons with what had been permitted before; they talked about what would be permitted in the future and focused upon the relatively small proportion of residentially zoned land . . . where limits higher than 40 feet were being proposed.

"For all the fireworks at the hearings, the overall effect of the testimony was constructive and persuasive. Most neighborhood organizations presented their arguments well, and some made detailed written proposals for map changes."[9]

Three of these proposals are worthy of note. One came from representatives of the Mission Coalition, who packed the house at one meeting and demanded lower heights along a main commercial artery, Mission Street, especially at the two rapid transit stations. Their presentation was bilingual, in English and Spanish, and they submitted drawings to show clearly what they wanted. Even where the planners had proposed moderately high limits to allow subsidized housing to be constructed with greater economic ease, coalition spokesmen objected. They would allow exceptions only for specific, socially oriented housing projects. Later, they would choose the lower limits for all projects. They saw no reason, they said, why lower income people should live under environmental standards different from anyone else's.

Although most of the very well-to-do Pacific Heights had had no height controls in the past (except for a 105-foot limit in one section), neighborhood residents wanted limits now. They were unconcerned about the facts that there was no earlier record of dissatisfaction with existing standards and that the department's new standards would be much more restrictive of future development. At the public meeting, testimony came from an entirely new neighborhood group that had been formed to supplant the more traditional group in the area. The new group wanted drastically reduced heights, arguing that they were necessary to protect the character of the area and to prevent a jarring contrast of building scales. They wanted limits that were more restrictive than what the planners proposed.

Russian Hill residents argued in a similar vein. At first, they had seemed to be satisfied with the prospect of staff and commission consideration and discretionary review of a few more tall, slender towers. This was, after all, some of the most expensive residential land in the city, much of it in long-term ownership, and many owners feared a drastic decrease in values if there were blanket 40- or 50-foot limits. It was the approval of the Haas Towers and one other high-rise proposal that led the Russian Hill residents to doubt that their interests would be protected by politically pressed planning commissioners (and staff as well) with discretion. At an evening meeting on the hill at the end of March, the staff reviewed the situation and posed alternatives. The outcome was that at the April 12 public hearing, the president of the Russian Hill Improvement Association presented a petition to the commission requesting a flat 40-foot limit.

There was very little testimony at the first four hearings in favor of increases in the heights proposed. Two owners of commercial property near a new transit station in Glen Park made a concentrated effort to raise a height limit, and there were a few other requests for increases by individual property owners. But for the most part the testimony was either in favor of the planners' height proposals or for even more stringent limits.

Surprisingly little testimony related to the bulk proposals. The business and labor groups, including the chamber of commerce, that usually made strong pro-development presentations were notably quiet. Perhaps they were taken aback by the strong neighborhood feelings and were waiting for a better time to present their views, such as before the Board of Supervisors or privately to commissioners. Their energies may have been concentrated on combatting the newest Duskin height initiative. Possibly, the planners' meetings with downtown and labor interests were having an effect.

Commission president Newman had long since advised the staff that the ordinance was the most important work of the commission as far as he was concerned. He felt it would be a major and lasting hallmark. As the hearings got under way, Newman suggested private meetings with labor and business officials in order to seek their support or at least keep them neutral. Newman and the director had lunch with Walter Shorenstein, a very influential real estate and political figure, with whom the director had tangled on previous occasions. The discussion seemed to center on the possibility that neither Shorenstein nor the planners were terrible people and that neither would knowingly destroy San Francisco ("and by the way, Mr. Shorenstein, the proposals are reasonable"). No deals or concessions were asked for or offered. The planning director met alone with top officials of another downtown real estate and management firm and with Daniel Del Carlo of the Building Trades Council. With Del Carlo, the discussion was as much about their backgrounds and credentials as fine human beings as it was about the proposed ordinance. Although the mayor was kept informed during this period, there were no significant discussions about the content of the proposed ordinance.

If the mayor, supervisors, and any members of the public not actively involved with the proceedings were getting their sense of the proposals and of citizen reaction to them from the press reports, they might have been misled. The press reports at the time gave the impression that the city planners were out of touch with the desires of the people and that they were oriented toward development. In their accounts of the first four public hearings on the ordinance, the press reports concentrated on the testimony for lower heights than the department was proposing. The speakers for lower heights seemed to recall every development proposal that the department had ever approved, whereas those who were pleased with the department's proposals expressed their approval more succinctly and less loudly. The result was that a generally anti-planner, anti-planning commission point of view was reflected in the press. One or two commissioners expressed concern that they were being forced into a too restrictive posture.

The first hearings were concluded on April 26. In his article, Peter Svirsky noted that these hearings gave the commission and the staff an "excellent reading of public concern and opinions," adding that "over the next several weeks, the staff analyzed every point raised and produced a lengthy report which recommended revisions in the mapping proposals." The staff's recommendations included widespread height reductions where they seemed warranted, including some that went further than what speakers had requested. The blanket 40-foot height control for Russian Hill was accepted.

In the end, the planners had concluded that a uniform scaling-down was better than haphazard amendments. With only a few exceptions, the new proposals remained consistent with the urban design element of the master plan. The most notable difference was the elimination of those few specific locations that had been designated as possible sites for tall buildings. The sites were chosen in order to accent hilltops, create strong focal points, and permit increased densities. The planners had always questioned, however, whether this generalized urban design concept was capable of implementation through zoning. It implied a "floating," or undefined, zone and a lot of discretion by the commission. Before making their newest recommendations public the planners met with a group of Pacific Heights residents that was pressing for greater height limitations. A special restudy of Pacific Heights resulted both in a proposal for lower heights and a second public hearing for the district. The staff also met with representatives of the University of California Medical Center (who agreed to lower height limits) and with the president of the Board of Supervisors, both to let her know what would be coming and to seek her support.

To ensure unanimous commission approval of the ordinance so that it would go to the Board of Supervisors with strong backing, the staff met with the commissioners to give them details of the proposal and to solicit their agreement. Two or three commissioners were present at each meeting, and on the whole they were agreeable. However, a few, most notably Julia Porter, expressed misgivings about the stringency of the proposals. John Ritchie felt that there was too low a limit on some of the industrial property near downtown. Several commissioners rejected a staff idea for establishing a procedure for automatic review of all large site development proposals, and eventually the idea was dropped. Ultimately, with a few exceptions that would be voted on individually, there was commission agreement.

The revised proposals were made public on May 25, just 12 days before the second Duskin height initiative was to be voted upon. Earlier, the commission had voted unanimously to oppose the initiative, and the staff had aroused the anger of the Duskin forces by publicly announcing that this proposal, like the earlier one, had a flaw: it would actually raise height limits on some residential property, extending existing 30- and 35-foot restrictions to 40 feet. The public was to vote on the initiative before the commission would have a chance to act on its staff's proposals.

Public response to the report was good. The neighborhood-oriented weekly newspaper, *San Francisco Progress*, reported that, except for the height of buildings to be permitted downtown, even the Duskin group was pleased with the modified proposals.

The second Duskin initiative lost with 43 per cent of the vote on June 6, and in the short period between the election and the commission's vote on the height-bulk ordinance, support for the staff's proposals began to erode. Clearly, the attitude of the commissioners was changing. They were more willing to listen to individual requests for increased height and paid more attention to the persistent Glen Park request for greater height. Up to this point, nevertheless, the commission still wanted very few changes. One commissioner now stated that if any more height reductions were proposed, he would start proposing some increases. The staff concluded it was important to get the commission to act as quickly as possible and pressed for a vote at the June 29 hearing. The vote was unanimous in favor of the ordinance.

The vote of the Board of Supervisors was yet to come. There were two fearsome possibilities. One was that, with summer just starting, the board would delay consideration of the matter, with the possible consequence of diminished citizen support. The other possibility was that the board would insist on amendments, which would force the return of the ordinance to the commission for the start of what might well be a long ping-pong game. The result might be a much weakened ordinance.

Fortunately, the planners would be going to the board with strong allies. By this time, most neighborhood groups were behind the department. Recognizing this, the staff asked for their active support in lobbying for an early hearing and in testifying before the board. The planners reminded the neighborhood representatives that they had gotten most of what they had asked for and that it was now time to be counted in support of the department. Most of the groups agreed readily.

The planners also met with Supervisor Roger Boas, head of the Planning and Development Committee and a strong supporter of planning legislation. The point of this meeting was to impress upon Boas the thoroughness of the work to date and the importance of early action.

Boas's committee met on the evening of July 18. The audience was filled with strong supporters of the ordinance. Some neighborhood representatives made further pleas for more restrictive amendments. Residents of Glen Park, for instance, were ready to oppose a lessening of restrictions in that area. Anticipating questions about particular proposals, and points raised in opposition, the planners had prepared cards with short answers and rebuttals. Quickly putting the cards in order, they could have fast, accurate responses to each point. There were no surprises. Some supervisors showed sympathy for requests for more restrictive amendments, but they also were aware that such efforts might delay board action or cause a voting deadlock. The committee members were prepared to recommend the ordinance as it was and have those possible amendments sent back to the commission for further consideration once the ordinance was passed.

By this time the ordinance seemed a sure thing, but the staff continued to run hard. The planners made telephone calls to the supervisors until the needed six votes were assured. One or two other supervisors, who knew they would be absent the day of the voting, were prevailed upon to write letters saying that the matter should not be postponed on their account and that they were in favor of the ordinance. On July 31, the Board of Supervisors voted unanimously to enact the citywide height and bulk ordinance.

By its action in passing the ordinance, the board had carried out a significant part of the master plan. It had responded to an issue that was of considerable concern to residents. From a city planning perspective, the new law represented a direct and immediate step toward implementing a plan.

We have been advised that the part of the city planning process that calls for plans to be adopted and carried out by a series of actions, including legislation, rarely runs smoothly. In this case, however, that part of the process worked in the way it was supposed to; the ordinance derived directly from a plan and, with very few exceptions, its final substance reflected the plan. Moreover, the theory of the city planning process which outlines a step-by-step procedure from initiation to adoption or rejection of implementing legislation, including provisions for citizen input along the way, also worked. Citizen involvement was strong and articulate, and it influenced the substance of the ordinance as well as its final acceptance. As might be expected, some of the main reasons for the success of this implementation effort were the same as those that accounted for the ready acceptance of the urban design plan.

The urban design plan was timely, and it was responsive to public awareness of an issue. And the proposed zoning controls were just as opportune. "Both the growing general awareness of environmental questions and recent episodes involving single building projects," Svirsky wrote, "contributed to that concern. Widespread notice of the hearings was given, and people were able to organize and lobby as neighborhoods. Because of the common suspicion of government and the importance attached to concrete controls, as evidenced by the two initiative campaigns for height limits, the outpouring of sentiment was unusually strong."[10]

Had the ordinance been less timely, and had fewer people been concerned, it is unlikely that it would have been passed so quickly. The commission had not expected citywide legislation of this nature as the urban design plan was nearing completion. This is not to say, however, that timeliness and widespread public awareness are always critical in passage of legislation to carry out a plan or that such efforts should never be attempted in the absence of these conditions. If there is little opposition, the absence of massive support may not be critical. Also, debating an ordinance is a way of increasing public awareness of the long-range implications of an issue. What is not timely today might be very timely tomorrow. And at times, the planner's vision of what is and is not timely may not be altogether clear. An obvious consideration, too, is the amount of staff effort and resources that this kind of undertaking requires, assuming that funds will always be limited. Nevertheless, it helps if the ordinance is timely, and in this case it was.

"On several occasions," said Svirsky, "the San Francisco procedure of providing for *interim controls* in rezoning has aided in adoption of new zoning measures. With the proposed controls in force in the interim, the workability and severity of them can be tested during the study and hearing period. If defects are seen in actual practice, refinements can be made before adoption, avoiding the need for later amendments. A race for building permits is thwarted for the most part, and delaying tactics need not be employed. On the contrary, the use of interim controls may build up pressure for final action so that both developers and the public at large will know where they stand for the long run." Given the timeliness of the proposals under consideration, it is reasonable to conclude that in this case an ordinance would have been passed without the interim controls. But they helped, especially when there were special problems like the Russian Hill situation, where the original proposals would not suffice.

Thorough professional work was as important to the preparation of the zoning proposals as it was to the earlier plan. The approach was considered, systematic, and detailed. It is hard to say whether or not mistakes in drafting the two Duskin height initiatives hurt those measures at the polls or, if so, by how much; but the mistakes could not have helped. On the other hand, it is not always easy to find competent professionals. Often, a city attorney's office does not have people with the detailed knowledge of city planning related matters. Even assuming that there is sympathy with the nature of the proposals at hand, there is no guarantee that the proper zoning ordinance drafting skills will be there. It was far better to have those skills in the planning department, with the city attorney as a backup.

Good organization and simple, understandable language were critical to the success of the San Francisco ordinance. So was an effective statement of purpose. It was important as well to know how to fit the new proposal into the existing machinery of government. The use of objective standards with minimum chance for arbitrary discretion also helped considerably. Had the work not been done as thoroughly as it was, and had it not been based on a plan, it is most likely that lawyers, architects, and the public as well would have found fault with either its content or its general approach. If the ordinance had been passed at all under those conditions, the process would have been more drawn out.

The initial plan was prepared in anticipation of implementation. That made it much easier to prepare an ordinance. Also, without the plan it might have been impossible to enact the interim controls that came from it with minimum required changes. The aspects of the plan that could be implemented directly, through legislation, were easier to achieve than those that were out of the planners' immediate control; public works programs, for example. The planners were, after all, accustomed to dealing with zoning. Thus, they produced a plan in the first place that could be implemented most easily by means which they could readily control.

Knowledge of the administrative machinery and legislative processes of government was all important in getting the ordinance passed. The planners understood that interim controls were possible; they knew something about the public hearing process (including how and when to send notices and to use hearings as a sounding board for public views); and they understood what the Board of Supervisors could and could not do with the ordinance. Citizen groups came to understand the mechanisms as well, and they used them. For instance, the Pacific Heights group, midway through the process, made its own specific proposals, thus forcing their consideration. The planners, with their own knowledge of the process, integrated the neighborhood action with their own proposals.

All of the knowledge and professional work of the planners might well have gone for naught had they not also been able to recognize opportunities and had a willingness to be involved in the politics of city planning. Conflicts over cases like the Transamerica building, the U.S. Steel proposal, the Holiday Inn, and the Russian Hill towers, especially when they had been approved, all gave the planners a chance to push their plan and ordinance. The height initiatives represented similar opportunities. Both before and during the public hearings the planners were not above meeting with potential supporters or old adversaries if that might help their cause. Nor were they beyond countering one group's demands with another group's fears. And they called upon their friends when they needed to do so, as they freely admitted when the two major proponents of greater height in Glen Park accused them of soliciting neighborhood support in opposition.

Although the work associated with preparing the ordinance was intricate and time-consuming, the zoning itself required relatively simple action. It was also action that could be easily understood by the public. The zoning studies were handled by existing staff. The planners did not try to deal with issues that were not directly related to height and bulk, even though many people urged them to do so. They did not deal directly with city growth, for example, nor did they attempt to solve questions of residential densities, transportation, or historic preservation, important as these might be.

It is interesting to note, too, that other city agencies were not actively involved, so a minimum of coordination was required. There was also little involvement on other administrative levels—federal, state, and regional—although some of their lands were at issue. Thus, the planning department was in a position to implement, on its own, a major part of the plan it had prepared. The planners were more sympathetic than anyone else to the measure, and they knew what they had in mind when interpretations had to be made or arguments forwarded to defend the proposals.

All along, government was responsive. As Svirsky put it, "If public views had not been thoroughly aired before the commission, analyzed by the staff, and incorporated in the final proposals, a height and bulk ordinance would not have been enacted." Despite the criticism that has been directed to the planning commission, its staff, and the Board of Supervisors, the fact is that they were remarkably responsive on this issue.

What if the city planners had not been as responsive? What if they had concluded that popular sentiment as expressed at the hearings was neither consistent with the plans they had prepared nor beneficial to the long-range development of the city? In regard to neighborhood views in a few specific areas they did indeed come to that conclusion. Their way of dealing with those situations was to prevail upon the board to pass "their" ordinance and then to fight out decisions on the isolated cases, separately, at a later time. The planners' views did not always prevail at the later board hearings, and height limits went lower than had been recommended in one or two cases. Overall, however, the planners felt that these decisions had only minor consequences. Had the disagreements been major or widespread, the story might have been different. A number of options would have been possible. For instance, the planners could have stuck by their guns; they could have insisted on whatever ordinance they had prepared. The result could well have been defeat for the proposal and no legislation at all. But what is more likely in that kind of situation is that the board would have proposed its own amendments, which would then have had to be considered by the commission. A long back-and-forth process would probably have resulted, with the board having to muster a two-thirds vote to overcome a negative vote on any zoning map change by the commission. Ultimately, something might have been passed, but it would have had little resemblance to a plan.

Alternatively, the planners might have chosen to compromise their position and to get the best ordinance they could on the grounds that something is better than nothing. That sort of thing frequently happens. It could be argued that the ordinance finally adopted represents a plan as much or more than the original document. One compromise approach would have been to pass legislation for only those geographic areas where there was agreement. Faced with major dissatisfaction with their proposals, the planners could also have tried to punt: to divorce themselves from the issue and the process that had been started and to wait for a more propitious moment to pursue their concerns. But, while that might be a reasonable strategy with some proposals, it does not seem likely that it would have proven successful in this case, where so many people were concerned. Again, it is more likely that piecemeal legislation would have resulted after considerable time had elapsed.

Moving still further into the realm of speculation, one could query what might have happened had there been no governmental response to the issue. What if there had been no plan and no ordinance following from it? Might one of the Duskin initiatives have passed? In the past, these kinds of situations have prompted requests from the board to undertake zoning studies to deal with the issue. (For instance, a downtown zoning study started this way in 1965; the zoning ordinance that resulted was passed by the board in 1968.) Without a plan to start with, such studies can take considerable time and the nature of the problem might change by the time the proposals are ready to be heard. If an ordinance results, it is not one that comes from a plan, with the purpose of plan implementation.

It is no more reasonable to expect that zoning enacted to help achieve a city plan will go unchanged than to expect the plan itself to remain forever intact. People's values, ideas, and perceptions of reality will change, and what may seem eminently desirable today may seem less so tomorrow. Nevertheless, it might be expected that, after all the effort involved in its preparation, the height and bulk ordinance would not undergo serious challenge or amendment immediately. And indeed, by late 1977, there had been but one change to the ordinance since the flurry of early, minor adjustments.

During the summer of 1976 the planning staff, commission, and supervisors agreed to raise the height limit in a small area, a fairly isolated site near the Candlestick Park stadium at the southeast entrance to the city, to permit offices up to 240 feet in height. The change was supported by people who testified from the nearest residential areas. The action represented the first time that a height restriction, once enacted, had been raised in San Francisco. Whether or not that act portends a rush of future changes is anyone's guess, but it is doubtful, and certainly no prediction can be based on one or two actions. The act did require modification of the urban design element of the master plan. It is clear that that document remains one of the major reference points for height and bulk zoning.

On a more day-to-day level, it will be recalled that one reason given for all the controversies over individual development proposals was the absence of a plan and follow-up legislation stating clearly what the community wanted to protect and what it wished to prevent. The difficulty that city planning has in dealing with significant individual ad hoc development proposals of private developers in conflict situations has also been observed. City planners will usually lose those battles. It has been held desirable to have clear development guidelines, zoning, and a governmental process that reduces the likelihood of conflicts developing in the first place and, if they do, assures that decisions are made in the best long-range interests of the city.

Since 1972 there have been fewer controversies over major building proposals and still fewer related to the height and bulk of buildings. (It is true, of course, that such factors as high interest rates, over-building, and decreased demand may have slowed the number of such proposals to start with.) Also, with the guidelines of the urban design plan and the height and bulk zoning as backup, and with the strong possibility of a discretionary review hearing by the commission over individual proposals, the project review section of the planning department may have more influence than it did earlier. It is significant that the major controversies over continued development of the University of California Medical Center and other hospitals, over the Yerba Buena redevelopment project, and over the nature of development on key sections of the waterfront, all long-standing issues in the community, do not center on the design characteristics of individual buildings. Rather, they have to do with public policies related to the uses of public lands and with large, complex sites. Although the urban design plan recognized problems inherent in development of large properties in San Francisco, no special efforts were made to address them as part of the ordinance. The commission stayed away from that issue.

Any number of critical observations can be made of semi-autonomous planning commissions and the long process of preparing a plan, trying to direct actions (including zoning legislation) toward its realization, and then starting the cycle all over again. The critics argue that planning commissions organized like San Francisco's are out of the mainstream of political decision making and therefore unresponsive and ineffective. Zoning is held to be rarely responsive to a plan, too time-consuming, a diversion from more important work, and a tool of the "haves" to discriminate against and exclude the "have-nots." This case study would not support those conclusions. If anything, it seems less likely that legislation such as the height and bulk ordinance would have been prepared, enacted, and then administered under an organizational framework that placed city planning under the executive or legislative branch of local government, or that directed it from on high (regionally), or from the neighborhood level.

The urban design plan and the height and bulk ordinance derived from concerns of both citizens and city planners over the quality of their city's physical environment. Both the plan and the legislation sought to retain some of the timeless qualities of an urban place. Both plan and ordinance were concerned with preservation as well as development, with a definition of urban environmental quality based upon human needs.

This case study and the one that precedes it point to the reality that, even under the most fortunate of circumstances, it is difficult to prepare and adopt a meaningful, responsive plan and the legislation to help carry it out. The matter of political climate aside, it took about three years to prepare the plan in the first place and another year to get the ordinance passed. An able, dedicated, professional staff working for the public at the level of local government was required. So was assistance, or at least empathy, from the outside professional community. Even then, notions of how to proceed were skimpy, and the planners, and citizens too, had to feel their way, knowing less about how to define what they wanted and about the possible consequences of their actions than they would have liked. No one yet has developed a surefire way for the public and its employees to communicate their needs, desires, ideas, and visions. San Franciscans, perhaps more aware and caring about the quality of their physical environment than the people in other cities, nevertheless exist in a national milieu that is not necessarily wedded to the idea of city planning as the approach to better communities. The notion that it is possible, or even that it is a good idea, to control or direct development of the physical environment is alien to many—including many San Franciscans. Finally, city plans and ordinances, even after they are adopted, can be very fragile. It is difficult to know how long they will act as meaningful forces.

Problems and difficulties notwithstanding, these two cases indicate that a rather classical approach to city planning can work. It can produce a plan that is responsive to immediate issues and that deals with the broader issue of the future of the city.

# Notes

1. Peter Svirsky, "San Francisco Limits the Buildings to See the Sky," *Planning*, January 1973, p. 11.

2. Marvin Markus and John West, "Urban Design Through Zoning," *Planners Notebook*, October 1972.

3. San Francisco City Planning Commission minutes of September 16, 1971, Resolution 6755.

4. For accounts of this case, especially in relation to the temper of the times in regard to urban design issues generally and the urban design plan in particular, see Tom Emch, "The Battle of Russian Hill," *California Living*, February 13, 1972; and Ralph Craib, "The Russian Hill Towers Win O.K.," *San Francisco Chronicle*, January 14, 1972. The Russian Hill towers were held up in court contests for years. As of the summer of 1978, they had not been constructed.

5. Gruen and Gruen Associates, "Four Working Papers on the Economic, Social, and Fiscal Effect of Highrise Buildings in San Francisco," 1971.

6. "Vote No, No, No, A Thousand Times No on Proposition T," *San Francisco Chronicle*, October 12, 1971. This advertisement was paid for by Citizens for San Francisco.

7. Herb Caen, *San Francisco Chronicle*, January 18, 1972; "Too Much Power in Jacobs' Hands," *San Francisco Examiner*, January 24, 1972.

8. Memorandum from Allan B. Jacobs to city planning commission, February 17, 1972, "Presentation of Proposed Permanent Height and Bulk Controls." See also "Guide and Summary for Proposed Ordinance Text," of same day.

9. Svirsky, "San Francisco Limits the Buildings," p. 12.

10. Svirsky, "San Francisco Limits the Buildings," p. 13. Svirsky expanded on his article in a lecture at the University of California, Berkeley, in the spring of 1976.

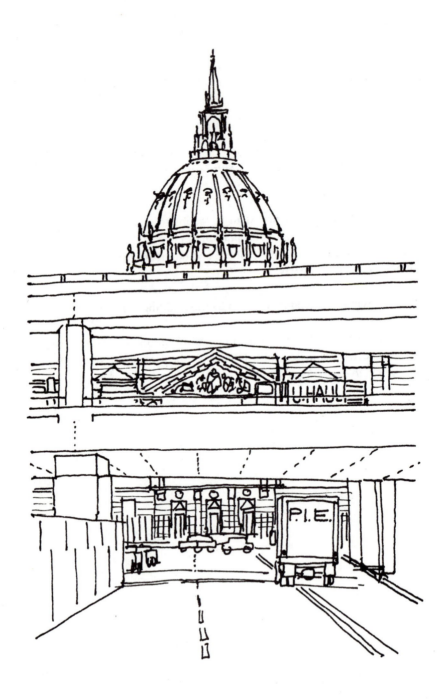

# Chapter 10
# 1972-1974: Power Brokers

As the past gets closer to the present, it gets fuzzier, not clearer, as one might expect. Thoughts, conversations, and confrontations that took place in 1967 and 1968 are sharper and better documented than those that took place six or seven years later. Why? Because there was so much going on in more recent years that it's harder to sort out? Because there has been too little time to gain perspective? I wish it were so. More likely it is because the more recent years were less comfortable and less to my taste than the earlier ones, too often painful, or with more pain relative to the joys. My mind was beginning to be somewhere else. So these years are harder to recall or to relive with sureness.

The years between early 1967 and late 1972 were optimistic, achieving, often cocky, and always striving years. Certainly, the planning department had a sounder base than I had originally thought. Nevertheless, in the years since, we had grown, establishing ourselves as competent, caring, professional city planners. The plans we were producing for the physical development of San Francisco were responsive to the concerns of residents, and our involvement in the programs to carry out those plans was increasing. In 1972, the planning department was a stronger force in the community than it had been earlier. People saw it as being relevant to the city's decision-making process. We did not always get our way, but defeats, though they always hurt, were momentary incidents. For me personally, the period was one of growing influence and security, and this was true for my staff as well. We all cared very much about the future of our city, and we were willing to take chances by speaking out on issues that were important to us. In the heat of a battle I could make such a stupid comment about organized labor's support of the massive building project proposed by U.S. Steel as, "They'd be in favor of building gas chambers if they thought it would put a few people to work," and still survive.[1] My refusal to appear in a television ad with Mayor Alioto to support his reelection campaign and the coolness that understandably ensued had made me a lot less sure of myself. But that incident had taken place a year before. Overall, one could be forgiven a sense of growth and accomplishment.

As always, during this period, the planning department did not exist in a vacuum. The Nixon administration continued to wind down and stop the federal programs that were intended to solve urban ills. The Viet Nam war ended, but that did not mean that war monies would be turned to local peace purposes. Funds were withheld or cut off for redevelopment programs, for low- and moderate-income housing, and for housing conservation. Local officials scurried around, trying to nail down as much money as they could, all the while explaining to waiting residents why they would not make good on their promises.

There were local effects, too, of the fearful, inward looking, centralized government geared to strong, insulated, executive leadership that characterized Washington (the kind of government that Watergates are made of). My earlier misgivings over the prospect of a vastly expanded mayor's office, with a new, federally funded Office of Community Development as part of it, were being confirmed. To me, the government of San Francisco was being changed in large part by forces from the outside, without its citizens knowing what was going on. The changes were certain to have an effect on the planning department.

I was changing, too, although I didn't always know it. As happy as I was with the state of city planning in San Francisco, its role in the community, and the overall quality of the staff, I was much less willing than earlier to accommodate and to work around bureaucratic and government hurdles. I was especially out of sync with the mayor and his top staff. The attraction and challenges of San Francisco remained strong, but now they competed increasingly with other enticements— not with the pull of other places, but of new ideas to be explored, new activities, and forces undefined.

Would that the continuing forces and momentums of city planning and plan implementation in a dynamic city, the internal political warfare over where city planning should be located and whose model would prevail, and the changes in my own priorities and values—would that they had existed separately. It doesn't happen that way. One force affects the others, and it is not always certain what planning program caused what personal point of view or what pique of a planning director brought about what new proposal for a change in organizational structure. The major streams, and many minor ones, traveled parallel to each other, sometimes together, sometimes apart, all certainly affecting one another.

We had completed plans for residence, transportation, and urban design, and we were working on plans for recreation and open space and community facilities and services (fire, health, library, police, social services). We were also working on detailed studies that would lead to plans for commerce and industry. We were beginning to think, too, of putting down in succinct but explicit form—perhaps in an opening section of the master plan—the basic assumptions that governed all the separate elements we were preparing. To date, these assumptions had been implicit in our work, and we had spoken of them with reasonable clarity. They boiled down to keeping San Francisco largely as it then was. Improvements and changes would be marginal and conservative, responsive to problems and opportunities—but made largely within the existing physical framework. Regularly, newspaper reporters asked me for my vision of San Francisco of the future, but I was never able to come up with anything very different, physically, from what existed. And so our plans for housing spoke of the desirability of providing for a wide range of life styles at existing and slightly higher densities; the plan for transportation reflected our emphasis on public transportation; and much of the urban design plan was oriented toward conservation and maintenance, toward improving what we had rather than making major changes.

Although we had not come to grips with the issue of city size, neither were we pushing growth. We saw San Francisco as the principal city in a compact, highly urban region with limits to its physical expansion. We saw the nearness of open space and agricultural land as significant factors in the well-being of all Bay Area residents. We hoped that other cities in the region would develop more densely so that the landscape would not be covered with tract homes and thus made less accessible to city residents. All these matters would, presumably, be made explicit in an opening section of the master plan.

Instead of working at our own pace, we were increasingly being sidetracked to work on plan elements that were mandated by state legislation.[2] Unfortunately, the state's priorities were not always consistent with our own priorities, and preparing the plans required by the state often took people and funds from more important work. When that was so, I spoke against complying with state law.

For instance, I argued with the city attorney and with members of my staff that we should not prepare the conservation element, a requirement that was mandated in 1970. It was to be completed by the end of December 1973. My reasoning was that, unlike rural counties, San Francisco had no rivers, no water with potential for hydraulic power, no minerals, no forests, and no significant wildlife to preserve. Conservation in an urban area should be considered part of the urban design and historic preservation programs.

I argued against the scenic highways element too. At our meetings, city residents had made it clear that they did not like the idea that was expressed in the legislation. They did not want to attract more drivers, especially out-of-towners. The city attorney's response was simple. The law, he said, was the law. Someone might go to court asking that all building permits be held up until we prepared the plans. Banks and insuring agencies might not back loans if there was a danger that a building could be stopped midstream in the courts; therefore, we had damned well better get on with the job. So we jumped through the state-held hoops, and if we did the work beautifully, it was more because of pride than desire.

Two other state-required plan elements dealt with noise and seismic safety. Although no San Francisco resident was unaware of the likelihood and possible consequences of a major earthquake (memories of the 1906 earthquake and fire, as well as pictures, predictions, and yearly commemorations abound), there was very little to indicate that people were prepared to take special steps, beyond those included in a regularly updated building code, to minimize loss of life or property from an earthquake or to plan their city differently because of the prospect. Preparation of plans dealing with noise and seismic safety would require considerable time, money, staff, and outside technical expertise. I wanted to do the job right. I went hat in hand to the planning commission, the mayor, and the Board of Supervisors for the considerable funding the work would require. By design, the city attorney was never far away, to advise reluctant officials that they had better allocate the money. Once Commission President Walter Newman was convinced of the necessity he was concerned only that we get the best help and do the best possible job. We got the money, hired consultants, and assigned staff to the tasks. Both the *Plan for Transportation Noise Control* and the *Community Safety Plan* were completed in September 1974. Although the work on both of these plans was as sound as that which produced the plans for housing and urban design, these plans were not soon recognized or used. The subject matter was not timely, and the fiscal and legal means of implementation were not readily at hand. Perhaps we failed to present our conclusions in a way that conveyed the feeling that the plans would be useful. In any case, the public showed little interest at the public hearings. Both plans were adopted quickly by the commission, in some solitude.

As reasonable and desirable as some of the state-mandated planning elements might have been, they were also an increasingly burdensome weight. Money was hard enough to come by for all the projects we wanted to do locally and for which there was a demand. If we got money to do the things that were required by the state, we could not get the money to do what we actually thought we should be doing. We stood a chance of losing stature in the community if people perceived us doing make-work that was of no particular interest to them. The part that weighed most heavily was a sense that we were less and less able to be our own people, that someone else, the state in this case, was calling the shots. We had to dance to someone else's tune. Being the city's planning agency was one thing; being an agent of the state, doing work to satisfy an unseen client and some undiscriminating legislation, was another. The net effect was to take some gusto out of the job.

Our plan for recreation and open space was also a state-mandated plan element, but we had started it because it made sense to us, not because it was required. Both the draft plan, *Improvement Plan for Recreation and Open Space—A Proposal for Citizen Review,* which appeared in September 1972, and the final version called for unbroken open space along the city's western shoreline and major new public facilities on the northern and eastern shores. We called for the preservation of existing open spaces throughout the city; elimination of non-recreation uses from parks; and creation of new, small parks, especially on hilltops. We designated what we termed "high-need" areas, usually the denser, older neighborhoods where low-income and least mobile people lived; and we called for new, small parks there too. We also called for a regional open space agency and a regional system of open space that would be accessible by public transportation.

The most strident participation in the recreation and open space planning came from the low-income areas. People living south of downtown demanded that they be provided with the two parks that they had long been promised. The parks were to replace those that had been taken as part of freeway and public building projects years earlier. We had no problems working with those residents and adapting the plan to meet their demands, but we did have problems with the general manager of the Recreation and Park Department. He didn't like the idea of small parks because they were more expensive to maintain than large ones, and he refused to go along with a policy that would prohibit new construction or expansion of existing structures in open space areas, especially in places like Golden Gate Park. He wanted to keep the options open. I spent more time trying to get agreement with him on wording that could satisfy us both than with citizens over their disagreements. We retained a strong statement in the plan that presumed against development on public open space, despite the manager's views. The commission adopted the plan—*Recreation and Open Space*—in May 1973. My concern shifted then to carrying it out, for in recent years, almost no public money had been spent on acquisition and development of public open space.

We had mixed results in carrying out all of these plans. The preparation and presentation of citywide plan elements was accompanied in most cases by a set of programs to implement them.[3] The programs were usually over-ambitious. We found that some of the other departments disliked the idea of even thinking about performance targets, let alone seeing them in print so the public could hold us accountable. But the programs did serve as public guides to citizens, especially those who wanted to pursue them at city hall.

We continued to put a lot of resources into housing programs. When the feds began to close down the FACE program, we worked with the Bureau of Building Inspection to draft a locally based program with the same objectives. We continued to look for sites for development of low- and moderate-income housing.

However, we had almost no luck in persuading city officials to use surplus public properties for subsidized housing. To the contrary, the mayor on one occasion asked why we shouldn't sell a particular housing project for nonsubsidized uses. The site was fine for public housing in the 1940s and 1950s when no one wanted it, but now interest sparked by Fisherman's Wharf tourism made people think of commercial and "artsy-craftsy" uses. Perhaps, the mayor suggested, the site was now too valuable for public housing. I told him that I didn't think the idea of selling the project would fly.

Our efforts to carry out plans continued to be reasonably successful where we were directly involved with the mechanisms for legislative implementation. For instance, the staff drafted an ordinance to ensure that any construction permitted on upper floors projecting over sidewalks would produce bona fide bay windows and not just give developers added floor space in the public right-of-way. This legislation, which was consistent with the urban design plan, was passed in early 1973. Early the next year, the Board of Supervisors passed temporary citywide legislation that would maintain most neighborhoods at existing densities while a residential zoning study was carried out.

At the same time, we started to work on new housing programs to replace the first set, which was becoming outdated with all the federal funding cutbacks and freezes. In 1974, legislation that we prepared was enacted to govern conversion of rental units to condominiums, protecting the rights of both tenants and prospective purchasers.

In 1973, I went to see State Assemblyman Willie Brown, head of the powerful Ways and Means Committee, to follow up on a letter he had written to the planning commission in support of our recreation and open space proposals. I asked for his help in carrying out our plan, especially the long-standing proposal for a shoreline park in the black, lower income South Bayshore, an area where we had been working for years. The assemblyman liked the idea and put his staff to work on it. Later the same year, Governor Reagan signed a state budget that contained $10 million for the purchase and development of the park. I was overjoyed. Over four years of effort to keep the land reserved and innumerable fruitless attempts to get funds to buy and develop a park were suddenly paying off. It seemed too good to be true.

Our attempts to carry out transportation plans involved a number of defensive holding actions. Forces for business-as-usual in regard to accommodating the auto still existed and had to be countered, especially where they had the wherewithal to frustrate major transit-oriented projects. And residents had become skeptical of any transportation project at all. In the Sunset district, residents joined traffic engineers in opposing a new streetcar line that the municipal railway proposed to add to much admired Sunset Boulevard. The line would take the place of an unneeded traffic lane. It would have answered the need of the area for more public transportation. In another case, we came up with a design that showed how the despised Embarcadero Freeway could be torn down and traffic handled as well, if not better, on the surface. But the state and local auto boys were not about to buy it.[4] Our staff, did, however, successfully oppose the plans of the state highway engineers and our own Department of Public Works to add traffic lanes to a major access route to the Golden Gate Bridge.

In an effort to carry out citywide transportation policy and agreed-upon projects, I initiated a transportation policy group, made up of myself, the general manager of utilities, and the director of the Department of Public Works. Our efforts proved to be only modestly successful, but in 1973 we did produce a report, "Transit Preferential Streets Program," that outlined a program for giving preference to transit vehicles on some key streets. The report was directly responsive to our earlier plans. With some reluctance, Public Works endorsed it and took some action to carry out the projects, but to this observer there seemed to be a lot of foot dragging.

We were beginning to make progress on projects that would discourage traffic from residential areas or that would at least slow it down. Prototypical improvements in one area that widened sidewalks, provided small sitting and play areas, and did a number of small, physical things to slow down traffic were proving successful. There was a problem when one neighborhood wanted more extensive constraints on traffic than my staff or I thought were warranted, but we went along with the residents.

Although more staff time was being directed to neighborhood planning, it was not the sort of an effort that produced well-documented, researched reports like those that came out of the South Bayshore and Chinatown projects. Rather, we were involved increasingly in a supportive relationship with neighborhood organizations that were attempting to do their own planning, with or without professional assistance. For areas like the Sunset, the Mission, and Richmond, I saw our role as one of providing information and offering a citywide perspective on problems and opportunities to local planning efforts. There was no point in competing with or duplicating their work. Also, our planners were charged with bringing back local information and concerns so we could keep up-to-date and, when necesary, respond.

Neighborhood-initiated planning produced more petitions for downzonings. Although I agreed with most of what was being proposed, I could not always support some requests of the sort that would result in large numbers of multi-unit apartment buildings being zoned for considerably lower densities. That seemed both inequitable and unrealistic. A few years earlier I would almost always have supported such neighborhood downzoning requests before the Board of Supervisors. Now it seemed that the neighborhood people and I were often adversaries, and I didn't find the position comfortable. It was easier for me to fight uncompromising people when they were developers.

I was never very comfortable, either, with our planning in the Haight-Ashbury. The Haight was an area of very liberal, would-be intellectual, middle-class whites, flower children, and graduate hippies, all of whom would be happiest without any government at all. There were also striving black residents, some of whom had been forced out of redevelopment areas to the east. I concluded early that the Haight people were the local equivalent of the Bengalis I had worked with in Calcutta. To both, matters of the mind were more important than those of the body. They could think of a million reasons why any proposal we came up with would not work or was inequitable. They could supply reasons for not doing anything faster than we could come up with solutions to problems. It wasn't hard to get agreement against something like urban renewal, but getting support for modest improvements to Haight Street was painful at best. In a situation where more people were requesting planning assistance than we could satisfy, it made sense to stay where we were wanted. Somehow, however, I got suckered into making a major commitment of staff time preparing a plan for the Haight-Ashbury. We were attacked most of the way at public meetings for all manner of terrible motives and imagined wrongdoings. Convinced that those who showed up at the meetings (and who were most vociferous) had intimidated the others in the neighborhood and that they did not represent most of the people, I was also aware that my views were the classic ones of every would-be despot who could not have his way and who was "misunderstood." We worked in the Haight for two-and-one-half years, finally producing a plan in July 1973—
*Haight-Ashbury—Improvements Recommended by the San Francisco*

*Department of City Planning.* In truth we did some of our best detailed planning there in the areas of commercial market analysis, traffic, and housing. But we fought over everything. There probably would have been major disagreement if I had suggested that the sun rises in the east. Some of our younger staff members learned a lot in the Haight, but for me there was very little enjoyment in the effort. Nor did the promise of carrying out parts of the plan bring satisfaction.

The area southeast of downtown, known as South of Market, was another place on which I could never get a handle. Between 10,000 and 15,000 people lived there (many of them Filipino), amid office buildings, cheap hotels, warehouses, factories, parking lots, and truck terminals. By 1972 we had developed decent relations with some of them. We met most often with elderly, poor activists and their younger and probably just as poor advocates. On a number of occasions we had been asked to do a plan for the area. But I was concerned about the probable outcome. Given all the other legitimate needs and interests that would have to be represented in any planning endeavor (an expanding business district, light industrial uses, traffic and parking demands) and given the meager implementing mechanisms (usually spelled m-o-n-e-y) for meeting the needs of poor people, I feared that residents would be forced out of the area faster as a result of a concentrated planning effort than if there were none. There were too few governmental resources and programs, local or national, that could be directed toward solving the problems of the people in that kind of area, while other interests could probably look out for themselves. Further, I doubted government's commitment to deal with that kind of marginal area without causing major hardships, and I told the people of my fears. Aside from minor programs and improvements, we would wait until there seemed a reasonable chance, with workable strategies, to help the people who lived there.

These were busy years. The planning and implementation efforts took place in a day-to-day working environment that involved the planning department in a host of large and small issues. The new Market Street began to take shape—plazas, brick paving, street furniture, trees, and new signs. At the mayor's request we worked on plans for a new Golden Gate Promenade to extend along the waterfront from the Golden Gate Bridge to Fisherman's Wharf, and I walked its length with him and thousands of San Franciscans on a Sunday morning. We evaluated many proposals to designate buildings as historic landmarks. Usually we agreed with the proposals—but not always. The staff learned to prepare the newly required environmental impact reports. I opposed a massive expansion of St. Mary's Hospital because I felt that it would provide commercial office space for doctors at the expense of housing. The planning commission heard and decided some 200 issues during fiscal 1973-74, and the staff was involved in many more.

My relations with the commission since the publication of the urban design plan and passage of the height and bulk zoning legislation had been amiable. Both staff and commission had emerged as winners in those matters. I was spending more time with President Newman, usually at lunch meetings where we discussed upcoming issues. We got along very well together, I felt. My friendship with Mortimer Fleishhacker continued, and my admiration for this tireless commissioner grew. He and his wife attended countless evening meetings in Chinatown. Often publicly abused because of his wealth and hard, questioning manner, he was in fact the most liberal of all the commissioners, and, at a time when no one else would even hear of it, he once indicated a willingness to consider rent control if it would solve problems.

I did have a problem with one commissioner who involved himself, without a word to me, in the hiring of a new assistant director. Also, his constant concern about the dress and grooming of my staff bugged me more than it should have, probably because I was not the neatest person myself. Indeed, another commissioner, Julia Porter, observed more than once, in response to my propensity to shed clothes during meetings, "When Allan gets all of his clothes off, he will plan the next millenium."

My relations with the Board of Supervisors were a far cry from the early days when I could expect to be berated regularly. Now my staff and I were respected, sought out, and listened to, if not always agreed with or supported. Individual supervisors knew that we could generate a major phone or letter campaign to support us on a number of issues, and they respected that. On environmental matters I sensed more support from the board than from my commission, the mayor's office, or other departments.

My relations with the mayor were cordial if not warm. They were characterized by a feeling of mutual respect but not one of ready or strong support. It was clear to me that I was no longer one of his major advisors. He or his aide, Jack Tolan, went directly to my commissioners on matters where we might disagree. I sought fewer meetings with the mayor than earlier; but when we did meet, he seemed to be interested in what I had to say, and he listened. I knew his views on most major development issues, so there was little point in discussing them. It was ironic that our period of greatest influence with the people and with the supervisors came at the time of our greatest problems with the mayor's office.

Press coverage continued to be extensive and fair for the most part. The two major dailies assigned top reporters to planning and they covered all of our meetings, often on the front pages. It was easy to get publicity when we wanted it by calling a press meeting or by talking casually with reporters, who were friendly, while at the same time challenging. The educational television station also gave us sympathetic coverage. The commercial television reporters were much less knowledgeable and up-to-date than their press brethren, but we got good coverage from them too.

The staff of the department was beginning to change. Some of the younger people that I had hired were beginning to leave, mostly, I sensed, for broader experience and higher level positions. Some were simply restless. They were not going out of dissatisfaction with the department, although my ability to advance deserving employees to salaries and job titles commensurate with their skills continued to be hampered by the civil service system. It was a system, by the way, for which I had less patience than ever; it seemed to lose all humanity as it strove for objectivity. The new employees were as eager and bright as those they replaced, but they needed guidance that I had less time (and possibly less inclination) to give them personally, and we did suffer from a lack of professional leadership and positive role models. Nonetheless, the staff remained a great strength and point of personal pride.

By 1972, I had come to appreciate San Francisco's no-power-to-anyone government. Whether that was because it really did suit the place or because I now knew how to work well within it, or both, will never be entirely clear. In any case, I had long since given up my illusions about a centralized government led by a strong mayor. That form of government had once seemed so efficient, but San Francisco was a different place than Pittsburgh, New York, or Chicago, and it seemed right that its government should be different as well. It was not so necessary here to make drastic physical responses to changing social and economic issues. In size, it was an understandable city, and its people took part in governing it. All the governmental checks and balances made things move so slowly that sometimes I was almost driven to distraction, but the slowness also meant that no one could give the place away, at least not with ease. Even if he was serious when he asked me one day what would be the matter with beautiful, tall, slender apartment buildings, built by unions and spaced at intervals along the northern edge of Golden Gate Park, *in the park,* Mayor Alioto could not have pulled it off, given San Francisco's governmental structure.

It was also true that San Francisco's governmental structure gave me some independence and the opportunity to expand a constituency that generally supported what my department was doing. If my views about what the electoral process produces in the way of centralized leadership were somewhat cynical, and if they labeled me as an elitist, I was prepared to live with the marking. I was also prepared to live with and work in a system that withheld too much power from me as well.

My emerging views of government help to explain why I perceived the establishment of an Office of Community Development in the mayor's office in late 1972 as a threat to the Department of City Planning. Regardless of what they called it, I instinctively knew that it could easily become another planning department, one that might deal with more than physical development issues and that would have considerable overlap with the one I directed. With a city planner, my ex-assistant director, Dean Macris, at its helm, some encroachment seemed assured. It took no genius to figure out which planning agency would come out on top in any disagreement—the one closest to the mayor would win, hands down. On the other hand, the mayor never had more than a handful of people working for him. This small staff was consistent with the city charter, which bestowed little power on the mayor. If that situation remained—and there was little to suggest that the board would fund new positions for the mayor—then the establishment of one or two people in his office might not be of great consequence.

Although I was not always fully aware of it at the time, the changes that were taking place in the city's government were to a considerable degree the work of federal and local power brokers working together.

They were achieving what the voters had rejected by defeating the charter revision proposals of 1969. Strangely enough, in some ways I would be a party to making those changes occur.

From a local perspective, it was clear, in the early 1970s, that the feds were cutting down on the plethora of often overlapping categorical programs that had been devised since the late 1940s to solve urban problems. Lyndon Johnson's Great Society had created a rush of new programs in the 1960s. Some had been poorly conceived. Escalating costs, program excesses, doubtful effectiveness, and mounting bureaucratic red tape were reasons to stop or slow down some of them. To some of us, however, the single most compelling reason was that the Nixon administration was basically unsympathetic to what these programs were trying to achieve.

The categorical programs that were being wound down—renewal and code enforcement, for instance—had permitted considerable entrepreneurial hustling on the part of local officials as they competed for funds with their counterparts in other cities and even sometimes among themselves. There were ever increasing federal hoops for locals to jump through in order to justify funding. But the effort was usually worth it, even if it was made with considerable moaning and groaning. What the hustling for funds meant was that federal representatives had to deal with any number of different local agencies, often in regard to the same federal program. By way of example, a Department of Housing and Urban Development official might have to deal with both redevelopment and building inspection people in regard to housing rehabilitation loans. HUD officials might be involved with as many as seven separate city agencies at the same time (the mayor's office, Department of City Planning, Redevelopment Agency, Housing Authority, Bureau of Building Inspection, Department of Public Works, Model Cities Agency). Those contacts showed the federal officials that local efforts did not always have a coordinated and unified direction. The same could be said by local officials of federal coordination, especially if one city agency had to deal with more than one federal department.

Federal officials seemed to be forgetting that a coordinating device existed, the "Workable Program for Community Improvement." This federally required document was based on the organizational preferences of local governments. Its purpose was to assure, as a condition for federal funding, that local governments had some kind of comprehensive, coordinated program to prevent physical development and housing problems and to solve them when they did occur. When push came to shove, however, the feds showed little inclination to enforce the requirements of the program, especially if that meant stopping a redevelopment project. The political pressures that were sometimes associated with individual projects were much too strong to be stopped by longer term, less tangible considerations. The federal officials seemed unwilling to take the requirement of a workable program seriously and to insist that it be used.

Instead, even before revenue sharing and block grant legislation was enacted to replace the categorical programs (presumably to let local officials use federal funds more freely), the feds began looking to some central, single office with which to deal locally. It seemed to make no difference to them that some local governments, including San Francisco's, were not organized around a strong central power. They wanted local chief executives to take direct control of federal programs. To that end they funded local management studies and co-ordinating devices, and they established offices of community development in the office of the mayor or the city manager.

One of those federally sponsored management studies was carried out under my direction. Early in 1972, I was advised by Jack Tolan of the mayor's office and Dean Macris, my assistant director, that the feds, in the form of the newly created Federal Regional Council, were prepared to fund a $50,000 study that would address our changing relationship with the federal government. The study was to focus on the development of an "annual development program" for improving coordination between planning activities and budgeting in the city and improving the capability of the mayor and Board of Supervisors to review and program city activities.[5] We were also to come up with recommendations for facilitating dealings with the federal government.

Tolan asked us to take over the study. There could be any number of valid reasons, not the least of which were our planning, coordinating, and capital budgeting roles. Furthermore, we had access to the talent that was necessary. I was somewhat uneasy, though, about our doing the study—or anyone else's doing it for that matter—but I did not take the time to explore the feeling. Macris thought it to be a fine opportunity for us, since we weren't all that close to the mayor's office those days. The study that was finally completed called for the mayor to provide guidelines for the allocation of funds for improvement programs, to establish a central clearinghouse in his office for all applications for federal funding, and to propose greater administrative flexibility in budgeting.

Well before the study was concluded, the Office of Community Development had become a reality. Seven new positions were created, and Macris had decided to take the job as its first director. Other new city planning-related positions also moved to the mayor's office from federally sponsored programs; from the Model Cities program, for example. The mayor's office was growing in other ways too. New federally funded positions opened up in areas like law enforcement and economic development. All the while, the Board of Supervisors seemed to pay little attention to the expansion of the executive function. Little or no local money was involved, and no one seemed to be keeping track of what positions were moving where. To me, the balance of power in the city seemed to be shifting, from one that favored no person or group in particular, to one that benefited the mayor at the expense of the board and the departments.

From the start, I did not get along well with the budding bureaucracy in the mayor's office. I was sure that the city planners over there would soon have their hands in some of the kinds of work that had always been our domain, or that the mayor's city planners would soon be second guessing us. Certainly my ego was involved. I did not take kindly to the people who used to make requests and who now were giving directions—particularly if they were people who had recently been working for me. By the latter half of 1973 we were engaged in quiet warfare with the Office of Community Development, the kind of battle where the combatants know what is going on and what is at stake but rarely confront each other directly, and where the general public is not privy to the action. It was the kind of conflict that I did not handle well.

My apprehensions had proved well founded. By 1973 we were being cut out of federal planning funds that had previously been used solely by the planning department. The mayor's office first wanted just a part and then increasing amounts of the federal planning monies. Since the mayor's people worked with the feds and since we could no longer apply directly for those funds, we were cut off at the pass. I could bellow in anger, and we would still not get those funds. In 1973, too, there had been at least one case of staff raiding, although there was an agreement not to do that. There were conflicts over which agency represented San Francisco on planning matters in dealing with the regional government association. Attempts to come to agreements, in writing, that would define our roles and minimize conflicts were not terribly productive. The mere fact that we were going through the exercise would tell any astute observer that a major conflict existed.

Things got worse as time passed, and by 1974 one heard reports, some confirmed, some not, of intentions to move the city planning function into the mayor's office, and of the possibility of a November charter amendment that would leave the planning commission to deal only with zoning matters. There were assertions to my staff and others (from people in the Office of Community Development) that "the mayor's office is going to have a city planning staff whether you like it or not." Barbs that I would have considered petty in other times became attacks. Whenever I wondered whether I was making too much of my differences with the mayor's growing planning staff, the answer always came out the same: they would love to see us done in, and they did not share our concern for planning the physical environment of San Francisco. Federal and local power brokers were changing the place and nature of the city's government, and they were trying to change the nature of city planning. At a time when there was substantive work to be done, too much of my energy was being directed to painful and tedious bureaucratic power games.

I was not handling the matter with particular aplomb. Going public with the issue did not seem a fruitful course. Shouting "power grab" or something like that would sound like sour grapes. I did not go directly to the planning commission either, partly for the same reason. I felt I should be able to handle the matter myself. While I kept Commission President Newman advised of my concerns, I did not ask him to take any specific action. I sensed that he and most of the other commissioners were not anxious to confront the mayor, and I was not even sure they would see things the way I did.

I did meet with Mayor Alioto more than once during this period. On those few occasions when I could get his sole attention, I told him of my concerns. He seemed to understand and even to agree with me. No, he did not want to weaken the planning department. Yes, we should be able to meet with and deal directly with federal agencies. Yes, we should have access to funds that had been "ours" in the past. Yes, we should continue in our role as planning representatives to the regional planning body. No, the Office of Community Development should not overlap or duplicate the planning department's physical planning capability. On one occasion I told him that, with federal help, power was becoming more and more centralized in his office and that this was bad for the city. I made references to consequences similar to those then so apparent in Washington in the last hours of the Nixon administration. The trouble with those meetings, regardless of how attentive and agreeable Alioto seemed to be, was that nothing came of them—the damage had been done by the time we got together. I could walk out of one of those meetings feeling good, with a sense of progress, and then nothing would happen.

My concerns did not appear to be shared by others. The one or two supervisors to whom I spoke listened and nodded their heads knowingly, but they did not seem terribly interested. The leadership of the San Francisco Planning and Urban Renewal Association reacted similarly. I sensed their wish to remain aloof. Here was another bureaucrat being gored in the never ending internal political wars. Why should they get involved? I had off-the-record meetings with reporters from the two dailies to advise them of what was going on and to suggest some in-depth reporting. Their responses were similar—and they wrote nothing. Only the *Progress*, then a twice-a-week, shopping-oriented neighborhood newspaper printed a story, but there was no follow-up. Maybe, indeed, I was somewhat paranoid on the subject.

Finally, in early 1974, I put together a list of particulars and discussed them at considerable length with President Newman. Other commissioners also were genuinely concerned, for the commission's role, too, was at stake. In late April, the commissioners met with the mayor, who apparently assured them that, while there might be personality conflicts and differences of opinion between some of his staff and me, he did not intend to weaken either the commission or the department. They seemed satisfied.

Earlier, I had said to anyone who cared to listen that my bags were always packed. And a lot of freedom comes with that point of view. If you don't really give a damn whether you're fired or not, then, presumably, job security is not a hindrance to saying what you want. I felt that such a position was a major key to successful, effective city planning. In 1972 I moved into a new house, one that I had built—until then I had rented. It is possible that my bags were no longer packed, that I was beginning to give a damn if they fired me. If, instead of worrying how to handle the growing conflict with the mayor's office, I had simply stated my concerns clearly, or shouted them, in a very public way, without worrying about how I would be heard, the situation might have handled itself. Perhaps, at some level, I was beginning to care about the personal consequences of my professional position.

My decision to leave the planning department was related to what was happening in the mayor's office. But that unsatisfactory relationship was by no means the only determinant, probably not even the most significant. It didn't happen either, as I had always thought it would, that some picayune issue, a hassle over a civil service regulation or over a typewriter would be the straw to break this camel's back. Instead, starting as early as 1971, the pull of other places and other ideas was becoming increasingly insistent.

If I did not respond positively to job offers starting in 1971, I did on occasion listen to and consider them. There were other pulls, to do other things. I had never done much professionally related travel, not even to Washington, preferring to stay home and mind the store. But in late 1973 I accepted an invitation to visit cities in Germany, and I was accepting engagements in far-flung places to lecture on city planning, particularly urban design. These were pleasant interludes.

With a grant from the National Endowment for the Arts, I began a photo essay of San Francisco, an effort that would take me from the office on some days. I accepted positions on advisory boards of organizations outside of the city. Without quite knowing or even thinking where it might lead, I was looking for other things to do. Discreetly, I let people know that I might be interested in returning to teaching. By 1973, when I was sounded out by people from the University of California about a possible teaching position at Berkeley, I was receptive.

These attractions of other places and other things were stronger than they might have been in more satisfying times. I found myself less patient and less willing to deal with personnel issues. The civil service hassles involved in getting, keeping, and advancing top-quality people and in preventing the professionally wounded from getting the best jobs were driving me nuts. A city planning director doesn't do much city planning himself, even in the best of circumstances, but I had been involved in some of our earlier plans, and besides being personally satisfying, that had made dealing with administrative matters bearable. But now administration was taking over. Management demanded more time, and I was less willing to give it. I also sensed on one or two occasions what I called a vested interest in earlier decisions. I might, for example, fail to come up with a new idea or proposal or fail to respond positively to someone else's, because I was still defending a proposal I had prepared earlier, even though it was inappropriate now. That was a dangerous position to be in.

Of the reasons for leaving, perhaps the most difficult to deal with was the kind that came as a result of success. I had felt from the start that one reason for citizens' distrust of their government was the remoteness of top level officials. It was important for department heads to be available, to be in the neighborhoods, taking part in whatever their department was supposed to do. I had been accessible, and I had enjoyed the involvement. I had expanded our neighborhood planning program. But success can bring failure. How many neighborhood meetings can one planning director attend, and how much personal attention can he give to how many neighborhoods? I also found that some of our neighborhood planners would not ask me to attend meetings in "their" areas, although I had told them that I was available. It made sense for them not to. They were anxious to learn and to do their own thing, to take charge of planning in areas where they had been assigned. I would only inhibit them, and people's attention naturally would go to the top man. Further, some did not find my style complementary to their own. So they reported what was going on at meetings and asked me to attend only when there was a major issue to be resolved. On the one hand, all of this was part and parcel of building up a quality staff. On the other hand, I was not doing some of the things I had most enjoyed, and I was aware that I, too, was becoming less accessible to residents than might be desirable.

The strongest reason for staying was the staff. I had become close friends with many. We were working for the same thing. I did not want to let them down.

Nonetheless, by early 1974 I had pretty well decided that, if the university position materialized, I would take it. If not, it was only a matter of time before I would make some move. An evening meeting in Bernal Heights helped confirm that evolving position. We were being "mau-maued" by neighborhood activists *for* designation of a new subsidized code enforcement program in their area. That was a far cry from the way people were responding to some public programs at the time. Hell, it was our program and nothing would have pleased me more than to see it used all over the city. But there were no funds available, and I was not about to promise something I couldn't deliver. I was also not sure that the group that had been arriving unannounced at my office, filling the halls, and demanding meetings represented all the people of the area. Sure enough, on the night of the meeting I was greeted by not one, but two groups. The second, equally militant, though smaller, was opposed to the project and had managed to put out a cartoon flyer in two languages accusing me of proposing all kinds of terrible things for the neighborhood. I think they had me pictured riding a bulldozer. While I was waiting to answer the first, well-prepared "have you stopped beating your wife" question, I had the strong feeling that at that moment I hated everyone in the room, even those few who "understood." At the same time, I knew that feeling to be unreasonable, that they were doing what they were supposed to do, that they were participating. I had been in situations like that a hundred times before, and though my adrenaline might have been going pretty well, I had not felt anger. Then why did I hate them?

I felt sure I would raise hell that night, that I would lose my temper. But, as a middle-aged lady read that first terrible question that someone had prepared for her, something clicked, and I knew I had the evening made. I got up, talked, and answered questions for over an hour. I laughingly told them everything that was on my mind and that we were all in a "no win" situation. I explained my position and suggested some things they could do, if they wished. Positions may or may not have changed by the time I left, but I sensed there was a lot learned and a lot more understanding than when we had started.

I thought about that night. What had happened? Prone to exaggeration, I concluded that maybe I was becoming like a punch-drunk fighter, brain slightly addled, sitting in his corner. The bell had sounded and I came out and did my thing. It was time to do something else.

Bill Wheaton, Dean of the College of Environmental Design at Berkeley, called me one day that spring, not to tell me that the teaching position had been confirmed, but to advise me that a student-faculty committee had invited me to speak at the upcoming commencement exercises. I accepted, and then pondered at some length what to say. These were not the best of times for university graduates. The sadness of Watergate was unfolding. Each day brought a new onslaught on the

sensibilities of reasonable people. One could be excused a large measure of cynicism about our governments and the people who worked in them. We were walking away from urban problems rather than challenging them. Jobs were becoming difficult to find.

I was not feeling terribly optimistic about city planning just then, either, but it did seem to me that for the budding design professional, concerned with the quality of the built and natural environment, there was plenty to do. At an understandable, local level, where people live, where satisfactions are most intensely felt, and where changing the physical environment has a tangible impact on people's lives, it was possible to do what one was trained to do. It was possible to concentrate on local issues, large or small, and to achieve solutions. The reward was a feeling of immense satisfaction. It was, in short, possible to be effective as a city planner. To make the point to that graduating class, there were plenty of examples to choose from. San Francisco had more than its share.

## Notes

1. Herb Caen, *San Francisco Chronicle*, November 17, 1970.

2. The following are the required elements. In parentheses are the year the requirement became state law and the deadline for prepara-

tion. Many of the deadlines were originally earlier, but they were extended by legislative amendment.

Land use (1965; no deadline); Circulation (1965; no deadline); Housing (1967; no deadline); Conservation (1970; December 31, 1973); Open Space (1970; interim plan by August 31, 1972); Seismic Safety (1971; December 31, 1976); Noise (1971; December 31, 1976); Scenic Highway (1971; December 31, 1976); Safety (1971; December 31, 1976).

3. For examples, see San Francisco Department of City Planning, *Housing Programs—Recommendations for Carrying Out the Plan for Residence*, May 1971; and *Programs Recommended for Carrying Out the Improvement Plan for Recreation Open Space*, 1972.

4. San Francisco Department of City Planning, *A Transportation System for the Embarcadero Area*, 1974.

5. See agenda and notes for first meeting of the Technical Advisory Committee of the Annual Development Program Project, October 2, 1972; and "Recommendations for Program Development and Management in San Francisco," July 1973, p. 4.

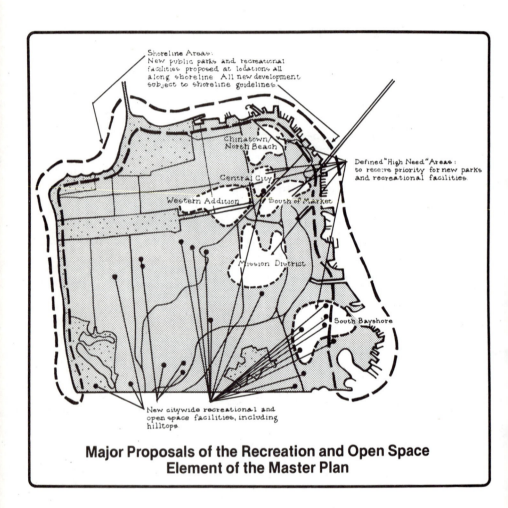

Shoreline Areas:
New public parks and recreational facilities proposed at locations all along shoreline. All new development subject to shoreline guidelines.

Chinatown/North Beach

Central City

Western Addition

South of Market

Defined "High Need" Areas: to receive priority for new parks and recreational facilities.

Mission District

South Bayshore

New citywide recreational and open space facilities, including hilltops.

## Major Proposals of the Recreation and Open Space Element of the Master Plan

# Chapter 11
# Case Study: Proposition J—
# Implementing the Recreation and
# Open Space Plan

In late 1972, the staff of the city planning department was completing a first draft of the recreation and open space element of the city's comprehensive plan. This particular effort, started in mid-1970, was part of a step-by-step, subject-matter by subject-matter approach to revising and updating the existing master plan. It was to set forth citywide objectives, policies, principles, and priorities for the location, number, and nature of recreation and open space facilities in San Francisco. Other master plan elements dealing with housing, urban design, and transportation had already been adopted, and work on still others was under way.

The city planners were not worried about getting the plan adopted, but they were concerned about implementing those parts of any plan that would require major expenditures for land acquisition and physical improvements.

There was a clear need for additional public open space, as Commission President Walter Newman observed at a meeting of the planning commission on October 12, 1972. "Public interest in preserving open space has grown tremendously," he noted. "At the same time pressures on remaining open space are increasing. Major opportunity areas exist, especially along the shoreline, but it is often difficult to take advantage of them. There is a growing demand for recreation, yet many of the city's neighborhoods lack adequate facilities."

Demand and need notwithstanding, the city planners saw little in recent local history or on the horizon to make them optimistic about obtaining public funds to purchase land for open space and recreation. They recalled the earlier efforts that had resulted in Golden Gate Park and McLaren Park, but that kind of undertaking seemed beyond the scope of the built-up San Francisco of the 1970s. To be sure, the western shoreline and part of the northern shoreline might soon be included in the federally sponsored Golden Gate National Recreation Area, but that involved a transfer of lands from one jurisdiction to another. The city would gain little new open space in the transfer. State agencies did not indicate that they were prepared to help purchase open space in San Francisco. Indeed, the state's park representatives shunned the idea of a new state park in an urban area. Locally, recent bond issue proposals for recreation and open space development and improvements had failed, and proposals to purchase land as part of the capital improvement program were never funded. The Recreation and Park Department had precious little in the way of funds to maintain what park land existed. The department feared that new open space would only increase its burden. Gifts of open space were welcome, of course, but there was no assurance that they would coincide with areas of greatest need, and they were few and far between anyway. Elected officials might be sympathetic, but new open space was not one of their highest priorities.

This case study has to do with plan implementation. More specifically it describes a successful effort that was initiated by the planning department to carry out its citywide plan for recreation and open space. The effort came down to asking the voters to tax themselves for a 15-year period to purchase the city's last important open spaces and to add new ones where they were most needed.

The recreation and open space proposals that the planners were working on were by no means the first for San Francisco. In the 1860s, Frederick Law Olmsted had prepared plans that led to the creation of Golden Gate Park. (William Hammond Hall prepared the original plans for the park itself.) Much more recently, in 1956, a "Recreation Area and Park Location Plan" was adopted by the planning commission and became part of the city's master plan. The newest effort came about for a number of reasons. The remaining open space in the city, some of it critically located, was fast disappearing, and the same was true throughout the Bay Area. The greatest need for recreation areas was in lower income minority neighborhoods; a plan could try to deal with the inequities. And in a city bounded on three sides by water, the recreation potential of the shoreline had yet to be realized. But with many demands for recreation and open space and with limited resources to meet them, the question of priorities was always present. Open space may not have been the most pressing issue in San Francisco in the early 1970s, but it was nevertheless an issue.

There were other reasons for preparing a plan. The urban design plan which was then being prepared was providing considerable information that was directly applicable to recreation and open space matters. It was information that could be used with ease. State legislation that was passed in late 1970 required local governments to adopt open space plans by 1972. Although the city planners had started their work before the legislation had passed and were not greatly concerned about the mandate, they were aware that it existed. Some impetus to the effort also came from the Recreation and Park Department. In addition, the planners cared a great deal about the subject matter of this plan and felt they had some expertise in the area.

Under the direction of Dean Macris, assistant director for plans and programs, at least five staff members worked on the plan from its start until October 1972, when a preliminary version was presented.[1] Only one or two of them worked full time on the project for extended periods. They worked closely with Tom Malloy, an ex-staff member of the planning department, who was then with the Recreation and Park Department (Rec-Park).

Rec-Park was the operating agency most concerned with a recreation and open space plan. In 1970, it had commissioned a "plan for action," which analyzed its facilities and programs. The two-part report criticized poor maintenance of existing facilities, and proposed changes that would require new funding.[2] It was as much a plan for streamlining operations and identifying areas of "high need" as it was a plan for additional space and facilities. Malloy was instrumental in getting planning department input into that study, especially in determining the areas of high need. He understood how the city planners would be helpful to him, for instance in dealing with the consultants who were preparing the report. Throughout the preparation of the open space plan, Malloy provided a critical link to the Recreation and Park Commission and its staff.

Members of the planning commission were not intimately involved in the preparation of the plan, at least not until the public hearings on the initial proposal. A commission committee was kept advised of the progress of the work, but for the most part the planning was left to the staff. Neither the mayor nor the supervisors played any significant role.

Contact with citizens and neighborhood associations could best be described as modest. Many of the ideas, policies, and proposals in the final document, however, derived directly from the plans that neighborhood groups had prepared (Potrero Hill, Bernal Heights, the Richmond, and Oceanview-Merced Heights-Ingleside, for example). Other input came informally, in meetings or from people's comments at zoning hearings and other meetings of the commission. Planners who were working in the neighborhoods also provided information. But there was no citywide citizens advisory committee to help prepare the plan and no preliminary reports from which to get feedback. There was, in fact, no formalized process of citizen participation in the preparation of the plan until the preliminary plan, including a proposal for citizen review, was drafted and distributed in September 1972.

There was, however, relatively continuous input from city and regional organizations that had conservation or recreation and open space interests. These included official agencies such as the Bay Conservation and Development Commission and the Association of Bay Area Governments, and activist groups like People For Open Space and California Tomorrow. In the city, the names of two organizations give an inkling of the kinds of counsel the planners sought: San Francisco Beautiful and the Citizens' Waterfront Committee.

The preliminary plan that was produced in September 1972— *Improvement Plan for Recreation and Open Space: A Proposal for Citizen Review*—outlined policies relating to recreation and open space at both the citywide and neighborhood levels, including the more than 20 mile shoreline, and at the regional scale. The plan was accompanied by locational maps.

The first policy stated was simply that existing public open space should be preserved. An obvious, uncontroversial proposal, it would seem. Not so. Public space, in the form of reservoirs, grounds of public buildings, and dedicated but undeveloped street rights-of-way, was often in the hands of agencies that cared little for open space. This policy said to those agencies and to the city that such land should be retained as open space unless there was a very good reason to the contrary, that public parks should not be used in any nonrecreational way, and that there should be a presumption in public open space against the construction or expansion of recreational and cultural buildings. Rec-Park was opposed to such a policy. In accord with its charter-mandated responsibilities, the general manager and some of his commissioners did not want to be told how to use their land. They wanted to be able to put a facility on property they already owned without having to pay the price for new land, or at least that was the way the city planners viewed Rec-Park's position. The planners would not compromise as Rec-Park wished, and the policy was proposed over the objections of the operating agency.

Another policy, to eliminate nonrecreational uses in parks and to reduce auto traffic in and around public open space, was also geared to making the most of what existed. Two other policies, to acquire additional citywide open space for public use and to require usable outdoor open space in new residential development, were directed to increasing the supply. The first was directed to privately held sites that had long been regarded as public open space and to hilltop locations and other land with unique natural characteristics. Proposed sites were located in the plan.

On the neighborhood level, where the problem of acquiring new land and financing new facilities persisted, the city planners proposed a policy of making more intensive use of existing facilities by means of additional staffing, improved maintenance, multiple use, and increased accessibility. The planners also proposed new space and facilities, including use of street space and portable facilities. They gave priority to the high-need neighborhoods.

A significant part of the plan was aimed at increasing the recreational use of the city's shoreline. However, the planners recognized the importance of the port facilities and water-related industries. Their recommendations included creation of a special shoreline zone to insure that all new public and private uses conformed to the plan, improvement of existing public facilities, and creation of new shoreline parks. The parts of the plan that dealt with the shoreline were presented in considerable detail, because much of the land was in the hands of one public agency or another, most notably the federal government, which owned the Presidio army base, and the city's port commission.

The planners understood that San Francisco was a part of the larger Bay region. The city could not meet all of its recreation and open space needs within its own boundaries, and a city-centered Bay Area plan would not be realized without a permanent regional open space system to guide development. Much of the regional open space was also owned by San Francisco in the form of watershed lands. With these considerations in mind, the planners called for the city to support the establishment of a regional agency responsible for open space regulation, acquisition, and management; to increase accessibility of regional parks by locating them near population centers and providing public access to them; and to place a high priority on the acquisition of lands with unique natural qualities. In a sense, the planners were providing city officials with policy guidelines for relating to a particular regional concern, one that was shared locally.

Together with their preliminary plan, the planners published a set of of programs to carry it out—*Programs Recommended for Carrying out the Improvement Plan for Recreation and Open Space*. The programs dealt with such matters as state and local legislation, specific public improvements to reduce traffic, changes to the city's zoning ordinance, specific locations and designs of new facilities, staffing, and maintenance. They included proposals for specific sites in high-need neighborhoods. Although stress was placed on preserving and making better use of existing resources, acquisition of new lands and construction of facilities could hardly be avoided. But the city planners avoided saying with any specificity just how much these proposals were likely to cost or where the money was to come from. In fact, they did not know.

The preliminary plan and implementing programs were presented in October 1972 before a joint meeting of the city planning and recreation and park commissions. Four hundred copies were distributed before the meeting. The presentation was uneventful, and the next day it was reported without fanfare in the two daily newspapers. By the time of the first public hearing in mid-November, another 250 copies had been distributed and the planning staff had met with a number of citywide and neighborhood groups to discuss the contents. These were important meetings in that they gave the staff and the representatives of the community groups a chance to iron out differences in regard to specific proposals. People began to understand that the planners were not wedded to their initial plan and that they did listen and respond to reasonable alternatives.

Public commentary at the three public hearings followed a pattern, most of it favorable to both the broad policies and the specific recommendations. Most often, people wanted more than was proposed, and a couple of groups—the Mission Coalition was one—prepared detailed reviews of the plan in relation to their areas.[3] Only one group, from a lower income area, spoke against buying up new open space, but the neighborhood it represented was in a unique position, having recently been provided with additional open space by a redevelopment project. It was not alone, however, in stressing that the maintenance of existing facilities was at least as important as acquiring new ones.

Considerable testimony dealt not so much with the plan as with the means of carrying it out. One line of testimony held that the programs should be part of the plan and that both should be adopted by the Board of Supervisors as well as the planning commission. Only then, it was held, would there be full commitment to implementing the plan. The planners were criticized for not speaking to the question of how the new facilities were to be obtained, and for not adequately addressing the matter of costs.

The suggestions that came out of the hearings ranged from zoning land for open space (without compensation to owners) to simply increasing the budget of the Rec-Park Department from the city's general fund to permit acquisition of what was needed (not very likely given the history of that budget). There were proposals for a regional open space agency that would carry out local as well as regional recommendations of the plan, for mini-assessment districts at the neighborhood level, for neighborhood fund raising campaigns, and for new open space agencies with their own funding sources like those that had been created in nearby counties. Another idea was to create a new open space acquisition and development fund that would be a source of matching funds for federal and state grants. These ideas often came in the form of criticism: "Why haven't you proposed such and such?" or "Why do you bring us all the way down here when there's no way to . . . ?" Whether the planners or those testifying knew it or not, they were participating in the start of an idea to carry out the plan as much as in the plan itself.

With the end of the first round of public hearings, the staff started to review testimony and to meet more frequently with the people who had new proposals or who found fault with the work. It would take until mid-April to come up with a revised document. In the meantime, the planning director was feeling increasingly that the prospects of implementing any part of a plan that called for expenditures for new land or facilities were dim at best. A regional open space agency was years away, and there was little hope that a two-thirds majority of the voters could be mustered to pass a local bond issue for open space. Neighborhood fund raising efforts would raise nickels and dimes at best, and mini-assessment districts would not address citywide needs even if they were successful. And they were not likely to be successful in poor neighborhoods where the need was greatest.

There was the possibility of a citizen-led effort that would set up some kind of special open space districts with its own taxing powers. The special open space districts in Marin and Santa Clara counties had been the result of the dedication of grassroots, activist, citizens' groups that had worked long and hard to get their ideas adopted via petitions, referenda, and special elections. The director sensed that they had succeeded despite official bureaucracies, that is by by-passing the established governmental institutions rather than because of them. A similar grass-roots effort in San Francisco might work. It would require a simple majority rather than a two-thirds vote to pass. Also, the threat of a citizen-led petition drive to get such a measure on a ballot might be effective with elected officials. Supervisors might want to be on the right side of that issue, not appear to be opposed to it by refusing to put it on the ballot themselves. But it seemed very unlikely to the director that the planning commission, part of the administration after all, would advocate or endorse a citizen-led charter amendment or petition-signing campaign to set up a special district government or an agency to buy and develop new open space.

In late February 1973 the planning director and Emily Hill, the staff planner most responsible for recreation and open space planning, called a meeting to discuss implementation of the recreation and open space plan. They were convinced that a special effort was needed, one that would go outside the more usual methods of plan implementation to which city planning departments were accustomed. Sixteen people were invited to the Saturday morning, Saint Patrick's Day meeting in the planning department's offices: representatives of city and regional planning and open space groups, well-known open space activists such as Dorothy Erskine and Margot Patterson Doss (a prolific and popular writer on San Francisco), people from lower and moderate-income neighborhoods, a member of State Assemblyman Willie Brown's staff, a representative from the Levi Strauss firm whom the director knew to be sympathetic on environmental matters, and Tom Malloy of Rec-Park. Many of the people did not know each other. The planning commission's president, Walter Newman, had been advised of the meeting.

At the meeting, the planning director told the group that nothing was likely to come of the plan that was soon to be adopted unless some special effort was made to implement it. He hoped that the people who were present would form the nucleus of a group that would make that effort. He outlined two or three approaches and said they should be prepared to take their case directly to the voters if the mayor and Board of Supervisors or even the planning commission would not support them. The group that made this effort would have to be a dedicated, narrowly focused one. Would they form such a group to work privately to come up with the best of alternative methods, and then work publicly to achieve it? Emily Hill would be at their disposal whenever they wished, and they could call on the director when they felt so inclined. In response, they formed a steering committee of nine members and got started.

The steering committee took to its task with zest. One month after the initial meeting at the planning department, it was considering a proposal by Malloy for creation of a new open space advisory board to advise the Rec-Park Commission on open space acquisition and for earmarking a predesignated amount of property taxes, yearly for 15 years, for open space acquisition and development.[4] Two weeks later the committee was debating the pros and cons of five additional possibilities, including mandatory use of a local real estate transfer tax for open space acquisition, use of pending state legislation and funding for beautification of local streets, and formation under state law of a new regional park district, the "region" being the city and county of San Francisco in this case. The committee had been enlarged by at least one member, Howard Chickering, a lawyer representing the San Francisco Bar Association.

The role played by the planning staff during this period leading to a firm proposal was significant. Emily Hill helped the committee in its research, kept it informed of the progress of the plan and of related city issues, and acted as a liaison with the director. She, together with the director and George Williams, a lawyer-planner who had recently become an assistant director, reviewed and debated alternative proposals and made substantive suggestions to the committee. Williams's legislative drafting skills became more important as time passed. The director's major concern was that the committee's efforts stay directed toward a secure funding and organizational mechanism to carry out the plan. In addition, the director tried to dispel the members' distrust of the Rec-Park hierarchy (including its commissioners).

At some point in June, the steering committee rejected the idea of a San Francisco regional park district, because that device would require state legislation as well as action by the San Francisco Board of Supervisors, or by the people, through an initiative. (Existing state law required that a regional park district be formed by at least two cities and/or counties. The city and county of San Francisco constituted only one unit.) The members concluded that it would be better to pursue the idea of a special agency with a reserve fund, as an addition to the charter.

Between early July and the end of November, an initial draft and at least four significant revisions of a charter amendment were prepared. The steering committee met regularly to consider the changes, and the parent group met on occasion to ratify the steering committee's endeavors.

The charter amendment that was proposed would create an open space acquisition fund for 15 years, to be financed by a tax of 10 cents on each $100 of assessed property valuation. The fund would be used only for recreation and open space purposes determined by the planning department to be consistent with its recreation and open space plan. Expenditures would also have to accord with an action program, to be endorsed by the planning and Rec-Park commissions meeting jointly. Funds could be used for development of the purchased lands only in designated "high-need neighborhoods" as defined in the plan. There were other stipulations; for instance, a certain percentage of funds in any five-year period had to be used for land acquisition, and staff size had to be limited. But the proposal would join two key city commissions in a common task. It would give them money to spend for a clearly defined goal.[5]

By the time the committee finished the first phase of its work, the planning commission had adopted, on May 24, 1973, the revised improvement plan for recreation and open space as the recreation and open space element of the master plan. The commission had also, on July 19, endorsed the *Recreation and Open Space Programs: Recommendations for Carrying Out the Recreation and Open Space Element of the Comprehensive Plan* and authorized the director to "take all reasonable steps" to implement the programs. By that time, too, the staff, working directly with Assemblyman Willie Brown's office, had

seen the state budget $10 million for the acquisition and development
of a park in the largely black, low- and moderate-income South Bayshore area, a proposal that had first appeared four years earlier in the
department's plan for the South Bayshore.

Until this time, the work of the open space group and its steering
committee had been remarkably low-key. It is doubtful that as many as
100 people knew of their existence or of the details of what they were
proposing. Nor could their members be called heavyweights in the
usual, political, "movers and shakers" sense. There were no elected
officials involved to this point, no state or national representatives
(except Willie Brown's assistant), no well-known business or media
names, none of the big names usually associated with power, politics, or
fashion. Rather, it was an effort of conservationists and open space
advocates, representatives of low- and moderate-income neighborhoods, young lawyers from established firms working in public advocacy roles, League of Women Voters people, and city planners. Although their names were not exactly household words in San Francisco,
many of them had long been active in city affairs, and they were known
and respected by those in power. Now the committee decided it was
time to test the waters in a more public way, to seek support from
elected political figures and the influential people who helped put them
in office.

Early in December, Robert Kirkwood, a lawyer and civic activist
working with the steering committee, advised the mayor's director of
community development of the proposal and asked for advice on what
steps to take in the mayor's office. At the same time, the committee
invited 200 people to a meeting to discuss the plan. The presentations
spoke to the need for saving scarce open space, for providing parks in
high-need neighborhoods, and for implementing the plan that had been
approved. The fact sheet prepared for the meeting stressed the relatively low cost of the proposals.

Copies of the proposal for a charter amendment were then sent to
all the supervisors, along with letters requesting their support. By the
first of the year Supervisor Ronald Pelosi, an ex-planning commissioner,
who was considered to be a friend of the department and of open
space-conservationist groups, introduced the charter amendment to
the full board. The timing was important, since, if the board chose to put
the matter on the ballot in June, a long and costly petition-signing
campaign would be unnecessary. Moreover, the public debates leading

to the final legislation might produce a more universally acceptable document than if the sponsoring group had to guess at what would satisfy diverse interests. If the group were to solicit signatures on petitions in favor of a specific charter amendment, it would not be able to change the language of the proposal without starting a new petition geared to the precise new language. But going through the Board of Supervisors, with its public hearings, would provide a chance to sharpen the language and make it acceptable to a wider audience.

Before it could be heard by the board's Legislative and Personnel Committee, the amendment was referred to the city planning commission, the port commission, and the recreation and park commission for comments and recommendations. Within two weeks, the Rec-Park commission had approved it, with only minor changes. A week later, the planning commission did the same. The Legislative and Personnel Committee made more minor changes and approved the proposal in early February. A last-minute attempt by Joseph Caverly, the general manager of Rec-Park, to allow two new executive appointments was beaten back by the steering committee and one or two supervisors. (Members of the steering committee were reported to have been aghast when Caverly stood up to say he could not support the charter amendment unless he got his wish![6]) One month later the full board approved submission of the proposal—Proposition C—to the voters on the June ballot. The first rounds had been successful, and a campaign for voter approval was on.

By most big city funding standards, the campaign to pass Proposition C, the open space measure, was small. A new six-member steering committee was formed—San Franciscans for Open Space/Recreation—and it set a budget of $32,000 for the effort.[7] Some three years earlier, the chamber of commerce was rumored to have amassed a war chest of 15 times that amount to fight an initiative to limit building height. What the committee lacked in money it hoped to make up in energy. It had influential cochairmen, including Supervisor Pelosi; it had a good issue, and it had or soon would have a lot of people working on its side.

The three-month campaign, with a general theme of "Save Something [Open Space] For Yourself," had all the trappings of a major San Francisco vote-getting effort: fund raising; direct mailings; advertisements on transit vehicles; staged media events at threatened open space sites; posters on houses, stores, and fences; literature handouts at shopping centers; telephone campaigns; evening meetings with neighborhood organizations. On weekends, groups went door-to-door in neighborhoods where demographic data and the record of previous elections suggested that person-to-person contacts would be helpful.

Without being officially assigned to the effort, Emily Hill worked with the committee on a nonstop basis. The assistant director, George Williams, also spent considerable time in the effort, mostly after hours. The director offered his time and services in whatever capacity the committee wished, but at this stage his involvement was limited to occasional public speaking appearances and meetings with editorial writers of the two daily papers.

Efforts to gain support of noted individuals and important organizations were successful. In one way or another almost every locally based elected public official, including the mayor, a congressman, and state legislators, publicly supported the proposal. Nineteen citywide and neighborhood organizations and well over 100 individuals supported the measure in the voters handbook that was distributed just before the election. Only two people signed an argument against Proposition C.

The committee was less successful at getting favorable wording for the measure in the voters handbook and on the ballot itself. Wording on the ballot started out, "Shall a tax of ten cents ($0.10) for each one hundred dollars ($100.00) of assessed valuation be imposed...." The first words that greeted the reader, then, were those having to do with cost rather than with the objective of the amendment.

There were other problems. The *San Francisco Examiner* opposed the measure, as did the influential neighborhood-oriented *San Francisco Progress* and a major radio station, KCBS. The chamber of commerce also opposed Proposition C.

Internal dissension among its members made the committee less effective than it could have been. The dissension centered on disagreements between the people paid to direct the campaign (one of whom had earlier been a member of the committee) and the volunteer members. They disagreed over the best ways of spending the limited resources and where to concentrate them for maximum effectiveness.

What bothered the planners most, however, was that people in some neighborhoods, most notably Chinatown, felt that the proposal wouldn't serve them because it didn't provide money for recreation programs (as opposed to open space) and new indoor facilities. This was unfortunate in that the plan had designated Chinatown as one of the high-need, high-priority neighborhoods. The plan appears to have been poorly presented in that area (and perhaps others); the committee did not call upon the top people of the planning department to present the proposals in areas where they might have been most effective.

Regardless of the problems, the committee and the planners approached election day with hopeful anticipation. There had been a lot of hard work and enthusiasm, and there seemed to be strong support for the proposal. They thought they would win. They were wrong. Proposition C lost by a vote of 73,865 to 78,018, a margin of 4,153 votes out of a total of 151,983.

Less than 24 hours after Proposition C lost, the planning director and staff members George Williams and Peter Svirsky decided they should try again. The election had been so close that any number of small changes could have made it successful. Immediately, even before any changes were made in the wording of the amendment, Supervisor Pelosi was asked to reintroduce the proposal before the board so that it could be placed on the ballot in November. On June 6, two days after the election, the planning director suggested to the commission that it encourage another try. Pelosi reintroduced the measure on June 10.

Some changes would have to be made, but given the time and effort that had been put forth on the first proposal, the planners felt that they should be as few as possible. Any changes that were made should be designed to pick up new supporters without losing the support of those who were in favor of the original measure.

The big change would be to earmark 25 per cent of the revenues for renovation of existing parks and recreation facilities, part of this to be matched by private funds. This change was in part a response to those opponents of Proposition C who felt Rec-Park could not adequately maintain the facilities it had and who also wanted to encourage private initiative in the provision of facilities rather than to depend wholly on public actions. Another change was to make any neighborhood (not just one designated high-need) eligible for the renovation funds. Other changes were more semantic than substantive; for instance, altering the title of the proposed fund from "Open Space Acquisition Fund" to "Open Space Acquisition and Park Renovation Fund" to emphasize the fact that existing facilities were as important as new ones.

The planning director called editorial writer Dick Pearce of the

*Examiner* to see if the paper would support the effort if changes were made. While no firm commitment was made, Pearce was encouraging. The publisher of the *San Francisco Progress* was also contacted (by George Williams) to see what changes would be acceptable to him. Apparently, he was flattered to be asked.

Another strategy was to see if the city attorney would agree to change the wording on the voting machines from something that started "Shall a tax of . . . " to new wording to the effect of "Shall existing parks and recreation facilities be renovated. . . ."

At the invitation of Pelosi, 20 to 30 Proposition C supporters met at the planning department late in June to help rewrite the proposal and to discuss a campaign stategy for November. Most agreed that the planners' changes were in order. Representatives of Chinatown, which had not strongly supported the earlier effort, were still at odds with the proposal and wanted a guarantee that their area would get its share of funds. On the whole, however, there was a willingness to try again.

In early August, the amendment was approved for the November ballot. It would be known as Proposition J. The staff of the planning department had been instrumental in bringing the matter to its present state, especially in drafting the final amendment. It would be involved, too, in the second campaign.

The original citizens' committee had been reorganized to promote Proposition J, and it had a new name, The Coalition for Neighborhood Parks. Unfortunately, it was less well funded than the first effort and had fewer big names. Campaign coordinator Ken Hunter called for a "bare bones" election fund of $6,000. With that little money, the emphasis would have to be on media endorsements, handbills, door-to-door campaigns, support from office seekers in their campaign literature, and getting favorable wording on the ballot.

All of these things were done. The ballot wording was changed exactly as had been proposed by George Williams. This time it made only scant reference to money. Supervisor Pelosi was instrumental in persuading the city attorney of the appropriateness of changing the wording. Meetings were arranged between media representatives and Proposition J supporters. This time the *Chronicle, Examiner* and *Progress* endorsed the proposal as did the lesser known papers. KCBS was for it, but KRON-TV was opposed. This time the chamber of commerce endorsed the proposal as did the one supervisor who had balked previously. The same officials, organizations, and individuals that had backed Proposition C supported J in the new voters handbook. The only organization opposed to the measure in the handbook was the San Francisco Board of Realtors. The planning director debated with its president on television in what was thought to be an effective defense of the proposal.

Particular attention was paid to Chinatown. The staff of the planning department went to meetings and made sure that the measure was explained clearly, including the possibility of leasing existing structures for recreation purposes in that land-scarce neighborhood. In other neighborhoods, high school students distributed Proposition J handbills. As voting day came near, the Coalition for Neighborhood Parks found funds to sponsor some short television and radio ads.

Despite all the effort, the proponents were doubtful of their chances at the polls. The effort had been a penny-pinching one at best. The same basic measure had failed five months earlier. The national economy had deteriorated since June, and the 1974 city tax bills arrived in people's mailboxes on the day before the election.

But on election day Proposition J passed overwhelmingly—116,654 in favor and 64,527 opposed. The voters had approved a charter amendment that would provide an estimated $2.5 million a year, for 15 years, to implement the plan that had been prepared by the planning department. The amendment grew out of a meeting that had been called almost two years earlier by the department's staff for precisely that purpose.

On election day the voters also approved another charter amendment that would require a two-thirds vote of approval by the Board of Supervisors for most new construction in Golden Gate Park. That vote, too, was consistent with the plan prepared by the city planners. During this same period, open space advocates in Berkeley, across the Bay from San Francisco, passed a similar measure. The city's planners had reason to conclude that they were being effective.

It is worthwhile seeing what has happened, by mid-1977, with the funds generated by Proposition J. (In 1977-78, the allocation was slightly over $3 million.) To what extent have the funds been used to carry out the plan in the first two-and-one-half years since the voters passed the measure?

The charter amendment did not call for any special commission, board, or committee to oversee Proposition J funds. This was to be left to the city planning and Rec-Park commissions meeting jointly and in accord with their own administrative processes. Moreover, the board was to have the final say on any lands to be acquired. Some Proposition J committee members, neighborhood leaders, and Supervisor Pelosi too, thought some kind of new citizens' monitoring group to represent neighborhoods and to help set spending priorities would be in order.

It took the various interests approximately six months to agree to legislation establishing an "Open Space/Park Renovation Citizens Advisory Committee."[8] A basic responsibility of the 23-member group would be to assist and advise the general manager of Rec-Park and the planning director in establishing priorities for renovation, acquisition, and development of properties in accordance with the recreation and open space element of the master plan.

One of the early functions of the new committee was to serve as a watchdog. It prevented one supervisor from carrying out a move to divert Proposition J funds to cover the normal budget for recreation and park maintenance. This was a possibility that had been foreseen by the original committee. By early 1978 there were indications that other supervisors would try to divert or stop the use of those funds.

The Rec-Park and city planning staffs and commissions were reluctant to move until the committee was in place, and it was not until mid-1976 that the first acquisition through Proposition J funds occurred—a less than one-acre site purchased for $110,000 in the high-need Mission district. By the end of 1976, two other sites had been acquired for approximately $860,000: another in the Mission and one that was definitely not in a designated high-need area. By the start of 1977 two additional sites in high-need neighborhoods were being appraised and six hilltop sites were in various stages preliminary to acquisition.[9] No park renovation projects had actually started.

By mid-1977 there were indications that use of the Proposition J funds to implement the plan were moving ahead, but slowly. If proposals for fiscal 1977-78 were carried out—purchase of four properties in high-need areas, eight hilltop sites, two waterfront sites, and 11 renovation projects—the pace would have quickened. It is reasonable to conclude that the intent of Proposition J was being realized but that prodding and watchdogging would be necessary to implement the plan: constant prodding of all the agencies involved to get on with the job and watchdogging to see that less than high-priority sites and facilities not use scarce resources. Whether the planning department or the Citizens Advisory Committee fulfilled these roles was to be seen.

Looked at in a straightforward, matter-of-fact way—a plan followed by two efforts to help carry it out through a legislative-assured funding mechanism—there may be nothing especially remarkable about this case. It lacks some of the conflict and excitement associated with a Transamerica case, an urban design plan, or a citywide height and bulk ordinance. To some, there may be a certain blandness to it all. The city planners were doing what they were supposed to do, and in 1977 the results looked favorable in terms of achieving what was intended. That matter-of-factness may be the most significant part of the case. City planning was working and was accepted, as were the roles of the city planners, by many, many people. A rather important improvement program was carried out calmly and quietly as a normal part of government.

It is worth noting, also, that this was a purely local effort. Those involved had paid little attention to the state mandate of an open space plan. They were not looking for federal or state funds to carry out their plan. The plan was local, for local purposes, to meet local needs. That kind of planning and implementation was a lot more fun for the planners than responding to criteria and regulations set by others. Also, any number of people, both from Rec-Park and from the planning department, have noted that as federal funding for many programs disappeared and as budgets became tighter in the mid-1970s and as land prices soared with inflation, this program was well funded and was moving.

Many others, beyond the city planners who prepared the plan, were responsible for the success of Proposition J. But the planners' role was significant, and it is worth reviewing and assessing the factors that contributed to this success.

Without a plan in the first place there would have been little to

implement. Although more than one public improvement bond program has been proposed and passed without benefit of a plan, the city
planners would not have initiated and argued for an implementing
mechanism that was not related to a plan they had prepared or adopted.
Moreover, there is reason to believe that San Franciscans might well
have shunned a simple bond issue directed to recreation and open
space improvements and acquisitions. Three such proposals had failed
since 1965. Proposition J was based upon a plan that had been publicly
aired and debated. It was a plan that had been criticized for not being
tied to specific implementing mechanisms to purchase and improve
space and facilities. As such, it represented something to be achieved.

The nature of the plan was significant. It was and is a policy plan.
For the most part, the policies deal broadly with what the city ought to
do in order to achieve objectives set out in the plan document. Nevertheless, where it was deemed possible and desirable to be specific about
proposals for sites—along the shoreline, for instance, and for many
citywide spaces (especially hilltop sites)—the maps that accompanied
the proposals clearly showed them. Where it was more difficult and less
important to know with certainty where new spaces would be located
and more important to establish need and priority regardless of specific
location (as in the high-need areas), the policies spoke directly to that
issue and maps located the areas in question so there could be little
doubt. When people voted on Proposition J, they knew reasonably well
what they were voting for: the plan provided a good mix of generality
and specificity.

The location of the city planning function within a semi-autonomous city planning commission contributed to the effectiveness of the
city planners in implementing their plan. The planners were in a position where they could develop and respond to a city planning-open
space constituency with some ease. They could work with groups of
interested people to develop an implementing mechanism for their
plans. They did this within the existing governmental structure. Approval of the mayor or the supervisors was not required for the planners' early efforts to organize supporters. Located as they were under a
commission, the planners had a level of freedom to pursue their interests that might not have been so readily available had the planning
function been located under the mayor or the board. In San Francisco's
government there were any number of checks and balances to stop the
planners from running amok if they were to be so foolish. At the same

time, their freedom did not stop them from working with the mayor or the board.

Freedom to call a meeting does not assure that anyone will come or that those attending will take happily to a challenge, once it is made. It is reasonable to conclude that over the years a city planning-open space constituency had matured; there was considerable mutual trust and commonness of purpose between the planners and the people. Without those characteristics, it is doubtful that the cooperation and coordination essential to success would have taken place. The city planners were in a position where they could speak and be trusted by most of the involved groups.

What if the department staff had not taken the lead in 1972 to find a new method of implementing the plan they were preparing? One can never be sure about those kinds of "ifs," but it is not unreasonable to imagine that others would have filled the void. Similar movements in nearby Bay Area counties had been successfully initiated by what were largely citizen-led groups. And San Francisco was certainly not lacking for open space, conservation, and recreation leadership among its residents. Faced with an issue that concerned them or a plan they approved of, one or more groups might well have started a movement similar to the one that took place. And it could have been successful. Nonetheless, the department was critical to the effort. Its staff had comprehensive knowledge that few others possessed. Not all that many people knew there were such places as Martha Hill, or knew their locations. The staff also was intimately familiar with a wide variety of people and interests and could bring them together more easily than could most anyone else. And a citizens' group would have had little to implement if there had not been a plan.

Implementing a major part of the plan for recreation and open space required a knowledge of government and its administrative machinery. The city planners and open space advocates were painfully aware of the sad fate of recent general obligation bond proposals for recreation and open space. They concluded there was little likelihood of achieving the required two-thirds vote in the near future. Their knowledge of San Francisco's government led them to the device of a charter amendment, which only required a 50 per cent vote, as a more likely mechanism. They knew, too, how to go about getting their measure to the voters with reasonable ease and how to go about getting favorable wording for their proposal on the ballot.

It could be argued that implementing a plan via a charter amendment, including the funding, is a strange way to set public improvement priorities. And to the extent that the planners encouraged that mechanism, they were not exactly engaged in comprehensive planning or plan implementation. At best, the approach involved setting priorities sequentially, not comprehensively, certainly not by weighing the importance or value of one proposal against many (or even one or two) others or in relation to any public assessment of fiscal resources. And one does not normally think of a city's constitution as the best or proper place for long-range budgeting to take place. The planners would have a hard time convincing anyone that they had weighed recreation and open space priorities against others found in their plans. To be sure, bond issues are as sequential as Proposition J, but they at least require a two-thirds vote of the people, and they require programming as part of the capital improvement process. It could even be argued that the city planners were no less ad hoc incrementalists than those they so often oppose for just that reason.

In response, the planners could contend that their recreation and open space plan was not only comprehensive for the subject matter at hand but was also related to and coordinated with the other master plan elements. Clearly on the defensive, the planners might observe that comprehensive, long-range, assured funding programs for physical improvements simply do not happen very often. One could wait a long time to achieve that kind of comprehensiveness and unified priority setting, and by that time much of the desired open space would be gone. Comprehensive or not, this was the best available way of carrying out their plan.

In large measure, the critics were correct. The city planners had traded off some degree of comprehensiveness for what they held to be urgent and for what they reasoned to be effective.

The city planners did more than prepare a plan. They were willing to speak for it publicly and work with others to carry it out. They wanted it to work. It was the planning department's plan, regardless of whether the particular document had been prepared by the current staff or inherited by it. Advocacy alone might have gotten the planners nowhere, just as professional skills might have been insufficient by themselves. Together, they were very powerful.

As late as the first public presentations and hearings on the recreation and open space plan, the city planners had little idea of how they would implement some of its major proposals. They were criticized for that, for presenting a plan without detailed cost estimates and without specific implementation means. They did not know what the effective means were. But they felt what they were proposing was reasonable and that it was the kind of plan San Francisco should have. Later, they helped find a way to implement open space proposals and worked successfully to that end. What if they had not found a means? And what if their efforts with a particular means had failed? Would the plan have been less valid? The city planners would like to think not. They would like to think they would have found and successfully advocated another way.

## Notes

1. Emily Hill, Jim Paul, Beatrice Ryan, Dennis Ryan, John Sanger, and Jim White.

2. The first section of the final *Plan for Action* was by the Blyth-Zellerbach Committee; the second, on program evaluation, was by the Planning Research Corporation.

3. See San Francisco City Planning Commission minutes of December 12, 1972.

4. Document introduced to the steering committee by Tom Malloy on April 17, 1973.

5. "Revised Open Space Charter Amendments," November 29, 1973; and "Report from Steering Committee/Lowcost," October 1, 1973.

6. Caverly's reaction was reported by Joan Hockaday, a steering committee member, in comments on the first draft of this chapter. For more on the amendment, see Rec-Park Department memo of January 17, 1974, from Tom Malloy to Joseph Caverly; *San Francisco Examiner*

article of January 18, 1974; and San Francisco City Planning Commission minutes of January 24, 1974.

7. Robert Kirkwood, Dorothy Erskine, Howard Chickering, Joan Hockaday, Richard Park, and David Yamakawa.

8. Ordinance 148-75, March 24, 1975.

9. Recreation and Park Department, General Manager's Report, "Open Space Acquisition and Park Renovation Fund—Fiscal Year 1977-78," January 7, 1977.

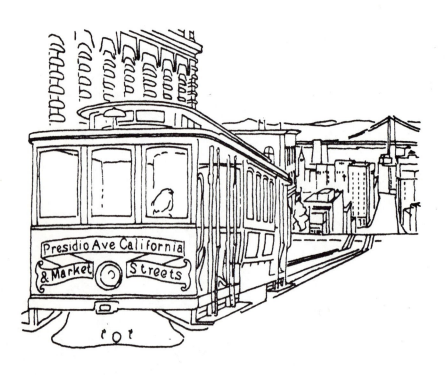

# Chapter 12
# Looking Back

Comprehensive, citywide, long-range physical planning is important and can work. The idea of a comprehensive plan that contains policies, principles, and visions of what a community wants to be in relation to its physical development, to serve as the basis for both immediate and long-range actions and for legislation geared to its achievement—the idea of such a plan as a foundation of city planning is valid, and it is borne out by much of the work that was done in San Francisco.

Measured against a demanding model of what a comprehensive plan should be, as best set forth in Jack Kent's *Urban General Plan*, our San Francisco efforts may be found wanting in some respects.[1] But failure to reach an ideal in its entirety does not make it less than worthy. It would be hard to say that the master plan documents adopted between 1971 and 1974 constituted what Kent describes as a "unified general physical design for the community." There was no single, overall, published, comprehensive framework or idea about the city to which all of the separate plan elements related. If pressed, I could verbalize such a plan. It would call for respect for and maintenance and improvement of the existing physical character of the city. It would respond to important social and economic issues within that framework. It would not be a plan that called for major, citywide physical change. But we never published such a document. We simply never got to it, although we had the matter on our agenda.

On the other hand, the master plan elements for residence, transportation, urban design, and recreation and open space go a long way toward meeting that part of Kent's definition. Moreover, the elements are consistent with each other or were made so as each new element was adopted. Further, the plans were based in large measure on an assessment of the social needs of the residents, particularly those for whom public support seemed most in order.

Long-range, citywide plans of the kind that have been discussed here can, of course, be responsive to social and economic issues. Maintaining existing residential areas and adapting them to contemporary living standards instead of tearing them down, addressing housing needs of low- and moderate-income people, providing recreation and open space facilities in high-need areas, emphasizing the use of mass transit, keeping automobiles out of neighborhoods, protecting and enhancing views and the physical scale and character of the city— these are a few of the kinds of people-felt issues that the master plan elements responded to. They were real. In addressing them I do not recall making major compromises with long-range objectives or visions.

Each of the master plan elements was accompanied by a set of recommendations for programs and actions to carry it out. The programs were successful in varying degrees. We have seen that the programs that were most directly under the control of the planning department, especially those that could be achieved through legislative action, had a higher success rate than those that required actions on the part of others. It was not always possible to get the mayor, the Board of Supervisors, or other departments to endorse our policies or to pursue the programs intended to carry them out. And the capital improvement program was never the priority-setting and coordinating tool that it might have been. It suffered from a dearth of funds, and I was never able to get the commission to assert itself strongly in the process. I could not effectively orchestrate the capital budgeting process with all the actors involved around city hall.

Nevertheless, the plans and programs were there. Their purposes were clear when they were followed, and their mere existence in print provided information and a starting point for those citizens who were concerned about the future of their city.

As time passed and with a growing and more solidly based set of plans to rely upon, individual short-range proposals—both public and private—could be viewed in the light of long-range considerations. As a result, we had fewer Transamericas and U.S. Steels. We could review the location of a subsidized housing development in the context of the housing plan element. We could measure a neighborhood rezoning proposal against the housing and urban design elements. When a piece of public land was to be sold or leased, we could check it against a policy of the plan, as we could the vacation or widening of a street. We could relate a small renewal project in Chinatown to both the citywide and neighborhood plans that we had prepared, and we could advocate such a project. City planning was especially pleasing when the projects and programs were clearly the outcome of our plans. We were exhilarated when all our research, meetings, presentations, reconsiderations, confrontations, and responses to demands led to concrete actions, or even when all we knew was that the ideas had a fighting chance of becoming reality.

We were not always effective, nor did we win all our battles. Often, our mouths were too big for our stomachs in that we simply proposed much more than we, or anyone else, could implement. And the dictates of our plans were not adhered to in every case where we had discretion. I was furious when the planning commission or the Board of Supervisors overruled my staff on an issue—a major development proposal for instance—about which I felt the plans were clear. We could at least do battle. As the plans became clearer, it became harder for the commissioners to overrule the planners, especially if the commission had voted for the plans. Increasingly, too, people became aware of what was in the plans, and they used them to advocate or oppose projects. And they demanded changes in the plan as well.

In some cases, the mere existence of a plan or a proposal for a plan stimulated debate over issues that would ultimately have to be decided; for example, the location of public facilities such as police stations, the distribution of low-income housing, and the height of buildings in outlying neighborhoods. That, too, is comprehensive planning at work.

In *Land and the Environment: Planning in California Today*, Paul Sedway and Thomas Cooke list six functions of local planning.[2] The first is "long-range goal and policy making," which I assume includes the kind of citywide physical planning I have been addressing. Another possible function is "middle range programming and assessment of alternatives," which I think relates to planning and assessing more detailed programs involving immediate community issues, physical and otherwise (perhaps our neighborhood plans and our involvement with the FACE and RAP programs fall into this category). Sedway and Cooke also refer to the function of coordinating the programs of other agencies; the function of compiling and conveying information; incremental decision making on particular issues as they arise; and a line function that includes such things as zoning administration, subdivision approval, design review, and master plan referral. If we add the design and implementation of large-scale urban development projects, we have a reasonably inclusive list of the kinds of activities that might normally engage city planners. All of these activities are important, but all but one—conveying information—are found wanting without some framework within which to function and make recommendations. That framework is the general or master plan. Without it city planners have a much harder time explaining why their ideas and their proposals are preferable to anyone else's. There were times when I might have argued otherwise, most notably in the early San Francisco months when I was impatient to get on with the action, to respond to the burning issues. But then, that has so often been our way, and we continue to have the same burning issues. Taking the time to decide what we want our communities to be and then acting to achieve those goals seemed more and more worthwhile in San Francisco as time passed. It was a route that proved more practical as well.

The emphasis of city planning upon the physical nature of the city is perfectly reasonable, although no one would deny for a moment that the man-made physical environment should be responsive to people and to social and economic issues and aspirations. Of course, economic well-being and social relationships and services are at least as important as the physical settings within which they get acted out. It is more than reasonable, too, that those concerned with planning the physical environment should have their marching orders determined by social and economic policies that they may not have planned. But this does not make a fundamental orientation to planning the physical environment unimportant or less than socially relevant if it is not so comprehensive as to include within its realm planning for all related matters.

Planning for the physical environment can be responsive to social issues without taking direct, formal responsibility for social planning. It seems to me that when city planners have not planned as well as they might—especially when they have not considered social imperatives and economic realities adequately (to their own everlasting criticism and guilt)—they have too often responded to their failings by extending the scope of their planning.[3] It would have been better to have been more systematic and rigorous in the first place, including as many relevant factors as possible but still focusing on planning for the urban physical environment—in short, to do better what city planning started out to do.

Ever since I was awarded a degree in city planning from a school that stressed, I thought, the worthiness of comprehensive, long-range physical planning for urban areas, I have heard that whole notion criticized. Repeatedly, I have heard the quality, content, usefulness, and effectiveness of the comprehensive plan challenged, as often as not by those who teach city planning. The critics say that the comprehensive plan is too vague, too subjective, too biased, too specific. It is elitist and divorced from the people, they add, full of end-state visions that are unrelated to the real issues of a dynamic world. Besides, it is impossible to achieve, "pie in the sky."

There are certainly elements of truth in these assertions. But, in general, they coincide neither with my sense of reality nor with the centrality of the idea. Comprehensive plans have always been policy documents, even if they have not been read that way. They have become less and less end-state, static pictures of the future. They regularly deal with pressing current issues: housing, transportation, jobs, public services, open space, urban design. Often they are prepared concurrently with programs that are geared to their achievement, and some of these are quite innovative. Far from being divorced from the people, comprehensive plans dealing with land use are required and demanded by citizens and elected officials alike. There is no reason that plans cannot be responsive to felt issues in any case. Any planning efforts are remarkable in a society that could never be accused of having a bias toward city planning in the first place, a society that has tended to look at land and urban environments as little more than high-priced consumable commodities. And isn't it grand that plans are visionary! Why shouldn't a community have a view, a vision of what it wants to be, and then try to achieve it?

For many years now, since Robert Walker wrote *The Planning Function in Urban Government* in 1941, a growing body of practical wisdom has been calling for city planning to be located in the office of the chief executive: the mayor or the city manager.[4] The federal establishment, increasingly involved in the nuts and bolts of local government, including its city planning, prefers to have city planning located centrally. But I would be very cautious about giving up the semi-autonomous planning commissions. If the objective of city planning is to be able to prepare plans and then to have them carried out, then it is not at all clear to me that such an objective can be most easily achieved by working from within the office of a mayor of a large city.

Most big city mayors are not oriented to planning, especially to long-range city planning. Furthermore, the business and labor interests that are most influential in electing and supporting big city mayors will not necessarily share the concerns of the planners, particularly when the latter are not hell-bent for maximizing development. Big city mayors and the interests that elect them are more often attuned to quantity of urban development than to quality or to moderation. In the best of circumstances, it is difficult for a mayor to be concerned with the "long run," especially when he holds office for four years and is besieged with problems that require immediate answers. There may, of course, be nothing wrong with that state of affairs. City planners should be expected to work with chief executives, as well as with legislators and others, on all kinds of physical development issues. But that need not be done from within the office of the executive. It might even be more difficult from within than from outside. It is possible to advocate a city planning position to the mayor from within that office, but that may be the end of the line if the mayor disagrees. Besides, what is there to lead to a conclusion that city planners will be given critical positions or listened to any more if they are in chief executives' offices than if they are not? Independence is required if city planning recommendations are to be made public as a matter of course.

Considering the always-present demands of the moment that occupied the mayor's office in San Francisco, I cannot imagine that we could have devoted adequate time to long-range plan making had we been a part of that office, certainly not to the extent we did. There would always have been more urgent things to do. Nor can I imagine that the plan elements addressed to housing, urban design, and recreation and open space would have come out the way they did. Long-range plans would have been milder, less far-reaching, more oriented to executive discretion. It would also have been more difficult to advocate their implementation as strongly as we did.

City planning under a commission need not be out of the main-stream of decision making if the commission and the staff choose not to be. There is little to stop them from being involved and responsive to the needs of the city. City planners under a commission can have considerable freedom to innovate and to work for their own plans and those causes they conclude to be consistent with their city planning charge. They can explore ways of implementing plans on their own, yet within the framework of the government that establishes the planning department in the first place. In the beginning, I looked at the commission as a somewhat unnecessary appendage to the city planning staff, as a barrier that prevented us from working directly with the mayor and the Board of Supervisors, with other departments, and with the people themselves. In time, I changed my mind, even when we disagreed most violently and when the commission failed to support the staff on what I felt were critical matters. Commissioners know things about a community that a staff will never know. Their views are not necessarily elitist, even when they come from the ranks of wealth and power. A commissioner can provide a buffer from the demands of the moment. Perhaps most important, as I have noted elsewhere, city planners under a commission have the freedom to respond to and build a citywide planning constituency as well as separate, issue-oriented coalitions. That can be pretty heady business. Ultimately, it means that the planners' proposals can come before elected officials with considerable force and that they can achieve strong backing, assuming of course that what the planners produce is worthy.

Mayor Alioto was not particularly oriented to city planning. Still, a lot of city planning was accomplished while he was in office. At least I would like to think so. Sometimes, the city planning position held sway, even over the mayor's opposition. As it was, he could have rendered city planning less effective had he wished to. If city planning did well under Mayor Alioto, it can be argued that its achievements were his. Fine. The mayor was benevolent in this regard and tolerated many points of view he did not necessarily share. As a person, I think he should be honored for that. My point, however, is that the opportunity to push strong, controversial points of view is greater—the chance for planning to be effective is greater—if city planning is located out of the mayor's office rather than in it.

Alan Altshuler, speaking of the place of the city planning function in government, said that he had "no doubt that any city can find a timid planning director if it wants, one who will be awed by the barrier that veto-group politics poses to the initiation of new ideas. The difficult problem is to give a bold planning director room in which to maneuver, to encourage him to take the risks of initiating. No administrative set-up can make the role of the initiator easy; all that can be done is to make the risks more bearable to bold men."[5] The words "city planners" might have been substituted for "planning director." I believe the risks are more easily and better taken outside of the mayor's office than in and that the planning commission is as good a place as any other.

Risk taking and effectiveness aside, there is a more compelling reason to have city planning located outside of a chief executive's offices. It has to do with the whole nature of centrality in government. People ought to have more than one place to go in government to get what they want, to have their grievances redressed, to complain, and to propose ideas. If a mayor won't listen, or won't start or stop something, then perhaps the city council will. Or the courts. The same should hold true at the departmental level. If the department of public works refuses to consider methods to restrict traffic in a residential area, then other arms of government, elected and appointed, ought to be available to people. In San Francisco, the planning department and its commission served that function. It acted as a sounding board, an advocate, an initiator within government, another place for people to go, including a place to complain about bad planning. By the same token, the city planners could be stopped from getting their way. They might be compelled by others to do things they might not wish to do. But that is a reality they should be willing to live with, while at the same time trying to gain more responsibility and to bring about changes in legislation and in the administrative processes of government that will make planning more effective.

If the San Francisco planning department had been in the mayor's office, people would have had one less avenue through which to pursue their concerns. We would have been forever associated with the chief executive. The people at the federal level who were associated with urban affairs never seemed to understand the beauty and health of decentralized government as they used their considerable leverage to encourage communities to copy their favorite model. It is true that government, and perhaps city planning and development, might have been more efficient if it had been centralized, but I do not believe that the main objective of government is to be efficient. Rather it is to respond to the democratically determined needs of its citizens. Responsiveness is more important than efficiency, and I believe that responsiveness is more easily achieved if the planning department is not part of another office. Moreover, the San Francisco experience shows that city planning and plan implementation can indeed take place without centralized leadership and control.

Throughout this volume, I have stressed the importance of having a highly qualified, trained, and dedicated professional staff with expertise in a number of areas of city planning. That notion bears repeating.

My initial, generally unkind, assessment of the quality of the staff I found was probably overdone. It is all too easy for a new boy in town to forget that people and institutions were there before his arrival (they may not even have been awaiting his arrival) and that they had made important contributions to planning and to urban problem solving. Nonetheless, it was necessary to improve that staff. And it was possible to do so. Despite a perfectly terrible civil service system, we could attract bright, energetic, and skilled professionals, mostly young people. They came—as people like that usually do—because there was a challenge, a feeling that there would be a no-nonsense attack on problems. They saw that they would have a chance to direct their skills and enthusiasm to matters that they considered important. Existing staff, too, can and will respond to new challenges.

It is critical, however, to have some professional skills and knowledge. In the early San Francisco years, there were too many people, fresh from some of the best graduate schools, who responded to questions about their abilities by speaking of their understanding of the problems of the poor and of the minorities, of their desire to "work with the people." That was not enough. Those qualities should be everyone's.

As our abilities increased, our successes increased. Our most notable successes—with the master plan elements and the legislation prepared to help carry them out; with the various public programs that were prepared, particularly in housing and open space; and with the day-to-day zoning issues—grew from a systematic approach to the work at hand. We did best when we had staff members with the professional skills we needed. To some extent the specific skills of the staff determined the substantive areas we pursued. But even when the expertise was not at hand—in the areas of seismic safety and noise, for instance—we could still do well, with the aid of consultants. However, we could only work well with consultants if we had people on the staff who could relate the subject in question to land-use planning. We did not do as well as I would have liked in dealing with some ad hoc development proposals, with planning for the northern waterfront, and with planning for industry, because we did not have people with sophisticated knowledge about the economic analysis and fiscal management aspects of city planning. And we were never very good at traffic engineering.

I have always felt somewhat lacking as a professional for not having learned better the "nuts and bolts" of my art and craft. I wished I knew more about analytic techniques, land and market economics, utilities engineering, housing analysis, fiscal management—that I had worked enough with those areas so that they were more a part of me. A city planning director does not get to do very much city planning personally and directly, although that is where the fun is. Still, he ought to know in detail, in regard to a number of substantive areas, what is required. He ought to be able to show the way.

These misgivings notwithstanding, we did well in any area involving land-use law and in city planning matters that were related to housing, urban design, recreation and open space, neighborhood planning, information collection and analysis, and graphic communication. In time, our professional expertise was noticed and respected, even if our advice was not always followed. I have no way of knowing for certain, but I suspect that Mayor Alioto's continued tolerance of a city planning staff that often disagreed with him came out of his recognition of its professional quality.

I learned many times how important the dissemination of understandable, untampered with, factual information can be. I am sure, for example, that a major reason for our continuing role in housing was the information that we continually collected and published on that subject. During this same period, the Redevelopment Agency was putting out materials that people often found suspect. People tend to assign more responsibilities to an agency that gives them reliable information.

So many of the issues that city planners are involved in are like battles. Sometimes we won because of our professional skills, and sometimes we won because of our political acumen. We might not have been in favor of street widenings or turning a two-way street into a one-way street, but in a given situation we ought to have had the analytical skills to determine whether or not such proposals were necessary to move traffic or desirable in terms of their impacts on the lives of people and on activities that bordered the street. Traffic engineering is not so difficult, and analysts like Donald Appleyard have shown how to assess people's responses to traffic.[6] With or without those professional skills, we might also call upon friendly residents to help support our positions.

You never win all the contests and it is unpleasant to lose for whatever reason. But when you win because of your professional skills alone or even in combination with your political abilities, the victory is sweeter. When the *only* thing that stops the street from getting widened is your ability to "call out the troops," that is, your political skills, that is not a very good victory. It is a little bit shameful. The planning commission, the mayor, or the city council could as well hire anyone else; they don't need a city planner.

Certainly I was involved in the politics of city planning. Every city planner is. Overall, however, the best "politics" is top professional work, forcefully presented and defended.

It will come as no surprise that I believe city planners ought to have points of view and that they should be prepared to go to bat for them. They ought to have something to say about the quality of the urban environments they are involved in shaping. Being top-notch technicians is important, but it is not enough.

City planners should not be neutral, and I do not believe their clients, at the level of local government, expect them to be without values or opinions. After they have arrived at some position, some point of view, some desired direction, one would hope to see it reflected in both public plans and day-to-day recommendations. Why hide it? Further, city planners should be willing to stand up for their points of view if they want to be effective. They should be prepared to "mix it up." They must do more than recommend. Within a democratic process they should advocate and search for ways to carry out their plans. I believe, too, that they should value and nurture their utopian predilections. They are nothing to be ashamed of. I do not believe we have done these things enough. We have tended to be meek.

I am not suggesting for one minute that city planners do battle with every person with whom they disagree or with every interest that is different than theirs. Nor am I suggesting that *every* matter that comes up has a right and wrong side for the planners. Some matters have reasonable alternatives, not just one answer. Some will come out all right no matter what point of view prevails. In any event, the planners must do an honest job of evaluating various courses of action, and they must make their evaluations public. However, I am suggesting that there are many matters that do have right and wrong sides for planners and that when this is the case they should be prepared for conflicts, even with those interests they might wish most to serve. My experience with city planning in San Francisco indicates that everyone—elected and appointed officials, interest groups, and residents—appreciates, respects, and responds positively to strong advocacy, even if there is not always agreement with what is being proposed. I doubt that people in other places are that much different from San Franciscans in this respect.

The client, that is whoever literally or figuratively signs the city planner's paycheck, should have the right to fire the planner. The city planner would do well to have his or her bags packed. The worst losses are in battles that were never fought. We have points of view related to the way cities should be built and about the ways they should function. We might as well state them.

Planning cities can be a frustrating business. I do not think that Americans like cities very much. Planning them may be alien to our predispositions and to our habits. In the past, we could always move away from what we didn't like. Since we were a land of plenty, we did not have to plan. We have been more concerned with quantity than with quality. My observation is that when "how much" is in conflict with "what kind," the quantity bag men usually win. We see a continuous rush to bigness, but it may be a losing bargain. Private property rights and a growth-for-its-own-sake mentality have, for so many major American cities, produced a development cycle that results in ever-increasing intensities of land use—from rural to urban, urban to more urban—until we leave these cities or tear down large sections and start over.

Our patience for solving urban problems is short, and we get new problems before we have a chance to solve the old ones. Nothing, it seems, will stand still long enough for us to get a handle on it or to find a lasting solution. Victory today, over the wrong thing in the wrong place, does not ensure that the same battle will not have to be fought tomorrow or the next day.

Many of the problems that cities and their planners are asked to deal with require larger than local solutions. They have to be resolved at a metropolitan, regional, or larger scale, we think. Alfred Heller, longtime president of the conservationist and planning-oriented California Tomorrow, has said that for big cities like San Francisco, "all the major development decisions were made decades ago; and that all that is left today is to tinker with the remains by making 'urban design' rules."[7] But if he is right, then what are so many local people concerned about, and wouldn't the same thing be true at the state and regional level? In any case, the governmental structure to do effective city planning at a larger than city scale rarely exists. Besides, are the city planners (like the local people they represent) really sure they want to give planning powers to some super government? Can those fellows really be trusted? At the same time, people at the neighborhood or district scale think that theirs is the level at which to do city planning and to guide and control urban development. The city planner may have a hard time meshing neighborhood concerns with citywide plans and regional interests.

There is seldom enough time, or people, or information, or tools at the city planners' disposal to prepare the kinds of plans and implementing programs they would like. Often the tools and programs they do devise, such as zoning or urban redevelopment, get misused. There is never enough money (and the city planners rarely control its use in any case). City planners don't usually build things or run programs by themselves. They are always trying to get others to do what they want, and people are reluctant, if not ornery. More and more, it seems that someone from the federal or state government knows your business better than you and is telling you how to do it. (And will they cop out on you when the going gets tough? Better not to depend on them.) Just when you think you know your craft, your art, and what it will take to solve a problem and to plan for the future, there is yet another hurdle.

City planners may have a hard time knowing when they have been successful. It is hard to know what constitutes a good batting average. Very seldom does all of a plan get carried out. In many cities, success is measured by what happens, by what gets done, by what is accomplished. We are accustomed to thinking that way, but sometimes it is better to measure success by what does not happen. Any number of variations are possible and city planners, as well as their clients, may have a hard time identifying success when they see it. Success depends upon many variables—timing, people, laws, economics, you name it—and few of them are controlled by the city planner.

Nevertheless, the city is where the action is. It is the first line of government for most people. They feel their problems and frustrations where they live and work, and it is in their communities where people state their expectations and lodge their complaints. It is possible to do planning in cities within a context of specific faces and names as well as of places and things. It is possible to relate abstract policies and plans and programs to tangible experiences. The city planner can feel and experience what he is dealing with.

Even if city planners rarely design or build anything directly or operate a program, they can, working at the city level, have an impact on the environment. They can help a community decide what it wants to be and then help to achieve that future. They can see their successes and their failures, even those successes that are represented by something that did not happen.

The impact of local city planning may be more than local. When the solutions that are developed are truly innovative, they may be adopted and used elsewhere. But perhaps the most satisfying plans are the ones that respond purely to local needs and circumstances, those not required or mandated by any other level of government. Similarly, the best programs are the ones that are developed locally and carried out with local resources—because the community wants and endorses them for their own sake—not because of the availability of funds or aid programs, often illusory anyway, from some other level of government.

Certainly, there are frustrations. But if after many years you end up with one small park that might not have existed otherwise, one major piece of legislation, or one program that allows people to fix up their homes or live in sound and fairly priced housing in neighborhoods they enjoy, then the satisfactions can be very great. Such achievements will always be small in relation to the need. But there is always the chance of ending up with many parks and open spaces, a full transit system, a whole city of neighborhoods of well-maintained housing at prices that people can afford, and a host of facilities and services that together make a city what it can be. Those are very high stakes indeed.

# Notes

1. T. J. Kent, Jr., *The Urban General Plan* (San Francisco: Chandler Publishing Co., 1964).

2. Paul Sedway and Thomas Cooke, *Land and the Environment: Planning in California Today* (Los Altos, California: William Kaufmann, Inc., 1975), p. 139.

3. For an example of where city planning has gone and is going, see "National Policies for Planning," American Institute of Planners, revised draft, June 15, 1977, part I, pp. 1-3, on "The Role of Planning." This document, in its definition of planning, leaves considerable doubt as to whether planning has any roots at all in the physical environment or any particular relationship to urban areas. It is more concerned with government and "the planning process" than with the substance or focus of planning. Its only reference to the planning commission is in a historical sense, not as a desirable place to do city planning. A skeptic, observing the direction city planning has taken in the late 1970s, might say that since the definition of the field has become so broad that it includes all planning, for everyone, and that since everyone plans in one way or another, then everyone is a planner. That skeptic might well ask why a special planning organization or society should exist at all. (The final version of this document was adopted in October 1977 and released in 1978 under the title *AIP Planning Policies.*)

4. Robert A. Walker, *The Planning Function in Urban Government* (Chicago: University of Chicago Press, 1941).

5. Alan A. Altshuler, *The City Planning Process; A Political Analysis* (Ithaca: Cornell University Press, 1965), pp. 390-91.

6. For example, see Donald Appleyard and Mark Lintell, "The Environmental Quality of City Streets: The Residents' Viewpoint," *Journal of the American Institute of Planners*, March 1972. Also see San Francisco Department of City Planning (Donald Appleyard, consultant), *Street Livability Study,* June 1970.

7. Alfred Heller, "To Plan or Not to Plan," *San Francisco Bay Guardian,* April 14, 1977.

# Index

Weinstein, Sam, 83, 137
Williams, George, 287, 291, 292,
  293

## Z

zoning, 9-10, 11, 17-18, 43, 46-48,
  56-57, 99, 167-68, 181, 225-
  27, 231, 234, 235, 245-46,
  249, 251